Hollywood Dealmaking

SECOND EDITION

NEGOTIATING TALENT AGREEMENTS FOR FILM, TV, AND NEW MEDIA

BY

DINA APPLETON AND DANIEL YANKELEVITS

ATTORNEYS-AT-LAW

ALLWORTH PRESS
NEW YORK

14   13   12   11   10   5   4   3   2   1

Published by Allworth Press
An imprint of Allworth Communications, Inc.
10 East 23rd Street, New York, NY 10010

Cover design and interior design by Leah Lococo and Jennifer Moore
Page composition/typography by SR Desktop Services, Ridge, NY

Library of Congress Cataloging-in-Publication Data
Appleton, Dina.
Hollywood dealmaking : negotiating talent agreements for film, TV, and new media / by Dina Appleton and Daniel Yankelevits.—[2nd ed.]
p.   cm.
Includes bibliographical references and index.
ISBN 978-1-58115-671-3 (alk. paper)
1. Artists' contracts—United States.   2. Television producers and directors—Legal status, laws, etc.—United States.   3. Motion picture industry—Law and legislation—United States.   4. Television—Law and legislation—United States.
I. Yankelevits, Daniel.   II. Title.
KF390.A7A67   2009
343.73'0783848—dc22   2009038654

Printed in the United States of America

For my son and daughter, Adam and Ali. Remember to
always follow your dreams. And a special thank you to my parents,
Yigal and Diana, who have sacrificed without hesitation so that
I didn't have to, and who continue to encourage and inspire me;
and to my wife, Lori, who is the rock of our family.
— Dan

To my son, Jake (my pride and joy).
— Dina

★ ★ ★

ACKNOWLEDGMENTS

The authors are grateful for the assistance of the many individuals who offered their guidance in the preparation of this book, as well as to those who contributed their useful quotes. A special thanks to our agent, Andree Abecassis, for her tireless efforts on our behalf, and to Ron Reitshtein for his diligence. We are also indebted to our publisher, Tad Crawford, and his editorial team at Allworth Press.

★ ★ ★

DISCLAIMER

The information in this book is intended to help the reader better understand the dealmaking process in Hollywood. The material presented is neither exhaustive, nor is it presented on behalf of the authors' respective employers; all views and opinions are their own. It is not offered as legal advice, nor should it be construed as such. The authors strongly recommend that the reader consult with an experienced entertainment attorney to address each individual situation and any legal documentation.

★ ★ ★ Table of Contents ★ ★ ★

INTRODUCTION
to the
DEALMAKING PROCESS

*R*elationships play a key role in the dealmaking process in Hollywood. Not only does a good relationship ensure that a phone call will be returned or that a script will be read, but it helps cut through difficult negotiations when a deal is ready to be made. Once a level of trust is established between the negotiating parties, each side may more readily accept the other's bottom line.

THE PLAYERS

The major players in Hollywood routinely take part in power breakfasts, lunches, and dinners, cultivating their relationships with others in the business. Such principal players include the talent representatives (i.e., talent agents, personal managers, and entertainment attorneys), the buyers (studio executives and independent producers), and, at least indirectly, the guilds.

Talent Agents

A talent agent's primary role is to procure employment for her talent clients (i.e., the actors, writers, directors, producers or *below-the-line* crew who she may represent) and to negotiate such clients' employment agreements, possibly in conjunction with an entertainment attorney.

In California, talent agencies are regulated by the California Labor Code, section 1700 (also known as the California Talent Agency Act), and are required to be licensed by the State. This legislation requires that talent agencies post a surety bond in the amount of $50,000 prior to the issuance of their agency license. The regulations also require agencies to submit agents' fingerprints and references, to maintain a trust account and accurate records, and to submit the agency's form of talent representation agreement for approval by the Labor Commissioner.

Talent agents primarily make their living by commissioning the fees earned by their clients. Customarily, an agent will receive 10 percent of the client's gross earnings. For example, if an actor earned $60,000 for her acting services on a film, the agent would be entitled to a $6,000 fee. State legislation (mentioned above) and most guild regulations (discussed below) prohibit agents from taking a higher fee. In some cases, agencies will take a "packaging fee" in lieu of its standard 10 percent commission fee. This occurs in cases where the agency has "packaged" (or put together) a number of key elements in a film or television project (such as the writer, the director, a lead actor, etc.) and sold the project as a package to a buyer. In recent years, agencies have creatively sought out alternative revenue streams. William Morris Endeavor Entertainment, for example, provides marketing services to television networks and other clients.

Agencies representing guild members must be franchised by the relevant talent unions or guilds and must abide by the guilds' agency regulations. Most established agencies are members of the Association of Talent Agents (ATA), a nonprofit trade union comprised of companies engaged in the talent agency business. The ATA is the entity that negotiates the agency regulation agreements with the various talent unions and guilds (including Screen Actors Guild [SAG], the American Federation of Television and Radio Artists [AFTRA], Actors' Equity Association [AEA], the Writers Guild of America [WGA] and the Directors Guild of America [DGA]). It should be noted that the SAG/ATA agreement expired on October 19, 2000 due to the inability of the parties to agree on fundamental issues. The two sides continue to work together, despite the absence of a formal agreement. The various guild regulations not only restrict the terms of the agency representation agreements, but also give talent the right to terminate the agency agreement in the event that the agent is unable to secure any offers of employment during a set period. These guild agency regulations, along with the California Talent Agency Act, are the foundation upon which talent agencies operate.

Being represented by an agent provides legitimacy to a talent, and the more prestigious the agency, the better. It should be noted that many production companies will not accept literary materials unless they are submitted through an established agency or entertainment attorney with whom they have a business relationship. The theory is that if the project is represented by an agent, it must be of a certain standard, and hence, worth the investment of time needed to evaluate the material.

There are hundreds of talent agencies in Los Angeles and elsewhere (most notably, New York City), some representing several different types of talent and some that focus their representation on a particular niche (such as television writers or commercial actors). Moreover, some clients have more than one agent for different areas of representation. For example, an actor client may be represented by one agency for film and television and another for commercial work. In recent years, agencies have branched out and/or expanded, forming alternative divisions that encompass such areas as sports, branded entertainment, and new media. Mergers and acquisitions, such as the recent Endeavor/William Morris Agency merger, have consolidated power in the entertainment industry and representatives are seeing that their clients are looking to them to provide more services and create more opportunities, and agencies are responding by changing their business models to meet that demand.

Talent Managers

Unlike agents, managers (or "personal managers," as they are often called, so as not to be confused with business managers) are not required to be licensed or bonded by the State of California, nor must they be franchised by the guilds. In fact, anyone can, in theory, be a manager, since neither a license nor specific experience or training is required. In addition, managers are free to take as high a commission as their clients are willing to pay, since, unlike agents, they are not bound by state or guild regulations. Some shady or fly-by-night managers have been known to take up to 50 percent of their clients' earnings. Most reputable managers, however, take a 15 percent commission fee, and some charge just 10 percent.

In recent years, the line between agent and manager has blurred substantially. Traditionally, the manager's role was to provide day-to-day and long-term career advice for actors (and, less commonly, writers) and liaison with the client's other representatives, while the agent's role was to procure employment and negotiate the employment deal. Many managers, however, commonly solicit employment on their client's behalf and, in effect, act as unlicensed talent agents. In fact, some talent, such as Clint Eastwood and Leo DiCaprio (and, until recently, Sharon Stone), have reportedly dropped their agents to work solely with their personal managers and entertainment attorneys. This trend has triggered much controversy, as many agents are concerned that managers are encroaching upon their territory and threatening to make their role obsolete. The birth of Mike Ovitz's Artists Management Group (AMG) added fuel to the fire, particularly after some talent agents as well as talent clients left his former agency and current nemesis, Creative Artists Agency, for AMG. As a result, there have been pending proposals in the California legislature (and much lobbying on both the agent and manager side) to regulate personal managers and impose the same restrictions upon managers that agents face.

It should be noted that personal managers are not legally permitted to deal with the solicitation and procurement of their clients' employment, unless they become licensed "talent agents" pursuant to California's talent agency legislation (although the legislation doesn't prevent managers from counseling and advising artists). In fact, until 1982, the talent agency regulations subjected persons acting as unlicensed talent agents to criminal liability. Under the current law, the Labor Commission has the power to declare management contracts void and possibly order restitution of commissions earned under such contract if the artist can demonstrate that the manager acted as an unlicensed talent agent. Thus, unlicensed agents still stand the very real risk of having their management contracts declared illegal and unenforceable and losing all their commissions. This is true even if the talent agent services were only incidental to other services (i.e., directing and advising clients) provided as a manager. However, the labor code does permit managers to negotiate employment agreements if done "in conjunction with, and at the request of, a licensed talent agent."

Though talent managers are not subject to state regulation, the Talent Managers' Association (TMA) has created a Code of Ethics that its members are expected to uphold. Pursuant to such Code, managers' commissions should not exceed 15 percent of the client's gross income from the entertainment industry (excluding music and modeling, where commissions cannot exceed 20 percent). The Code also provides that the duration of the Personal Talent Management Contract shall not exceed three years (except in the music industry, where it shall not exceed five years). While the Code does not specify that managers will not engage in the procurement of employment, it does state that "a personal manager is engaged in the occupation of advising and counseling talent and personalities in the entertainment industry."

Entertainment Attorneys

The final member of the representation team is the entertainment attorney (also known as the "talent lawyer"). While not all individuals in the creative community retain lawyers to represent them, those involved in high-level deals are wise to do so. Entertainment attorneys may charge an hourly rate or, more commonly, take a percentage fee (customarily 5 percent) of their clients' gross earnings. While an entertainment attorney may assist a client in obtaining representation, meeting key executives, and even procuring employment, her primary role is to protect the client with respect to the legal aspects of the deal, which agents often fail to address. Often, entertainment attorneys negotiate a client's deal in conjunction with the client's other representatives.

It should be noted that entertainment attorneys are also hired by the studios as outside counsel and, more commonly, by independent producers who don't have in-house business affairs departments to prepare and negotiate production, distribution, and financing contracts for them. This can raise conflict of issues concerns if a law firm represents both the talent client and the production company, which is not all that uncommon in Hollywood.

Creative Executives

Creative executives at the studios dictate which projects will be developed, when such projects will be abandoned, and whether any such projects will proceed to production. Much of a creative executive's time (particularly at the more junior levels) is spent reading scripts and treatments. They also spend much of their week meeting with writers and producers who *pitch* their ideas to the studio executive. If a creative executive is passionate about a particular project, she will sometimes be able to persuade her superiors to commit some amount of money to further *develop* the project, such as by hiring a writer to write an outline or screenplay or hiring producers (who will be paid the bulk of their fees only if the project is eventually produced).

Junior level creative executives are sometimes referred to as "D-Girls" (the D stands for development). While not all such employees are female, there are a great number of young women working within the executive ranks of studio development departments. These D-Girls track the progress of the hundreds of film projects struggling their way through the development process at studios and production companies all over town (i.e., not only projects being developed at their own studios). If a writer or director falls out of some project and, therefore, becomes suddenly available, or if an option lapses or a project is put into *turnaround,* these D-Girls hope to be among the first to know and report such information to their superiors.

In addition to selecting projects suitable for development, studio creative executives (subject to the final authority of the studio or network chief) will collectively decide which projects to move forward to the production stage. From the perspective of the studio negotiators, or business affairs execs (as described below), the creative executives initiate the projects. Once they determine whom they would like to employ on a particular project, the business affairs executives will become involved and negotiate the terms of such employment.

Business Affairs Executives

Most studios and production companies employ several "business affairs" personnel to negotiate talent and production agreements on behalf of the studio. The majority of business affairs negotiators are attorneys. This is the case because a legal background is generally considered useful when structuring agreements. However, a law degree is not crucial, and several respected business affairs executives have never attended law school.

Business affairs executives essentially play the role of middleman, negotiating agreements on behalf of their studio's creative executives, who actually make the hiring decisions. The business affairs executive's job begins with an instruction from the applicable creative executive, requesting that the business affairs exec negotiate the terms of employment of a particular director, writer, actor, or other individual. The function of the creative executive, as more fully described above, is to make creative decisions (take pitches, read scripts, decide which director or actress is best suited to a particular project, etc.). The common thinking in the entertainment industry is that since creative executives tend to become quite passionate about their projects, they would not be best suited to negotiate the financial terms of production agreements. There is some element of truth in the foregoing, as a creative executive will generally be rewarded for overseeing hits. It is, therefore, in the creative exec's best interest to secure the most desirable talent in connection with any given project, regardless of cost. Consequently, studios felt it necessary to separate out the negotiation function and entrust such duties to a discrete level of executives, whose job was to be fiscally responsible.

Thus, in the ordinary course of business, a business affairs executive will be instructed by a creative executive to attempt to negotiate terms of employment for a specific individual. Very often, the first thing the business affairs executive will do will be to call the creative executive and attempt to ascertain the background of this hire (the nature of the project and any other relevant information). Most commonly, the next step will be for the business affairs executive to contact the representative (i.e., agent, attorney, or manager) of the potential hire and ask for some applicable quotes (i.e., what this person has been paid for similar services in the recent past). At times, the talent may not have applicable quotes, as such talent may not have rendered similar services in the recent past. To the extent that there are applicable quotes, the agent (or other talent representative) will generally provide the information to the studio executives.

Once the business affairs executive is provided with the relevant payment history of the talent representative's client, the executive will usually undertake efforts to confirm those figures with the applicable studio employers. This is not necessarily because the business affairs executive does not trust the agent (although this is sometimes the case), but the agent may possess incorrect information or have made an innocent mistake. In any event, the business affairs executive needs to practice the corporate technique of CYA (cover your ass) and will not want to be faulted for not confirming an erroneous quote.

Studios are, in most instances, expected to make the first offer. Thus, after the appropriate creative executive makes a decision to try to hire someone, the business affairs person will (after performing a bit of research, consulting the budget, discussing the particulars with the creative executive, etc.) call the talent's representative (again, usually the agent, but potentially the manager or attorney) and make an offer, setting forth terms of compensation, exclusivity, and credit, as well as any unique issues that may arise in any particular negotiation.

Once the business affairs executive and talent representative believe that they have reached a principal agreement on all material terms, the business affairs executive will typically draft either an internal memo to the legal department setting forth such principal deal points or send a confirming letter to the agent, with a copy to the legal department.

At this point, the studio attorney will plug such terms into a first draft contract and send it off to the talent's attorney (if the talent is represented by legal counsel) or to the talent representative that negotiated the deal.

It should be noted that most of the major talent agencies employ in-house attorneys, which are similarly referred to as business affairs executives. While such talent agency executives sometimes negotiate entire deals opposite their studio counterparts, they more commonly provide advice to the talent agents and assist such agents in structuring and negotiating agreements. In addition, these agency-employed attorneys frequently review and comment on long-form contracts generated by the studio's in-house legal department (discussed below), providing many of the same services that are typically rendered by talent attorneys (particularly in instances where the agency's client has not independently retained an attorney).

In-House Legal Department

Some studios separate their business affairs department from their legal department. Even when such departments are combined, however, their functions are often distinct. Business affairs negotiates the deals, most often opposite talent agents (as opposed to other attorneys), while in-house attorneys draft and negotiate the contractual language.

The in-house attorneys at the studios generally get involved in the deal after the business affairs executive has already negotiated the material terms of an agreement with a talent representative. Although, in most cases, an agreement will not be reduced to written form until the in-house lawyer drafts a contract and the parties take the position that an agreement already exists, albeit an oral agreement. Other times, an abbreviated deal memo will have been exchanged, summarizing the principal terms of the agreement in written form. Notwithstanding the foregoing, there are many issues that are typically not addressed prior to the contract stage. Often, these include modifications (potentially significant ones) to the net profits definition. Although the business affairs executive will have negotiated the percentage of the profits to be granted to the talent, the attorneys (on both sides) will often spend considerable time negotiating the finer points of the definition.

The primary function of the production attorney is to draft and negotiate contractual provisions based on the deal concluded by the business affairs executive. A deal memo (such as those we are providing) can be relatively brief—as little as two or three paragraphs. The contract based on such a deal memo may be thirty to forty pages long. This is mainly due to the "customary" or "standard" terms and conditions that are necessary to flesh out most talent deals. The in-house attorney will generally draft provisions relating to representations and warranties, indemnities, insurance, events of default, as well as supply a detailed net profits definition, if applicable.

In addition to drafting such "long-form" contracts and modifying the contract's language in response to comments generated by the talent lawyers, many studio attorneys also handle issues relating to clearances (whether a particular production has the legal right to use copyrighted logos, artwork, music, or other material).

The Guilds

The main guilds (i.e., talent unions) in Hollywood are:
* ★ The three key actors' guilds: Screen Actors Guild (SAG), Actors' Equity, and AFTRA
* ★ The key screenwriters' union: Writers Guild of America (WGA)
* ★ The director's union: Directors Guild of America (DGA)

★ The below-the-line talent union: International Alliance of
Theatrical Stage Employees, Moving Picture Technicians,
Artists and Allied Crafts (IATSE)

While there is an organization called the Producers Guild of America (PGA),
it is not a union, but merely a trade organization.

Through independent negotiations, the PGA has secured agreements with
the television and motion picture academies to determine academy award
eligibility.

The PGA assists qualifying members in accessing benefits under the
Motion Picture Industry Pension and Health Plan—trust funds established by
collective bargaining agreements and primarily supported by industry employers. Additionally, while not yet established, one of the fundamental goals of
the group is to provide insurance and retirement plans to all of its members.

Union Membership

Union membership offers talent the protections stipulated in each guild agreement, including minimum fee requirements as well as the support of the guild in
enforcing compliance with its rules. As mentioned earlier, these guilds also protect talent vis-à-vis their own representatives. Each guild has specific membership requirements, ranging from merely paying a registration fee (as is the case
with AFTRA) to gaining a certain amount of practical experience. Following are
basic membership requirements for the three major Hollywood unions.

Writers Guild of America. In order to become a member of the WGA, a
writer must accumulate an aggregate of twenty-four units of credit (within the
three years preceding his application), which are obtained by entering into
agreements with signatory companies to perform services or to sell literary
work. Different types of work are allocated different numbers of credit units.
Each of the following works (in and of itself) constitutes twenty-four units:

★ A screenplay for a feature-length film, television program, or radio
play ninety minutes or longer in duration
★ A bible (i.e., a long-term story projection for a television series) for
a prime-time miniseries or television serial of four hours or longer
★ A bible for a specified term, or an existing non–prime-time serial
appearing five times per week

In addition, there is an initiation fee (currently in the range of $3,000).

For more specifics on membership, writers should contact the WGA's
membership department at (323) 782-4532.

Screen Actors Guild. A performer is eligible to join SAG if he renders services as a principal performer in a film, television program, or commercial for a signatory company or if he renders a minimum of three days of "extra" work on a SAG signatory production. Alternatively, a performer can join SAG if he has been a member in good standing of a sister union (such as AFTRA, AEA, ACTRA) for at least one year, has worked at least once as a principal performer in that union's jurisdiction, and is current in dues. In addition, there is a small initiation and annual fee. SAG members are not permitted to work for non-guild companies (discussed immediately below) except in limited circumstances and are subject to disciplinary action (and possibly termination) for doing so. For more specifics, call the SAG membership department at (323) 549-6757.

AFTRA. The union affiliation for a pilot and the subsequent series is determined by the method of filming: film for SAG and digital for AFTRA. The digital revolution that swept TV production for the 2009 pilot season has strengthened AFTRA as an actors union (vis-à-vis SAG). Because of the prolonged period of uncertainty resulting from the possibility of a SAG strike, as well as the appeal of less expensive—and at times, more flexible—digital production, the transition from film to digital has been growing at an accelerated pace. In 2009, at least four of the studios produced 100 percent of their television pilots under the AFTRA agreement (using digital technology): Twentieth Century Fox TV (nine pilots), ABC Studios (fifteen), Sony TV (nine), and Universal Media Studios (nine). For CBS Paramount and Warner Bros. Television, the percentages were 92 percent and 79 percent, respectively.

Directors Guild of America. The DGA represents film and television directors, unit production managers, first assistant directors, second assistant directors, coordinators and associate directors, stage managers, and production associates. To join in any Guild category, you must obtain employment with a company that has signed a collective bargaining agreement with the DGA, such as the major studios and networks (e.g., MGM, Paramount, Universal, Sony, 20th Century Fox, WB, NBC, ABC, CBS). For further information, please call the DGA at (310) 289-2000.

Guild Signatories

As mentioned previously, agents representing guild members must be franchised by the pertinent guild(s). Similarly, producers or studios wishing to employ guild members on their productions must become *guild signatories.* As such, they are required to pay employees no less than the guild minimum fees (set out in the applicable guild agreement) and meet other guild requirements, including remitting pension, health, and welfare payments to the applicable guild on behalf of the talent. The major studios are all signatories to the key guilds. The Association of Motion Picture and Television Producers (AMPTP), on behalf of motion picture and television studios or producers, like ATA on behalf of its agent members, negotiates with each guild. This past year, two such negotiations (the WGA Agreement and the SAG Agreement) took place. These agreements generally provide for three (3) year terms, with mandatory minimum compensation increasing annually by approximately 3 to 4 percent.

STUDIOS VERSUS INDEPENDENT PRODUCERS

There are important differences in dealmaking with an independent producer versus dealing with a major studio. Of course, the independent producer is known to make "art films," while studios are notorious for producing big-budget blockbusters. In addition to those traditional distinctions, it should be noted that independent producers are often more flexible in dealmaking than studios, since they are usually working within much smaller budgets. As a result, they are likely paying talent salaries below quote, and thus, are often more willing to grant greater back-end participations and other perks to talent that they are trying to engage. Studios, on the other hand, have very rigid negotiation parameters set by the studio heads, and the studio negotiators will often refuse to "break precedent." On the other hand, when dealing with a studio, one is relatively certain he will get paid for his services. Such is not always the case when dealing with independent producers, particularly foreign ones who may be difficult to track down later. In addition, indie film productions are often outside guild jurisdiction, while most studio films are guild-regulated.

THE ART OF NEGOTIATION: TIPS FROM INDUSTRY PLAYERS

Every dealmaker develops his own unique style of negotiating. Set forth below are a few negotiating tips from industry professionals.

Norman Aladjem, Agent, Paradigm
Let the other person think he's gotten the best of you in a negotiation, especially if he hasn't. Everyone wants to feel like a winner, or at least that he was a worthy opponent in a hard-fought battle. In an industry where the same people negotiate against each other over and over, it's important that your adversary's dignity always be left intact. Resist the impulse to celebrate that you got

the best of a deal. Whether I've just closed a deal for $100 or $10 million, I always end a negotiation by saying something like, "Well, you got the best of me this time; hopefully, I'll get you the next time." It's good sportsmanship and, more importantly, will make it less likely that the next time your adversary will be gunning for you.

Daniel Blatt, President, Daniel H. Blatt Productions
There comes a time when you must close!

David Brownstein, Former Agent for James Gandolfini
The key to a successful negotiation is the willingness to pass on the deal— early and often!

Marti Blumenthal, Partner (Owner and Manager), Ampersand Management Group
What determines a successful negotiation is a solid understanding of what your client's bottom line is and, as importantly, a complete understanding of what your opponent's bottom line is as well.

Stephen J. Cannell, President, Stephen J. Cannell Productions (creator of *The A-Team*)
A deal works best when it's fair for both parties. The worst thing you can have is an uneven deal, because you end up arguing about the deal for the rest of the time you're involved.

Stephen M. Kravit, Executive Vice President, Business and Legal Affairs, The Gersh Agency
In short, clients are widgets—so know the process, follow the money (money out, money in), and know your leverage. You, as a negotiator, must know the product and the process of manufacture. How is the product made? How does your client fit into the process? What are the cost elements of the process? What are the income streams for the product? How critical to the process is your client? When you know these elements, you will know how to advise your client and how to make the best deal for your client.

Jeffrey Freedman, Legal Counsel, Creative Artists Agency
Every negotiation is a game of chess. A skillful negotiator will plan every offer/counteroffer, calculating how his opponent will react in each round. You should know before you begin what outcome you want to achieve. Furthermore, never negotiate against yourself. An old negotiator's trick is to

give the opponent a speech about how their proposal was outrageous, insulting, embarrassing, etc., and get him to come back with another offer, without ever making a counteroffer. Sometimes this ploy works, but it will almost never work against an experienced dealmaker.

David J. Matlof, Esq., Partner, Hirsch Wallerstein Hayum Matlof & Fishman
Preparation is an important key to any negotiation. Since studios negotiate based on precedent, it's critical to know how far they have gone on prior deals and what they will refuse to do categorically. For example, business affairs executives will often say simply, "We don't do that," or "We never . . ." Since these blanket statements are often false, it can prove very helpful to be able to refute them. It's equally important to know what not to request. If there is absolutely no way the studio will agree to a particular "ask," it only weakens your other positions.

Joel McKuin, Esq., Partner, Colden, McKuin & Frankel, LLP
Your power in a negotiation on behalf of a client comes from three places: the leverage you have by virtue of your client's desirability in the marketplace; your client's willingness to "blow a deal" that is not right, thereby testing the studio when it says it "can't do any better"; and your own credibility and skill as a negotiator in achieving the desired result. You sometimes can make a better deal for a smaller client with chutzpa than you can for a more established client who is afraid of walking away, and in all cases, the negotiator's reputation and quality of his or her relationships come to bear on the process.

Howard Meyers, Executive Vice President, Business Affairs, Focus Features
Relationships are key in the entertainment industry, including the legal and business affairs world where we often negotiate repeatedly with the same dealmakers. Get to know the people you negotiate with. Ask them to lunch. When you have relationships with the individuals you're negotiating with, and there is trust and mutual respect, you can often cut through a lot of the game-playing and posturing and quickly get to a deal that is fair and makes sense for both parties. A side benefit for those of us who negotiate deals all day long is that your job will be a lot more pleasant and enjoyable.

Dennis Nollette, Executive Vice President, Legal Affairs, Sony Pictures
In negotiating talent agreements, in-house lawyers at studios often find themselves fighting lonely battles. On the one hand are studio executives (speaking for their clients) chiefly interested in making their films and sometimes thinking of studio precedent and the legal department's concerns as an obstacle. On the

other hand are the agents and lawyers representing talent, and their concern, of course, is only getting the best deal for their client. It's like walking a tightrope sometimes, but in-house studio lawyers simply have to take a longer view, remembering that they represent an institution that is worth protecting, which may survive far longer than the careers of anyone involved in any negotiation.

Brett Paul, Executive Vice President, Warner Bros. Television Production
One of the unique aspects of being a negotiator involved in the network primetime television business is that you frequently face the same representatives over and over in your negotiations. The development and production dollars being put to work at the hands of a fairly small group of institutions and individuals is quite extraordinary. In that environment, I think that it is particularly important to make deals that fairly represent all of the relevant market conditions and variables. Over-leveraging a particular situation will undoubtedly come back at you in ways that may be unforeseeable at the time. The challenge for negotiators in making deals is to remain fully informed of the changes in the market conditions and evolutions in the business, so that the "fairness" of each situation can be appropriately evaluated.

Debbie Stasson, Owner, Media Strategies International
As a negotiator, I would advise the following:
- ★ Check your ego at the door. The deal is never about you, but your client.
- ★ Don't become emotional. Remember, it's only entertainment.
- ★ Always seek clarity about the best course for your clients and their individual needs.
- ★ Gather as much information as possible—you never want to be surprised by relevant information.
- ★ Anticipate where the right place is for the deal to close, as well as your client's parameters.
- ★ Trust your intuition.

Nicole Ungerman, Former Senior Vice President, Business and Legal Affairs, United Paramount Network (UPN)
My first tip would be—stay out of the business. . . . But if you're still keen on working in Hollywood, my suggestion is that you do so with integrity. Be someone who's known for being true to her word; it's the only thing that's completely within your control and that you can take with you wherever you go. It makes dealmaking more enjoyable—and looking in the mirror, too.

Amy Weiss, Executive Vice President, Business and Legal Affairs, Brillstein Entertainment Partners

As a negotiator, my biggest tip is to keep your adversary, as well as your colleagues, informed of the progress (or lack thereof) of every deal. People would rather have you call and tell them that you have no information than not to hear from you at all. That way, they are confident that you are working on closing the deal, as opposed to thinking that the deal may have slipped through the cracks.

THE NEW LANDSCAPE:
OBSERVATIONS OF INDUSTRY PLAYERS

Over the last seven years, since this book was first published, the landscape of the entertainment industry has changed dramatically. As you've likely noticed, original scripted television has been increasingly subjugated by reality television programming, and shows like *American Idol, The Apprentice,* and *Deal Or No Deal* take up primetime slots. Once-overlooked cable television networks such as USA and AMC, along with premium cable networks like Showtime and HBO, have attracted a loyal fanbase as well as critical acclaim and status, and such scripted programs as *Monk, Entourage, Mad Men, Weeds,* and *The Sopranos* have stolen much attention from the networks at the various award shows.

Meanwhile, TV series budgets are decreasing (one of the reasons for the growth of reality programming) as ad dollars once targeted for networks are being directed to a range of other media such as Internet, mobile, and cable in an attempt to try to catch the younger generation. It has become evident that these targeted viewers are spending less time watching TV and going to movie theatres and more time on the Internet (largely on social networking sites like Facebook [*www.facebook.com*] and MySpace [*www.myspace.com*]), texting on their cell phones and PDAs, and playing video games on their Wiis, Nintendo DSes, or Xboxes. Those who are watching TV are increasingly using TiVo or other DVR technology to skip over commercials. As a result, TV studios and networks are seeking alternative ways to generate revenue such as product placement and commercial tie-in deals, and talent agencies are hiring agents who specialize in these deals.

Strained union relations with the studios have further exacerbated the situation. In late 2007, the Writers Guild of America went on a one-hundred-day strike with issues such as DVD residuals, union jurisdiction over animation and reality programming, and compensation for new media at the forefront. With the writers on strike, the allure of reality television, often considered "unscripted" and traditionally non-union productions, intensified. A possible Screen Actors Guild strike was a looming threat throughout late 2008 until very recently as SAG members grappled with many of these same issues.

Like advertisers, studios are also now promoting their product (e.g., their film and television productions) with a major focus on digital marketing campaigns rather than just traditional print, TV, and radio ads. In addition, studios and producers are now interested in making original content intended for initial exploitation via the Internet or mobile. This raises many new issues for dealmakers, including what rights to ask for in their agreements and how these rights will be compensated.

Other changes in landscape include the rapid growth of branding and merchandising. Brands built around young stars such as Miley Cyrus and the Jonas Brothers have become a successful model for studios like Disney that everyone wants to replicate. These all-encompassing deals provide greater exposure and permeation into both new mediums and new demographics. Additionally, packaging a celebrity personality in such a way creates strong brand recognition, which further increases notoriety and sales. Celebrity product lines have become the norm, as everyone from Jessica Simpson to Jennifer Lopez to the Olsen twins has a clothing line and/or other product to offer. Such deals, of course, also spark a variety of new issues for negotiators.

Industry players are feeling the changes. The following quotes were provided by top dealmakers in different areas of the business—reality, film, new media—when asked to address the new landscape and the ways in which dealmaking has changed for them in recent years.

Jonathan Anschell, Executive Vice President and General Counsel, CBS Broadcasting, Inc.

The business and legal landscape impacting dealmaking has changed dramatically in recent years. Only a few years ago, online and wireless exploitation of audiovisual content was cumbersome and appealed primarily to techies; today, widespread exploitation on these platforms is a foregone conclusion at the inception of projects and figures prominently in the strategies of both sides to a transaction. All of this change has occurred against the backdrop of an evolving landscape in the relationship between the industry and the guilds, as reflected in the writers' strike that began in November 2007. As a result, force majeure provisions that once were regarded as boilerplate now receive considerably more attention. All of these developments suggest that the old forms and templates may not be the best fit for today's transactions, which call for some new negotiating, drafting, and thinking.

Craig Cardon, Partner, Sheppard Mullin Richter & Hampton, LLP

How do you make money in the free Internet economy? In nickels and dimes. There are a lot of nickels and dimes out there. The trick is identifying them and doing the right deals to pick them up. Where once content owners could do a single monolithic film distribution or network deal, now the key is to find all of the different ways to make money and make sure you are retaining the rights to do so. If your content is long-form, but has clip potential (e.g. talk shows, comedy, reality, etc.), retain the rights to monetize clips online. Are there related Web spinoffs, mobile applications, branded tie-ins, fan sites, etc.? Advertising still exists, but in different places and smaller denominations. In 2006, approximately $7 billion left certain categories of the upfronts, but online advertising increased by approximately the same amount that year. And in 2007 and 2008, online ad spends continued to increase. The world is consuming its entertainment content in a very different fashion than it has in the past. But advertisers remain willing to pay to reach those viewers in those different mediums. Premium professional content is what they are looking for, not videos of your cat dancing. The nickels, dimes, rupees, yen, pesos, etc., are still there to pick up. You just have to be prepared to do thirty deals instead of three, and be able to do those quickly and efficiently.

Denise Cooper, Vice President, General Counsel and Business Affairs, Virgin Mobile Canada

The intensity of competition faced by everybody in the film and television business—from creators to distributors to broadcasters—is unprecedented. Within the industry, a seemingly endless number of television channels compete for the attention of viewers. Meanwhile, audiences are migrating toward other forms of entertainment, such as social networking, video games, user-generated content, and short-form content created solely for the Internet and wireless devices. Those within the industry who understand interactive media and exploit these opportunities by rethinking the way content is produced, licensed and monetized will survive and prosper. The players who bury their heads in the sand and cling to the old traditional models will compete for an ever diminishing pie.

Robert A. Darwell, Partner, Sheppard Mullin Richter & Hampton, LLP

It's very clear that across all aspects of the entertainment and media business [that] we are in a new era, and the framework for negotiations has necessarily changed as a result. Studios, networks, and advertisers are all expecting more for their money, and talent precedent has never been less important. What matters now is performance and service, and with talent beginning to chase fewer available deals, the message has gotten through.

Nancy Derwin-Weiss, Partner, Wildman, Harrold, Allen & Dixon LLP

The growth of the Internet and, in turn, the expansion of online and mobile marketing campaigns for motion pictures and television shows, has fundamentally shifted the way in which entertainment deals are made. [Many] of these evolving marketing efforts require talent (actors, directors and writers) involvement early and over extended periods of time. Thus, talent agreements today need to contemplate these expanded duties, as the weekend press junket that talent has come to expect is only one piece of the "promotional" picture. Motion picture studios and television networks no longer confine their advertising to television and traditional print media. A well-executed online campaign builds product awareness early, harnessing fans that can translate into big box office numbers and ratings. However, it is not enough for a studio or network to simply launch a picture or show-specific Web site, which consumers often perceive as being too commercial, too promotional, and not as credible. In fact, most marketing activity happens outside the confines of the studio or network Web site in an effort to build product affinity in an increasingly fragmented world. Directors blog from the set and send e-mail updates, actors perform in Webisodes and participate in podcasts, talent likenesses are used to create online trading cards, and contests elicit user-generated "commercials," all of which is distributed virally and marketed on third-party social networking sites, where one can become a "friend" of the picture or television show. Studios and networks recruit fans to join online task forces where they can participate in word of mouth campaigns in an effort to create the perception of authenticity. Even advertising buys on third-party Web sites regularly include such add-ons as sweepstakes and advertorial content, which may feature live chats with the stars or director. For studios and networks, this means ensuring that the talent agreements require talent participation in these expanded and ever-changing marketing and publicity efforts and often with limited talent approval rights (where content is developed and launched within very tight timeframes). Attorneys assisting the marketing and publicity departments must also understand the subtle nuances of the various laws and regulations that govern online and mobile marketing, including the Communication Decency Act, the Digital Millennium Copyright Act, the Federal Can Spam Act, and the Federal Telephone Consumer Protection Act, as well as self-regulatory guidelines such as those of the Motion Picture Association of America, Children's Advertising Review Unit, Word of Mouth Marketing Association, and Mobile Marketing Association, all of which impact the manner in which companies conduct such campaigns.

Michael Grizzi, Senior Vice President, Legal, Paramount Pictures Corporation
In addition to the large variety of requests from high-level actors, we are now receiving requests at the major studios that were literally unthinkable a decade ago. For example, in certain very high-level actor deals, we are now being

asked to provide publicity material from a picture for use on an actor's personal Web site, or to agree to provide links to the actor's personal Web site from the official Web site of the film, or to agree to make advertising buys on Web sites owned by actors. I've even been asked to agree that an actor can film his own behind-the-scenes footage during principal photography of a picture for the actor to edit and post on his personal Web site as part of a blog of the actor's daily activities.

Such requests add additional levels of complexity to already complicated high-level actor agreements. For instance, a studio often strictly controls where publicity material such as the key art of the picture would be seen over time in order to maximize the publicity impact by using certain high-profile media outlets at certain times in order to reach specific market segments. Therefore, use of publicity material from a film on an actor's own Web site can blur and complicate efforts to promote a film effectively. In addition, attempts by actors to record their own behind-the-scenes footage raise additional clearance issues with respect to third party intellectual property that might be caught on camera, as well as the need to get the approval of other high-level actors who might be caught on camera in such footage. For all those reasons, studios are unable to agree to such requests, although that doesn't stop actor representatives from repeatedly asking, and I expect the chorus to grow louder and louder.

Daniel Grover, Television Business Affairs, Creative Artists Agency

In this era where the evolution of Internet, wireless, and electronic gaming media are having a profound impact on the motion picture and television media, one of the big challenges facing those who negotiate deals for film and tv talent is how to limit the studios' and networks' expanding appetite for talent's services beyond the traditional scope, often for little or no additional compensation. An actor's on-camera services for the project itself, along with the customary additional publicity and promotion services, are no longer enough. The studios and networks are attempting to expand the scope of required services to include on-camera and audio work for Internet, wireless, and video game projects related to the movie or series, "extended content" for VOD and home video, and still photo shoots for everything from computer wallpapers to Internet promotions. Writers, directors, and producers are being asked to render extended services to execute many of these same ancillary projects, again for nominal or no additional compensation.

Talent representatives have had to fight to make sure talent is compensated fairly for these additional services and also allowed to participate in the additional revenues generated by their work in emerging ancillary areas. And as these services are often expected outside production periods, we have had to fight to make sure they are subject to the artist's professional availability. And while we have to work to protect our clients' interests, we have to be realistic that there isn't a lot of money generated from these ancillary projects at this point, and we have to be flexible in making deals for these services. We have to be careful not to set precedents that can leave our clients without a fair share when these revenue streams grow. And yet we have to be more open-minded and forward-thinking than ever before.

Shelley E. Reid, Senior Vice President, Business & Legal Affairs, Fox Television Studios

The ever-changing landscape of entertainment practice demands that deal-makers adapt to the many new ways of doing business—the new business models as well as the new entertainment platforms. The digital age is here to stay and that means that every transaction, large or small, film or television, requires a new perspective and a new set of considerations. Today's dealmaker, regardless of who he or she represents, must be aware of the multitude of issues to be considered. With the explosion of the Internet, user-generated content, social networking, interactive television, and all other new and to-be-formed methods of communication and exploitation, the dealmaker must know how to navigate and protect his or her client in all of these areas. Every studio in Hollywood is involved in some manner with the new media component of its programming. This means that from production to marketing, the dealmaker must understand the commercial marketplace which includes addressing issues such as sponsorship and product integration, ancillary revenues, impression guarantees, usage patterns, collective bargaining issues, branding, nontraditional platforms such as online distribution, mobile, video games, streaming versus downloadable media, the Internet, revenue sharing, etc.

Rob Rieders, Associate General Counsel, Pixar Animation Studios

Exploitation of television shows and films—particularly animated films like those produced by Pixar—continues to grow rapidly. New media distribution platforms quickly fill whatever vacuum that may exist in consumer demand. Once the audience indicates a taste for a film, it is presented with a seemingly endless variety of ways to consume it. Beyond the traditional markets for film-based toys, books, and video games, new media and the Internet provide marketing and revenue opportunities via digital downloads/streaming video (iTunes, Hulu), virtual worlds (Club Penguin) and social networking (MySpace channels), among others. Dealmakers need to be aware of all the emerging platforms and their implications before making their deals. That awareness, plus a bit of prognostication, will ensure that the dealmakers (and their clients) are not surprised down the road.

Adina Savin, Executive Vice President, Business Affairs, Disney/ABC Cable Networks Group

We are in the midst of a sea change from audiences having limited programming choices at limited times and therefore relatively common viewing experiences to audiences having relatively unlimited programming choices with platform and time-shifting opportunities and therefore diverse and customized viewing experiences. The business models are changing from scarcity of exhibition and windowing on successive platforms, realizing separate revenue streams from each, to concurrent, multi-platform viewing with the potential to cannibalize later revenue streams. Consumers have become hungry "beasts," demanding content how, when, and where they want it—often, for free over the Internet. Distribution companies are going to be sorting through this chaos for some time, but large content production companies will be advantaged to the extent they focus on original, quality programming, brands, and the leveraging of assets to engage in franchise-building to cut through the clutter.

The pressure will be on for original content negotiators and lawyers to gather the biggest possible bundle of rights and to seriously consider walking away from any deal that does not permit this. Unitary ownership of 100 percent of any new intellectual property will be vital to a company's ability to exploit it and create derivative works based on it on a worldwide, all-media, and all-platforms basis. This may eliminate or reduce coproduction deals with split or shared rights, but it may also lead to a more lucrative result for any back-end participant on a successful production. For onscreen talent and their representatives, this may mean they will need to commit to more promotional and marketing activities and to limiting their approval and consultation rights but it may also open up more opportunities for them to become the "face" of program-related merchandise and to realize a better merchandise participation.

Hans Schiff, Agent, Creative Artists Agency

In relation to the world of non-scripted television, the dealmaking environment has grown more and more difficult for the creators and producers of content. Slowly, and I would say since about 2000, the broadcast networks, have gained considerable sophistication in their dealmaking. They have come to realize that the rights that are available to exploit format and ancillary revenue are the key components of how they can add value on top of the initial broadcast. These revenues have contributed addressing the downside of non-scripted television's intrinsic non-repeatability. What unfortunately happens however is that the focus of the vertically integrated networks is on their film and drama properties and they fail to maximize this revenue, to the detriment of themselves and the content creators.

In the cable universe, the distribution and ancillary rights have consistently been hoarded by the networks. Ironically, those networks pay less money in license fees and demand a greater portion of the available rights in return. In fact the term "license fee" hardly applies given the fact that most of these networks seek to make deals on a "for hire" basis. If one compares the deals made here in the U.S. to those overseas, they suggest that producers and creators of content are much more highly valued and they are able to retain a far greater control and proportion of the available rights. There are various strategies that can be employed to retain the largest portfolio of rights possible on behalf of producers/content creators. These strategies include delivering ideas in as much of a "turnkey" manner as possible with thorough development and casting in place as well as a production company that has a proven track record before the idea is exposed to the prospective network. Additionally, producers and content creators with sufficient relationships can seek to sell ideas overseas before they sell to a U.S. buyer. This allows them to reserve rights on the basis that the property has been tried and tested in another market and is therefore a "format."

At the end of the day, regardless of the marketplace, leverage, in the form of multiple offers, is the only sure-fire way to achieve a high-value deal.

Bradley S. Small, Partner, Bloom Hergott Diemer Rosenthal LaViolette Feldman & Goodman, LLP

Reality television is the reality of television today. Nearly half of the primetime programming currently on television is made up of variety, competition, news, and sports shows (not all of which are considered reality shows). Dealmaking in reality television, often termed "non-scripted television," is no longer the "Wild Wild West" it was termed five or so years ago. *American Idol, The Bachelor, The Amazing Race, Iron Chef, Project Runway, Paris Hilton's My New BFF, Extreme Makeover: Home Edition, Superstars of Dance,* and *Dancing With the Stars* are just a few of the reality programs on television today, whether they be network or cable shows. The stars and hosts, as well as the executive producers, of reality shows are now able to command fees equal to, and in some cases in excess of, their counterparts on scripted shows. As Lou Dobbs of CNN explained when speaking about the new homeland security reality show, if you can produce a reality show for around less than $500,000 per episode, and have people watch, while a scripted show averages about two to three million dollars per episode to produce, reality television is here to stay and become even more prominent in the television business.

David Zitzerman, Partner, Goodmans LLP

The distribution and consumption of filmed entertainment has changed considerably in recent years, and dealmaking has had to adapt and evolve to properly address the new commercial environment. With the advent of new technology and the rising importance of the Internet in our daily lives, traditional film and television audiences have fragmented. Consumers today desire to view entertainment content that they select on their own time schedule (e.g., TiVo, the Internet) and via their own preferred devices (e.g., TV, computer, cell phone, Blackberry, iPod). Feature films and TV programs routinely compete with video games and user-generated content for audience attention. Digital distribution of entertainment content (e.g., Hulu, Amazon Unbox, Joost, iTunes, YouTube, MySpace) is increasingly common. Advertising dollars that only a few years ago were devoted exclusively to film and television are now being redeployed to new media. In this new environment, the dealmaker must focus carefully on every potential source of financing and consider every possible avenue of commercial exploitation (theatrical; non-theatrical; all forms of television, including Pay, Pay Per View, and Video On Demand; home video and electronic sell-through; online and digital distribution; cellular/mobile and wireless video distribution; live attractions; video games; music, including soundtracks and ringtones; publishing; merchandising; and commercial tie-ins, etc.) to make a proper deal.

RIGHTS ACQUISITIONS AGREEMENTS

*P*roducers and studios will often uncover an existing literary property (such as a completed screenplay, book, video game, short story, stage play, or magazine article), which they hope to turn into a movie or television or multimedia production. Rather than purchasing the property outright (and paying a hefty purchase price) they will, in many cases, acquire an *option* on the property (for a fraction of the purchase cost). An option, in this context, refers to the exclusive, irrevocable right to purchase a literary property or certain specified rights in and to a literary property (such as the film and television or Internet rights) at a set price within a prescribed period of time. During the term of the option, no one else may acquire the rights to the property in question. Thus, an option enables the producer or studio to control the property for a limited time, during which it can undertake development and financing activities with respect to the property without having to incur the full expense of the purchase price. That way, the producer or studio can reduce its up-front risk and develop more properties than it would otherwise be able to if it were required to purchase every property outright.

In fact, not only producers, but directors and actors have been known to option literary properties that they discover, with the intention of producing, directing, and/or starring in a production based thereon. In most cases, the owner of the property in question (usually the writer) would prefer to have her property purchased outright rather than optioned, so that she will receive a greater payment upfront. In most cases, however, only hot properties, such as *spec scripts* involved in bidding wars or bestselling novels, will be purchased outright, since the writer will, in such cases, have the leverage to require a purchase. At times, the producer or studio may engage in an outright purchase if it is certain that the project will be produced.

THE OPTION/PURCHASE DEAL

Option Fee

The first deal point to be negotiated is the option fee. This is the only sum of money that the owner is guaranteed to receive. If the option period expires unexercised, the owner will retain not only the rights to the property, but the option payment(s) as well. There is no standard amount for an option fee, as it is subject to negotiation between the parties. Customarily, the option fee will be in the vicinity of 10 percent of the purchase price. In some cases, the writer may be willing to grant the purchaser an option for free. Technically, in such cases, the writer will grant the producer an option in exchange for "the producer's efforts in setting up the project" (such as securing financing, attaching bankable talent, and further developing the property) and "other good and valuable consideration." In order for any agreement to be technically valid under contract law, both sides must give some form of consideration (i.e., something of value, whether monetary or otherwise) to the other. Thus, some "free" option agreements may specify a nominal option fee of $1. Free options are commonly granted to independent producers or to "friends" of the owner, who may be passionate about the project, but who may not have the resources of a major studio or production company. Other times, a free option may be granted if the owner finds no other "takers" who are interested in the property. Free options are rarely granted with respect to studio deals, where option fees can range from $5,000 to as much as $100,000 for a twelve- to eighteen-month option. Generally, the amount of the option fee (as well as the purchase price) will be affected by the following factors:

* The demand for the property (for example, are other studios vying for the property?)
* The "heat" on the writer (for example, is he or she a bestselling author?)
* The relationship of the owner and purchaser (for example, do they have a preexisting relationship?)
* The resources of the purchaser (for example, is the purchaser a studio or an independent producer?)
* The length of the option period granted (generally, the lower the fee, the shorter the option)
* The type of project involved (for example, option fees for television projects will usually be lower than those for feature-length motion pictures)

Option Period

An option period is the period of time during which the purchaser may exercise the option (and purchase the property) or forfeit his rights to do so, unless he has negotiated for the right to extend the option period. The length of the option period is subject to negotiation and may range from three months to two years or longer. Most commonly, the option period is twelve to eighteen months. In many cases, the option period for a "free option" will be shorter (three to nine months), since the property is being taken off the market for little or no financial consideration. It is in the producer's interest to have as long an option period as possible, so that the producer will have more time to secure financing and undertake development activities to assess the viability of the project. Conversely, the owner of property (in most cases, the writer) will want as short an option period as possible, so that the producer will be required to make a quick decision as to whether or not the property will be produced (and to pay the purchase price!). If the option is not exercised, the owner can then try to find another buyer.

Option Extensions

In many cases, the owner will grant the purchaser the right to extend the "Initial Option Period" for an additional period (usually referred to as the "Extended Option Period") upon payment of an additional fee on or before the expiration of the preceding option. Such extensions allow the purchaser to continue to retain the exclusive right to buy the property without having to exercise the option (preferably until the purchaser is certain that the project will be produced). In some instances, the purchaser will be given more than one right of extension. Consider the following example:

- ★ Joe Producer options Jane's script for $1,000 for eighteen months.
- ★ Jane gives Joe the right to extend the option for an additional twelve months by paying Jane an additional $1,500 before the initial option period expires.
- ★ Jane gives Joe a further right to extend the extended option period for twelve more months by payment of an additional $1,500 on or before the extended option period expires.

In some cases, the owner will only allow the right to extend if certain conditions are met. For example, the owner may require language stating that the option period may be extended "only if the project is in active development" (e.g., the screenplay is being written or talent has been given a *pay-or-play* offer).

Applicability of Option Fee Against Purchase Price

Another point of negotiation is whether or not the option payment(s) will be applicable against (i.e., be deemed an advance against) the purchase price should the option be exercised. In most cases, the producer will require that at least the initial option fee be applicable against the purchase price. For example, if the initial option fee is $10,000 and the purchase price is $100,000, the producer will only owe an additional $90,000 upon purchasing the property. If one or more extended option periods are granted, it is customary that the fees paid for those extensions will not be applied to reduce the purchase price. The rationale is that the initial payment was considered "an advance" against the purchase price. However, if the producer wants to continue to hold the property off the market, but is not yet willing to purchase it, then these fees must be paid in addition to the purchase price. This structure gives the producer the incentive to exercise the option, as opposed to continually extending the option period. Typically, the option extension fee will be higher than the initial option payment, for the same reason.

Option Activities

During the option period, the producer is typically permitted to engage in all customary development activities, including preparing or submitting treatments, screenplays, or other writings based on the property, attaching talent, and securing financing. However, in accordance with the terms of almost all option agreements, commencement of principal photography will be deemed exercise of the option, and the purchase price will then become immediately due.

Suspension and Extension of the Option Period

The producer will usually include standard suspension language in the option/purchase contract specifying that the option period will be suspended and extended in the event of *force majeure* (i.e., an unexpected and disruptive event, such as an earthquake, flood, or guild strike). Under such a provision, the option period will be deemed "frozen in time" for the duration of such event. Once the event is resolved, the option period will be automatically extended by the amount of time that the event lasted. The owner will usually want to cap any extension of the option period resulting from the events of force majeure to no more than twelve months. Some producers vigorously resist this request, arguing that a true force majeure event (such as a writer's strike) will hamper a studio's business operations for the entire duration of the event (in this example, the strike). Accordingly, the producer will maintain that any "cap" on extending the option is unfair. Sometimes, the two sides will compromise by agreeing to set a limit on extensions due to certain events of force majeure (e.g., weather-related events) and not others (e.g., work stoppages). The contract may include similar language allowing a suspension and extension of the option period in the event of a third-party claim against the property (i.e., if another party challenges the owner's rights to the property). If the claim is not resolved within twelve months, the owner may request the right to rescind the agreement and require the purchaser to refund any monies received.

Set-Up Bonus

In some cases, usually when the option was free or acquired for a relatively modest sum, the owner will request a *set-up bonus.* A set-up bonus is an additional fee payable if the purchaser enters into an agreement for the development or production of the property with a studio, financier, or production company or, in the case of a television movie or series, a television network. Clearly, set-up bonuses are often appropriate in instances where the purchaser is an independent producer. This is because independent producers frequently option properties at below-market prices, with the promise of a bonus in the event that a major studio takes on the project. Studios and networks frequently option materials directly, making a set-up bonus inapplicable. Sometimes, when the producer agrees to such a bonus, she will require that the option period be automatically extended for an additional period upon payment of such bonus. The producer will usually want the bonus to be applicable against the purchase price, while the writer will resist this position. This issue is subject to negotiation between the parties, and the final terms will vary from deal to deal.

Purchase Price

The purchase price, in most cases, is negotiated simultaneously with the option terms, since in order to exercise the option, the purchase price must be paid. It must be noted that an option agreement without an agreed-upon purchase price merely buys the purchaser the right to haggle with the owner in the future. If the purchaser desires to acquire the property upon the expiration of the option, the owner will possess an inordinate amount of leverage, as he can refuse to sell the property unless his price is met. The purchaser, therefore, will be in an extremely vulnerable position. If, for example, such purchaser offered a reasonable purchase price of $100,000, the owner could, in theory, refrain from selling unless he receives $200,000. Therefore, at least from the purchaser's perspective, it is necessary to negotiate the purchase price up front as part of the option/purchase agreement.

The purchase price will be due and payable upon exercise of the option, if ever, and is usually accompanied by a written notice of exercise. It should be noted that if the agreement were an outright purchase agreement (rather than an option agreement), the purchase price would be payable upon signature of the agreement, and the purchaser would immediately become the owner of the requisite rights. The purchase agreement will contain all of the terms discussed below relating to option agreements; the only difference is that the option provisions discussed above will not be included.

There is no set formula for determining a purchase price. The WGA doesn't set option prices, although it does set minimum purchase prices for acquiring original screenplays, which are currently in the range of $45,000 to $90,000 (depending on the anticipated budget of the production). In some cases, the owner will request that the purchase price of the property be "tied to" the budget of the film. For example, the owner may request that the purchase price be equal to a percentage (usually between 1.5 and 3 percent) of the final budget (usually with limited customary exclusions from the budget, such as bond, contingency, and overhead). However, in order to ensure that the purchase price meets certain monetary minimums, the owner will often request a *floor* (i.e., a minimum price). For example: "Owner will receive 2 percent of the budget upon exercise of the option, with a floor of $150,000." The producer will usually request a *ceiling* (a maximum price) to protect against situations in which the budget spirals out of control (like the budget for the motion picture *Titanic*). Even when the purchase price is tied to the final "approved" budget, a ceiling may be appropriate in the case of a mega-budget film.

Contingent Compensation

The owner of a literary property will usually request a profit participation. Customarily, the purchaser will grant a net profit participation, usually 5 percent of net proceeds. In addition, the owner may request box office bonuses payable at such time, if ever, as the picture generates a particular level of theatrical box office gross receipts. These points are subject to negotiation between the parties and will vary from deal to deal.

Credit

If the optioned property is an existing screenplay, the credit will generally be determined in accordance with the WGA Agreement (assuming that the production is subject to WGA jurisdiction). In general, the WGA Agreement requires credit to appear in the main titles, on a separate card, in a size of type equal to that of the director and producer, and in paid advertisements. If the production is non-guild, or the acquired property is not a screenplay (e.g., a book, article, play, etc.), all aspects of credit will need to be specifically negotiated. Screenplay credit is discussed in greater detail in chapter 3.

If the optioned property is a book or short story, and the picture has the same title as the property, credit will usually be in the form of: "Based upon the {book}{short story} by _____." If the title of the picture is different from that of the property, it would be: "Based upon the {book} {short story} '_____' by _____."

Grant of Rights

The option/purchase agreement must stipulate the rights that are being sold. For example, the purchaser may purchase all rights in and to the property or limited rights, such as the film and television rights. In some cases, certain rights may have already been exploited, and thus, only limited rights may remain available for sale. The precise description of the rights granted to the purchaser will depend on the work in question and the nature of the project to be produced. The producer will typically require certain subsidiary and ancillary rights, such as the right to publish synopses of the work for the purpose of promotion or advertising and the right to merchandise elements of the work. These days, most purchasers are careful to specifically include all Internet and digital rights (including mobile) with respect to advertising and promotion of the proposed production in such new media. In most option agreements, there is a catch-all: "in all media now known or hereafter . . ."

Reserved Rights

In many cases, the writer will attempt to reserve (i.e., retain) certain rights. If the optioned property is a book, the owner will almost always withhold the print publication rights (a must if the book is already published!). Similarly, if the underlying property is a play, the owner will ask to reserve live stage rights. Generally, when agreeing to option an original spec screenplay, a book, or a play, most owners will negotiate to retain the customarily reserved rights: print publication, live stage, radio, and live television, as further discussed below.

Print Publication Rights

The owner will, in most cases, ask to retain the right to publish and distribute print editions of the property in book form, as well as in magazines and other periodicals, including the right to publish the book in the form of a CD-ROM, DVD, videocassette, audiotape, or e-book. The retention of these rights is obviously essential if the property is a book (as opposed to a screenplay or stage play). Many producers are careful to limit the definition of such electronic media as inclusive of "text only," as opposed to interactive games on CD-ROM or on the Internet. Film studios will often want to acquire exclusive interactive rights, so that they can market games based on the film without competing products on the market. Recently, there has been an increase in the amount of negotiation necessary to clarify the definition of print publication rights as opposed to digital or media rights. Book publishers have become more aggressive in the agreements they enter into with authors, particularly first-time authors, and often seek broad rights in such print publication agreements. While most publishers have not gone so far as to attempt to acquire television or motion picture rights, it is not uncommon for studios to discover that the publisher's definition of "print" rights conflicts with the studio's definition of media rights in some respects. Frequently, the author's representatives will attempt to persuade the studio's lawyers to negotiate such issues directly with the book publisher. In any event, the purchaser will usually require the right to publish excerpts of the property for advertising and promotional purposes. Such rights will generally be limited to 7,500 to 10,000 words.

Author-Written Sequels

An author-written sequel is a literary property containing one or more of the characters appearing in the original property and whose plot is substantially different from that of the original property. In the case of an optioned book, for example, an author will usually insist upon reserving the right to write sequels. The purchaser will usually agree, provided that the author does not use any of the new characters or characterizations created specifically for the motion picture. Also, such rights will usually be subject to a holdback period (i.e., the author will not be permitted to exploit these rights until a specified date, usually five years from the first general release in the United States or seven years after the date of the exercise of the option, whichever is earlier). These rights are separate from the producer's right to make sequel films based upon the work that he has produced.

Live Dramatic Stage Rights

This is essentially the right to perform the property or adaptations thereof on stage. Up until five years ago, it was extremely common for studios to grant these rights to the author (or the creator of the work). Most major studios were not involved in the production of stage plays (other than in limited circumstances, such as outdoor amphitheater performances at theme parks). However, with the successes of *Beauty and the Beast* and *Shrek the Musical* on Broadway, studios have been less willing to part with these stage rights. The disposition of stage rights can lead to very intense negotiations, with some studios refusing to budge and insisting on retaining these rights. A skilled agent or attorney may be able to secure a "separate-pot" royalty for her client out of revenues that may be generated by the studio's exploitation of stage-play rights. In those instances where these rights are granted, the original rights-holder will be required to agree that he will refrain from broadcasting, telecasting, streaming, or recording the performance. These rights will usually be similarly subject to a holdback period.

Radio Rights

The right to broadcast the property (such as the reading of a play) on a radio by sound only may be granted, subject to the producer's right to advertise the property on radio.

First Negotiation / Last Refusal

The producer/purchaser will often demand the *right of first negotiation* with respect to any of the reserved rights. Essentially, this means that the producer will have the right to enter into good faith negotiations with the owner with respect to the acquisition of the reserved rights at such time as she is ready to sell. In addition, the purchaser may ask for a right of *last refusal* (also known as a "matching right), which gives the purchaser the right to match any other offer that the owner may be willing to accept.

Consider the following example:

Owner A wishes to sell the film rights to a sequel she's written to her novel. She approaches Purchaser B to enter into negotiations. No deal is reached because Owner A is insisting on a hefty price of $1 million. Subsequently, Owner A receives an offer of $600,000 from another party and wishes to accept. Before accepting such offer, Owner A must first give Purchaser B the opportunity to acquire the rights at that same price.

In many cases, an owner will agree to grant the right of first negotiation, but will attempt to knock out any right of last refusal. This is because such a right can hamper the owner's ability to negotiate the sale of the property to a third party. If the third party knows that there is a chance that any negotiation may be fruitless should the original purchaser decide to exercise its right of last refusal, the third party may not bother attempting to acquire the property.

In any event, if the optioned property is a spec screenplay and the deal comes under WGA jurisdiction, the *Separation of Rights* provision of the WGA Agreement will bestow certain reserved rights upon the owner, as discussed in greater detail in chapter 3.

Writing Services

In cases where the optioned property is a screenplay, the owner will want to ensure that she is guaranteed the right to perform specified writing services on the property (and be paid for such services). If the project falls within WGA jurisdiction, the writer of an original screenplay will be guaranteed the right to perform the first rewrite at a fee of no less than WGA minimum (see chapter 3 for a more detailed discussion of separation of rights). If the project does not fall under WGA jurisdiction, the writer will have to specifically negotiate for this right.

Even in cases where the optioned property is a book or stage play, the owner may insist on the right to adapt such novel or play for film or television. If the owner has no experience writing scripts, the purchaser may be reluctant to grant the owner's request. In some cases, the purchaser may allow the owner to write the first draft, provided that the owner understands that she can be replaced after that step.

In most cases, the purchaser will insist that the writing fees be applicable against the purchase price of the property. Although this is negotiable, such practice is generally accepted.

It is important to note that whether or not the option is ultimately exercised, all writing services will be deemed to be a *work-for-hire,* and thus owned by the purchaser (see chapter 3). Thus, if the option is not exercised and the owner wishes to sell the material to a third party, she would be permitted to sell the original property that was optioned, but she could not sell any of the subsequently written material based on the property. Many owners or owner representatives will, therefore, request a right of *reversion* with respect to any rewrites, in the event that the option lapses. If the producer agrees, the rights in and to any rewrites commissioned by the producer will revert back to the owner, usually subject to a lien in an amount equal to the sums paid by the initial purchaser for such writing services.

Warranties

The purchaser will typically insist that the owner make certain representations and warranties about the property and her rights with respect thereto. Essentially, the purchaser will want to be sure that the owner owns all the rights she is purporting to sell. Customary warranty provisions may read as follows:

★ The writer is the sole and exclusive owner of the property and has the unrestricted right and power to sell and assign the rights to the producer.

★ The property is wholly original with the writer, and no part thereof is taken or copied from any other source except for public domain material.

★ Neither the property, nor its use in any form, adaptation, or version, does or will infringe any copyright, literary, dramatic, or common law rights of any person, firm, or corporation nor, to the best of the writer's knowledge, in any way defames, libels, or invades the privacy of a person, firm, or corporation.

★ None of the rights herein sold and assigned to the producer have been sold, assigned, licensed, or otherwise transferred to any other person, firm, or corporation.

★ The writer will not take any action that would interfere with the producer's enjoyment of the rights.

The purchaser will prefer that the warranties above are absolute, while the writer will want many of them to be subject to the writer's best knowledge. That way, if the writer, in good faith and acting reasonably, believed that she did not defame or libel anyone, she will not be held liable.

First Right of Negotiation for Subsequent Productions

In the case of the sale of an existing screenplay, the owner will likely want to ensure her participation in any subsequent productions based on the property, such as remakes, sequels, or productions in other media. Thus, the owner will usually request that she be offered the first opportunity to render writing services on subsequent productions. The producer will likely agree, provided that the owner is at that time a professional writer in the applicable medium. In most cases, the compensation for such services will be subject to good faith negotiation at such future time, with the current deal often serving as a floor (or starting point) for such negotiations.

Passive Payments/Royalties

If the property is not a script or the owner is not guaranteed to be engaged to render writing services on the subsequent production, she will often request customary passive payments as follows:

In the event that a theatrical sequel is produced, the writer will usually receive an amount equal to 50 percent of her compensation (usually fixed and contingent compensation) under the original deal. In the case of a theatrical remake, the writer will generally receive a sum totaling one-third of the compensation paid under the original agreement. Royalties often will also be paid to the owner upon exploitation of other types of productions, such as television series and series *spin-offs*.

Reversion

The owner will often request the right to reacquire her property in the event that the purchaser does not produce a motion picture, television film, or series (as applicable) based on the property within a certain, negotiated time period (usually between three to seven years from the date the rights were acquired). That way, the owner can try to set the project up with another producer or studio. The purchaser may grant a right of reversion subject to the owner repaying the purchaser all sums that had previously been paid to the owner by the purchaser, with interest. In some cases, the studio may request a percentage of future profits as well. If the property is a screenplay and the owner is entitled to separation of rights, she will be entitled to a right of reacquisition, as discussed further in chapter 3.

Consultation/Approval Rights

Most owners of literary property will not receive consultation or approval rights over creative aspects of the film or television project (such as the cast, the director, or the screenplay), since the purchaser will not want to be restricted. However, certain high-level authors, such as John Grisham or Tom Clancy, may refuse to part with the rights to their books unless they are afforded a certain degree of control over the creative aspects of the film or television production based upon their work.

Miscellaneous

The owner of the property will likely request that she receive a DVD or Blu-Ray copy of the finished film or television movie. In addition, she might ask for a copy of the soundtrack and an invitation to the premiere plus reimbursement for expenses incurred in connection with her attendance at such premiere. The purchaser will likely agree to guarantee the owner an invitation to the premiere, but may or may not agree to provide expenses. The owner will also usually demand to be included on the purchaser's E & O and general liability insurance policies.

Optioning Books or Stage Plays

In addition to the issues discussed above, certain unique factors come into play when the optioned property is a book or stage play rather than a screenplay. It is important to note that the WGA does not cover the writing of books, articles, or plays, and thus some of the protections afforded to screenwriters optioning or selling their screenplays to a guild signatory will not apply. For example, all reserved rights, as well as royalties, passive payments, and issues of reversion, must be specifically negotiated by such playwrights and novelists.

Book authors can also negotiate for "bestseller bonuses" (i.e., additional sums payable if and when the book is listed on the *New York Times* bestseller list or some other specified list). Playwrights sometimes negotiate for bonuses based on their winning awards, such as the Tony Award. In addition, renowned book authors or playwrights may be able to negotiate for possessory credit. Examples include *Bram Stroker's Dracula* and *Wes Craven's Nightmare on Elm Street*.

Finally, it is important to note that most purchasers will require that the book option agreement be accompanied by a ***publisher's release,*** to be executed by the book publisher. This release acknowledges that the publisher does not own the film, television, or specified ancillary rights in and to the book and ensures that the purchaser is free to exploit such rights.

Short-Form Option and Assignment

Option agreements are usually accompanied by a short-form option and short–form assignment. These are one- or two-page forms that acknowledge the transfer of rights and are usually filed with the U.S. Copyright Office by the purchaser upon the exercise of the option. In the event that the long-form agreement remains unsigned, the purchaser will rely on the signed short-form option and assignment.

Applicability of Collective Bargaining Agreement

As with all entertainment industry agreements, it is important to determine whether or not the applicable guild agreement applies. As mentioned earlier, in the case of option/purchase agreements, if the underlying work being optioned is a screenplay, the agreement may fall under WGA jurisdiction if the purchaser is a signatory or if the parties agree to be contractually bound by such terms. If not, the terms generally addressed by the WGA Agreement will have to be specifically negotiated.

"Shopping" or "Attachment" Agreements

Sometimes instead of optioning a property, an independent producer will request and be granted the exclusive right to "shop" it (whether it is a completed screenplay or an underlying property, like a book) to "buyers" (such as studios, networks, production companies, or other financiers) for a limited period of time to see if they can get the project "set up." The producer, in this case, will not have the exclusive right to get people interested, and if this happens, the "Shopping" agreement will require that he or she be attached to the project as a producer (and in some cases, in other capacities as well).

LIFE STORY RIGHTS AGREEMENTS

Screenwriters often want to write scripts about "real life" stories involving "real life" individuals, and producers commonly make films about such people and events. Such writers and producers will usually need to obtain the rights to the depicted individual's "life story" or, alternatively, be extremely careful not to infringe on the rights of a subject who did not consent to be depicted in the writer's work. The first amendment may allow certain works to be created without the purchase of story rights, as long as the materials used are considered part of the public record (such as newspaper articles or court transcripts). However, in many cases, the portrayed individual may be able to make a valid claim against the writer or producer for defamation, violation of that person's right of publicity, invasion of privacy, or unfair competition. Even if the depicted person does not have a valid claim, it may, nevertheless, be beneficial to obtain her life rights in order to obtain her cooperation in developing the story. Each of these types of claims will be discussed briefly below.

Defamation

There are two types of defamation: *libel,* which is the publication of defamatory matter by written or printed word (such as a screenplay), and *slander,* which is the issuance of defamatory spoken words or gestures. According to the Restatement of Torts, in order to be defamatory, the communication must "tend" to hurt the reputation of the individual, so as to lower her in the eyes of the community or to deter others from associating with her. Such communications would be likely to expose the individual to "hatred, ridicule, and contempt." It should be noted that it is not necessary that the portrayed individual be named. It is sufficient that reasonable people would be able to identify the person in question.

Defenses to Defamation

Truth is an absolute defense to defamation. Thus, a screenwriter may publish a defamatory statement about an actual person (even with malicious intent) if the statement is true and accurate. In addition, it is important to note that one cannot defame a deceased individual. Defamation and right of privacy actions are personal rights and cannot be asserted by the heirs of the deceased. Thus, a writer can write or say whatever she wishes about a deceased individual, and that individual's heirs will have no remedy under the laws of defamation or right of privacy (discussed below).

Additionally, it is important to note that a story about a public person will be held to a different standard than that for a private citizen. If the defamatory communication refers to a "public figure," such as a rock star, a public official, or other individual who steps voluntarily into the public light, the depicted public figure must not only show that the statements were false, but must also prove that they were made with "actual malice" (i.e., the communication in question was known to be false or was made with reckless disregard to its truth). In some cases, it may be questionable as to whether the depicted person falls within the category of a "public figure" (for example, if the individual in question is the spouse of a public figure). Such concerns should be discussed with a seasoned entertainment attorney.

Another possible defense to an alleged defamatory statement is that it is a statement of opinion. Statements of opinion are permitted, provided that they do not contain specific facts that can be proven to be false. Likewise, insults and epithets are generally not considered defamatory and are viewed as outbursts of emotion. A defamed individual may seek both actual damages and punitive damages.

Right of Privacy

Unlike defamation, the right of privacy does not require injury to one's reputation. Rather, this action concerns the right to live one's life in seclusion without unwanted publicity. Right of privacy actions typically fall into one the following two categories.

Public Disclosure of Private Facts

According to the Restatement of Torts, one who makes public a matter concerning the private life of another is subject to liability to the other for the invasion of her privacy if the matter is of a kind that (1) would be highly offensive to a reasonable person, and (2) is not of legitimate concern to the public (i.e., the facts are not newsworthy). The scope of the right of privacy for public figures is restricted, since they have voluntarily placed themselves in the public eye. It is important to note that, unlike defamation, truth is not a defense to a privacy claim. Consent or constitutional privilege (such as when First Amendment speech issues come into play, e.g., the freedom to disseminate newsworthy information), however, are valid defenses. Like defamation, the right of privacy does not survive death (i.e., the estate of the deceased individual may not sue for a violation of her right of privacy).

False Light
This course of action relates to publicity that casts an individual in a false light. The plaintiff in such a case must show that material and objectionable false facts have been published that place the individual in a false light, hurting her feelings.

Defenses to Right to Privacy Claims
Unlike defamation, truth is not a defense to invasion of either of the privacy claims. Defenses to such false light claims include that constitutional privilege (such as most news reporting) and newsworthy statements are not actionable unless they have been made with intentional or reckless disregard for the truth.

Right of Publicity
The right of publicity is the right of an individual to control the use of one's name and likeness for commercial purposes. It gives the individual the exclusive right to license the use of her identity for commercial promotion. These types of claims don't typically arise in connection with a screenplay, but may arise in connection with the exploitation of such screenplay. Unlike defamation or the right of privacy, the right of publicity survives death if the individual has exploited her name or likeness during her lifetime so that an estate may pursue such claims (for example, the recent Jimi Hendrix case).

Making the Deal
Life rights agreements can be structured as outright purchase agreements, but more commonly take the form of option/purchase deals (for the same reasons discussed earlier with respect to books, plays, and existing screenplays). The agreement resembles the option of fictional literary material, except that the property in question is a life story.

Option Fee and Purchase Price
The option and purchase prices for life rights vary dramatically, depending upon the notoriety of the individual in question and her story. The life-story

rights for a famous individual could attract a fee of up to $1 million. Generally, purchase prices for life rights in connection with feature films will fall within the range of $100,000 to $250,000. For television projects, the range is usually $25,000 to $100,000. The option price is usually in the range of 10 percent of the purchase price (subject to the factors discussed in the Option/Purchase section above). In some instances, the individual may agree to grant a free option in consideration for the producer's efforts in setting up the property. Individuals selling their life-story rights will sometimes negotiate for a "consulting fee," either in addition to or in lieu of other compensation. Such owners may also negotiate for contingent compensation, such as a percentage of net profits and/or box office bonuses based on the success of the film.

Rights Granted

One of the key points of negotiation is the nature and extent of the rights granted. It should be noted that a life story may be divided and sold in parts, as opposed to in its entirety. For example, a producer may purchase the right to depict an individual from ages thirty to forty-five only. In addition, the rights may be restricted to one medium (for example, a life-rights holder may authorize a feature film only), as opposed to all media. Similarly, the rights to subsequent productions, such as sequels, remakes, or television series, as well as the acquisition of merchandising rights must also be negotiated. The purchaser will likely want as broad a grant as possible, while the owner may insist upon retaining certain rights, such as the print publication rights (so that she will have the opportunity to write her autobiography or hire someone to write her story). As mentioned previously, given the expansion of new media exploitation, purchasers want and need digital and Internet rights. Of course, such matters are subject to negotiation in each instance.

Consultation/Materials

Life-story agreements usually include the owner's promise to provide additional information and materials, as well as assistance in obtaining information or releases from relatives or friends who might be depicted in the story.

Fictionalization

The purchaser will also generally require the right to fictionalize or dramatize the individual's story to any extent desired by the purchaser. In some cases, depending on the owner's leverage, the owner may request (and may be granted) limited or complete approval rights over the story. Purchasers are clearly reluctant to grant such language, but certain individuals, such as Hugh

Hefner, are likely to receive approval over the treatment (i.e., story outline) and the selection of the screenwriter, although it is rare that any individual is granted approval over the final screenplay. In some cases, the owner will be able to negotiate for the right to determine whether the program will be billed as "based on a true story" or as a "dramatized account."

Representations and Warranties

The purchaser will, of course, insist that the depicted party warrant that she will not bring any claim against the purchaser in connection with the purchaser's use of her life story, specifically including claims based on defamation, invasion of privacy, or the right of publicity (discussed above). The owner will also typically be required to warrant that she has not previously assigned her life-story rights to any other party and that the information she provides does not defame or infringe upon the rights of any other individual.

Assignment

The purchaser will request the nonrestricted right to assign the life rights agreement to a third party. The owner will likely agree to this, provided that the purchaser remains secondarily liable for all payment obligations.

Depiction Release

Finally, the purchaser will require the owner to sign a standard *depiction release* and use reasonable efforts to obtain other third-party depiction releases for others briefly depicted in the film. The producer or studio will want a depiction release signed by anyone depicted in the story, no matter how briefly. (A sample depiction release appears in the back of this book.)

In sum, it is preferable to obtain a life-rights agreement when writing a screenplay based on someone's life story. However, when this is not possible, another option is to fictionalize the story. When fictionalizing, it is important to include an express disclaimer stating that the events and characters portrayed are fictional and that any similarity to actual persons, living or deceased, is entirely coincidental. In addition, as mentioned earlier, if the individual in question is deceased, the need to obtain her life rights generally no longer exists (provided such statements don't defame or otherwise infringe the rights of any living relatives of the deceased). Similarly, if the depicted individual is a public figure, there is less of a need to obtain her life rights, as the burden of proof to establish defamation or invasion of privacy is higher. In any event, one should consult with an experienced entertainment attorney about the risks involved in proceeding without obtaining a life-rights agreement.

Deal Point Summary:
OPTION/PURCHASE AGREEMENTS[1]

1. Option versus Outright Purchase
- Option Term/Fee
- Option Extension(s) Term/Fee/Conditions to Extend
- Applicability of Option Fee(s)
- Force Majeure/Claims
- Option Period Activities

2. Setup Bonus

3. Purchase Price
- Percent of Budget (floor/ceiling) versus Set Amount
- Contingent Compensation

4. Credit

5. Rights Conveyed

6. Rights Reserved

7. Writing Services—Fees

8. Warranties and Indemnities

9. Subsequent Productions
- First Opportunity to Write
- Passive Payments/Royalties

10. Reversion

11. Consultation and Approval Rights

12. Miscellaneous
- Premiere Invitations
- VHS/DVD copies
- E & O

13. Guild Applicability (Separation of Rights)

14. Short Form Option and Assignment

15. Book Publisher's Release

16. Bestseller/Tony Award Bonuses

---

[1]The deal point summaries in each chapter are intended to be used when coming up with a "game plan" for a particular negotiation. These lists serve as bullet-point reminders of issues to think about when strategizing prior to a negotiation, or to actually inquire about and discuss when negotiating or reviewing a proposal. Once the book is read thoroughly, the reader can refer to the summary to serve as a reminder of issues that need to be covered.

FEATURE WRITER EMPLOYMENT DEALS

*W*riter employment agreements are both the simplest and most prevalent types of industry agreements. They are so prevalent because practically every project begins with a script. As many writers like to point out, you cannot make a movie without a script (at least not a very good one!). Even in cases where the studio or producer purchases or options an existing screenplay, it will usually still hire a writer to perform one or more rewrites or polishes. Moreover, many projects never graduate from the *development stage* to reach a point where a producer, director, or actors need to be employed. Thus, any studio executive, independent producer, or entertainment attorney will likely see an overwhelming number of writer deals relative to any other single type of agreement.

Writer employment agreements are the simplest for two principal reasons. First, the entertainment industry has traditionally placed writers at the very bottom of the Hollywood hierarchy. Producers sometimes view writers as "fungible," or easily replaceable, and as a result, producers are often more reluctant to negotiate provisions outside the norm or the standard terms that typically govern writer agreements (except for very successful players). As one successful writer once said, "In Hollywood, the word 'writers' is always used in the plural, as in, 'I can always get more writers.'"

Additionally, in attempting to protect writers, their union, the Writers Guild of America (WGA), has comprehensively regulated most of the issues relating to the engagement of writers. For example, unlike producer or actor deals, the WGA Agreement governs credit provisions to such an extent that negotiations relating to credit (both on-screen and in printed advertising) are basically unnecessary. In fact, the WGA Agreement is sufficiently comprehensive to address not only credit, but writing fees, residuals, royalties, and reacquisition of materials (all explained below), as well as many other issues. Consequently, there are typically fewer issues to negotiate when hiring (or representing) a writer than there are in most other types of industry agreements.

However, it must be noted that even the WGA Agreement does not cover its member writers in all instances. For example, animation and low-budget, made-for-Internet productions are not yet regulated by the WGA (although the WGA is hard at work in its attempt to cover these areas). More importantly, not all writers are members of the WGA, nor are all production companies or studios signatory to the WGA Agreement, and thus bound by its regulations. Non-guild writers, however, can avail themselves of the protections offered by the WGA when contracting with entities that are *producer-signatories* to the Agreement, such as the major studios.

In any event, the WGA merely establishes *minimums* (financial and otherwise) and does not prevent its members from negotiating for provisions that surpass the minimum requirements set forth in the Agreement. Successful industry writers, for example, will often be able to negotiate for additional compensation and perks above and beyond WGA minimums in their studio writing assignment deals. This chapter will include a discussion of those types of deals, as well as the unique pitfalls relating to non-WGA writing deals.

MAKING THE DEAL

Most screenplay writing agreements include a number of standard provisions, regardless of the dollars involved. When negotiating these types of agreements, the dealmaker will confront the following issues.

Contingencies (a.k.a. Preconditions or Conditions Precedent)

The studio or producer will often insist that, before any of its obligations (most importantly, paying the writer) become legally binding, one or more conditions must be satisfied. The most common examples are set forth below.

Satisfactory Creative Meeting

A producer or studio will usually require that a satisfactory creative meeting take place early on in the development process in order to assess the writer's "take" on the project. Many studio executives have been faced with the following unpleasant situation:

A hot writer suddenly has a window of availability (an outside project fell through or certain rights could not be acquired). The studio executive sees this as an opportunity to engage the writer on one of his projects and insists that an offer to the writer be made promptly. The executive knows that if he delays, the writer might get snapped up by a competing studio or even get hired on a competing project within the executive's own studio. The writer accepts the offer (after heated negotiations, of course). Finally, the writer arrives at the executive's office to discuss the project. The executive is aghast to learn that the writer envisions this project as an edgy art house film, while the executive believes it to be a comedy along the lines of *American Pie*.

The conflicting visions described in the above situation are usually referred to as "creative differences." In an attempt to minimize the danger of the above scenario, studios and most independent producers often include language in agreements (not only for writers, but for directors and producers as well) explicitly stating that the employment agreement is subject to a satisfactory creative meeting between the studio chief (or applicable executive or producer) and the individual being hired.

Fortunately, this meeting usually happens very early in the creative process. Consequently, by the time the producer or the producer's lawyer sends out a draft of the agreement, this meeting is likely to have taken place, and upon request, the studio lawyer can acknowledge in the employment contract that this condition has been met.

Satisfaction of Chain of Title or Acquisition of Underlying Material

In instances where the writer's work is not based entirely upon her (or the producer's or studio executive's) original idea, the studio will justifiably insist that the deal cannot take effect until the studio acquires the rights to any and all **underlying material** that relates to the project. These materials can include book rights, life-story rights, rights to trademarked articles or names, etc. These underlying rights are required in order to satisfy the **chain of title** requirements. The chain of title refers to the history of ownership interest in a property, typically literary property, such as a screenplay. In order for studios to commit to millions of dollars in funds to exploit any property, it will want to ensure that the property has a "clean" chain of title (i.e., there are no potential owners or partial owners that can claim any proprietary interest in and to the property). Potential issues muddying up a chain of title include real-life individuals portrayed in a screenplay or past financiers of a motion-picture project that have not legally and fully released all claims to such property.

For example, the motion picture *Shine,* distributed by Fine Line Features, was based on the life of pianist David Helfgott, who is still living (if the person depicted is deceased, different issues come into play). The chain of title for this picture would include a signed release from Mr. Helfgott authorizing the filmmakers to depict him and use his name in the film. Producers typically purchase E & O (errors and omissions) insurance in order to minimize the risks associated with a defect in the chain of title. E & O policies are discussed in greater detail at the end of this chapter.

Note: While chapter 2 deals with the gamut of rights acquisitions, including the option to purchase or the outright acquisition of an existing (i.e., already written) screenplay, this chapter deals solely with the employment of writers to create a screenplay (or render rewrite services) as a work-for-hire on behalf of the studio or hiring entity. Such entity will not only control all exploitation rights to the screenplay, but will actually own the copyright. Under U.S. copyright law, a "work made for hire" is deemed to be owned by the hiring party. Chapter 2, dealing with the purchase of existing material, addresses the nuances of copyright law and the range of rights that may be acquired. However, when dealing with the hiring of writers, in all but the rarest of deals, ownership of the copyright in the writer's work is not negotiable. The studio might pay dearly for the copyright, but will insist on retaining complete ownership, subject to the WGA Agreement's Separation of Rights provision, which is discussed later in this chapter.

Concluding Other Deals Related to the Project

While most projects originate with the engagement of a writer or acquisition of a script (as described above), it is not uncommon for studios to hire a producer, director, or actor at the same time that the writer is hired. For example, a producer might discover a talented writer with a clever idea to pitch to the studio. The producer will bring her contacts and experience to bear, while the writer contributes the idea or written material. Thus, the studio is presented with this package, comprising both a writer and producer. Alternatively, a writer will already have found an A-level actor who is interested in playing a character in the script. In those instances, a studio might engage the writer on the condition that, for example, Susan Sarandon formally commits to the project. The project, on its own, may not be attractive enough to the studio, unless the star is involved. Similarly, there are instances where a director finds a particular script appealing, and that particular director represents a critical element that attracts the studio's attention.

In these instances, a studio might insist that before the writer is engaged to write a screenplay (in the case of a pitch) or rewrite a script (in the case of an existing screenplay or outline), the studio must first conclude agreements with other talent. While technically this is an issue open to negotiation, the leverage usually weighs heavily in favor of one or the other party. If the writer is relatively inexperienced, and the studio's interest was piqued primarily by some independent element (such as the interest of an A-level star), the studio is unlikely to agree to waive this particular condition. On the other hand, if the writer's idea or material was the subject of a bidding war by other studios or independent producers, the studio might agree to engage the writer without having firm commitments from third parties.

Miscellaneous

Other customary conditions include the requirement that the writer execute (i.e., sign) her employment agreement or, at a minimum, a short-form certificate of authorship, as well as provide the studio or producer with the appropriate IRS documentation.

Compensation and Services

Not surprisingly, this is the first item of discussion for any agent, manager, business affairs executive, writer, or producer. How much money does the writer need to be paid, and will the writer trade upfront cash *(fixed compensation)* for a profit participation or other deferred compensation *(contingent compensation)*?

The key factors relevant to this negotiation are as follows:

★ **WGA** *minimums*—For films falling within WGA jurisdiction, there are certain "floors" or **minimum prices** that must be paid for feature writing services. For a high-budget film (i.e., one with a budget of $5 million or more), the minimum is currently in the area of $110,000 for an original screenplay (including a treatment), approximately $30,000 for a rewrite, and about $15,000 for a polish. Low-budget films are those with a budget below $5 million and call for reduced minimum compensation for writers. First-time or relatively unknown writers will usually receive no more than scale payments; however, those minimums are often surpassed for experienced writers. Non-guild writers are obviously not guaranteed these minimum fees unless they are contracting with a guild-signatory producer, but such writers can nevertheless try to tie their fees to WGA minimums, or at least make use of the WGA minimums as guidelines when negotiating their deals.

★ **The writer's** *quote*—What the writer has been paid in the (preferably recent) past for the same or similar work will sometimes be the most crucial determinant in figuring out what to pay a writer (as well as what the writer and her representatives will feel is appropriate to accept). There are times, however, when a quote will have limited value. For example, when a relatively unknown writer is nominated for or wins an Academy Award or Golden Globe Award, her agents will never allow this client to work for her prior quote, as her value will have increased significantly as a result of the prestige associated with such a nomination or award. Other times, a writer has no quotes at all, or none that is easily applicable to the current assignment (for instance, the writer has written three television movies, but no theatrical movies, or written episodes of various television sitcoms, but no feature-length projects, etc.) As a general rule, the writer's quote is usually the floor or starting point for negotiations on the current assignment, subject to the other factors discussed herein.

★ **The nature of the particular assignment**—The writer's fee will usually depend, to a large extent, on the type of project being negotiated (e.g., whether the project is a big-budget summer blockbuster or a small independent film), as well as the history of deals made by the particular studio. For example, assuming Miramax Pictures can successfully argue that it has never paid any writer more than $200,000, a writer engaged to create a script for Miramax might agree to a reduction in her typical fee. Similarly, if the writer has an emotional attachment to a project or is eager to work with a particular producer or director who notoriously makes only low-budget films, the writer may be willing to work for a lower sum. One of the related issues to consider is the size of the intended budget for the film. If the budget is low, it will be more difficult for the writer to secure a high writing fee. Conversely, if the budget is high, the writer can more easily argue that she should receive her due share.

★ **The "heat" (or lack thereof) surrounding the particular writer**— A writer's compensation may also be affected by the success (or lack thereof) of his past projects and his recognition among those in the industry. An established writer may have had a run of bad luck, writing several flops over the past years. Alternatively, a writer may have even taken herself out of the market intentionally, in order to pursue personal or other professional interests. In such cases, there may be a perception in the industry that the writer's value has diminished, in which case a writer may be forced to work below her quote (with the only alternative being to refuse the assignment). Conversely, a relatively inexperienced writer may have recently sold a number of screenplays, treatments, or even pitches and suddenly finds herself to be in great demand. Similarly, she may have recently won a writing award or perhaps been mentioned in an article quoting Jim Carrey or Julia Roberts stating that this young writer is the "most talented writer to hit Hollywood in ten years." Whatever the source of the heat, if a writer is considered hot, a studio will be forced to pay a higher price to secure that writer's services.

In addition to the above, various other considerations unique to each particular situation will play a role in any given negotiation. Once the business affairs executive or the producer has considered all these factors and determined a number that he perceives as fair, another important question arises: Should the negotiator offer the number that he wants to "close the deal" at or something lower, allowing room for negotiation? If the latter proves to be a good strategy, how low can the initial offer be without risking insult to the other party?

Consider the following scenario: Jane Writer was hired one month ago by Warner Bros. to write an animated film for fixed compensation in the amount of $325,000. Paramount now wants to hire Jane to write a big-budget, live-action science-fiction film. In such a case, the Paramount executive might not be able to offer $250,000 with a straight face. The Paramount picture is seemingly higher-profile than the WB picture, and it would be hard to justify an offer so much lower than Jane's recent deal. Although there might be other considerations, the executive might feel that it would be unreasonable to offer even a penny less than $325,000, the precise amount of Jane's quote. As the negotiations progress, the Paramount executive must constantly revisit these issues in determining how much more to pay, if any.

Guaranteed versus Optional Writing Steps

Part and parcel of the negotiation relating to the writer's fixed compensation is determining precisely what the studio will be entitled to for that money—the number of writing steps (e.g., rewrites, polishes) that will be included in the writer's guaranteed fee and whether the writer will be working exclusively and immediately.

The basic writing steps for feature scripts are:

Treatment: A treatment is an adaptation of a story, book, play, or other literary material for motion picture use in a form suitable as the basis for a screenplay. An "original" treatment is an original story written for motion picture use in a form suitable as the basis for a screenplay.

First Draft Screenplay: A first draft is a complete draft of a screenplay, containing a sufficient number of scenes to constitute a feature-length motion picture.

Rewrite: A rewrite (sometimes referred to as a *set of revisions*) encompasses the writing of significant changes in plot, story line, or character relationships. A "page one rewrite" typically means that the script has been completely reworked.

Polish: A polish comprises changes in dialogue, narration, or action. Such changes would be more minor in nature than those included in a rewrite.

Guaranteed Steps

When a writer is guaranteed fixed compensation of, for example, $500,000, it is rarely for a single draft of a screenplay. A studio will normally contract for a first draft and one or more rewrites and/or polishes. The studio obviously wants to get as much out of the writer for as little money as possible, while the writer hopes to force the studio to pay separately for additional writing steps. Typically, as in any compromise, the studio and writer will agree to more than one writing step. Once the studio and writer agree on the amount and extent of the writing steps, the fees must be allocated among the various steps. Of course, the WGA Agreement sets out minimum fees for all of the writing steps, and the amounts allocated to each step must at least meet the minimum requirements if the deal falls within WGA jurisdiction.

In most cases, the studio's interest lies in deferring as much money as possible to a later date, while the writer wants to *frontload* the cash. Typically, the largest portion of the fixed compensation will be allocated to the first draft, as that usually requires the greatest effort from the writer. Even a second complete draft would require somewhat less work, so a lower portion of the overall fee would be attributed to that writing step. Although the writer will eventually receive the same overall payment, the allocation is sometimes an issue of contentious debate. The studio has a further interest in not inflating a writer's quote by attributing too great a payment to the polish or rewrite. In addition, once the studio agrees to the allocation, it could very well affect the price a studio will feel compelled to pay if it chooses to order additional drafts, rewrites, or polishes (beyond the number of writing steps negotiated for).

The guaranteed steps are typically guaranteed on a pay-or-play basis, which means that the studio, barring unusual contractual contingencies such as force majeure (i.e., an act of nature beyond the producer's control), material default, or breach by the writer, must pay the writer for each guaranteed step whether or not the particular step is actually ordered (i.e., the producer or studio may terminate the writer at any time, but would nevertheless be obligated to pay the entire compensation for each guaranteed step). In addition, even if the writer did complete all steps, the studio would not be obligated to actually use the writer's work in its film.

This differs from the concept of *pay-and-play,* which is very rare and is discussed in further detail in chapter 5. The concept of pay-and-play refers to the commitment by the studio or producer not only to pay the writer but to actually utilize her services. In other words (again, barring unusual contractual contingencies such as force majeure or the writer's default), the producer agrees that it will not produce the movie without the writer's full participation. In the rare instances where such a commitment is made, it is almost always made in connection with non-writing services, such as in cases where the writer is also a director or an actor. Consider the following example: A writer creates a marketable screenplay, but refuses to sell it unless the studio or producer agrees to allow such writer to render directing services if the project is produced. In such an instance, the studio might agree to engage the writer as director on a pay-and-play basis. In other words, if the project progresses to production, the studio must allow the writer to direct and cannot discharge its obligation simply by paying the negotiated directing fee. Rumor has it that Sylvester Stallone's acting deal in connection with *Rocky* was pay-and-play. Sly wrote the screenplay and reportedly refused to part with the rights unless the studio allowed him to star in the film.

Optional Steps

In the majority of cases, the studio will insist that a price be set in the writer's agreement for at least a limited number of additional writing steps, beyond what the fixed compensation covers. These steps are not guaranteed, but rather, the studio/producer has the option (or the right) to engage the writer for those services at a preset fee if the studio or producer so chooses. For example, if a writer is guaranteed $300,000 for a first draft and $125,000 for a rewrite, the producer will usually negotiate for the ability to require additional steps (likely a second rewrite and a polish) at a predetermined price, with first call on the writer's services if such services are required. These steps are referred to as "optional steps," and the studio may order some or none of these steps within certain time frames and will be required to pay only for those ordered.

Writer representatives will sometimes attempt to insert language preventing a studio or producer from ordering a particular optional step unless the immediately preceding optional step was also ordered. Thus, in a deal that provides for an optional rewrite and an optional polish, the writer's representative will argue that the optional steps should be dependent and consecutive, so that the polish cannot be ordered unless the studio first orders (and pays for) the rewrite. Studios will often resist this logic, claiming that if the script only needs a polish after delivery of the final *guaranteed step,* the studio should not have to pay for a rewrite it doesn't need.

Reading and Writing Periods

Another point of negotiation relates to the length of the writing periods (i.e., how many weeks the writer will have to deliver the work in question) and the reading periods (i.e., how long the studio/producer has to read the particular work and make comments before requesting that the writer commence the next writing step). Standard reading and writing periods will often conform with the following schedule:

★ First Draft: eight- to ten-week writing period, four- to six-week reading period

★ Rewrite: six- to eight-week writing period, four- to six-week reading period

★ Polish: four-week writing period, two- to four-week reading period

The writer will often try to negotiate for longer writing periods, so that she has more time to complete the work, and for shorter reading periods, so that payment for the next writing step is triggered sooner. Conversely, the studio will try to shorten the writing periods and lengthen the reading periods. The WGA does not set out specific writing/reading periods for feature writing services, provided, however, that the writer is paid no less than scale for each week in which the writer renders services. In other words, while $96,000 may be a permissible fee (under the terms of the WGA Agreement) for a feature-length script, it will not be recognized as sufficient compensation in an agreement specifying a twenty-five-week writing period, as WGA writers cannot be paid less than (approximately) $4,800 per week when rendering services on motion pictures.

In most writing deals, "time is of the essence." In other words, if a writer fails to deliver the work in question within the allocated writing period, she will be deemed to be in *default* or in *breach.* In addition, most producer or studio contracts require that the writer will render services on an "exclusive" basis during all writing periods (i.e., she may not render services for another party during that time) and on a nonexclusive, but "first priority" basis during all reading and option periods. In the event the producer (as opposed to the writer) wishes to extend the reading or writing period or postpone commencement of a particular writing step, the writer's representative will often negotiate for language requiring that the payment due on commencement of such delayed writing step be paid in accordance with the original schedule, notwithstanding the postponement. The writer should further attempt to limit the aggregate amount of time in which the studio or producer can postpone her services. Typically, studios will agree that a writing step cannot be postponed in excess of twelve to eighteen months from the date initially specified in the writer's agreement.

Payment Schedule

Feature writers are typically paid 50 percent of the fee allocated to a particular step upon the writer's commencement of such step and the remaining 50 percent upon delivery of the step. The payment schedule is not often modified, as this "half on commencement, half on completion" formula has become the industry standard. However, in cases where the writer is in dire need of cash, she will try to negotiate a larger upfront payment.

Contingent Compensation ("Back-End")

Prior to late 1999, it was practically unheard of for a writer to be granted a meaningful back-end participation in a feature film. While there are exceptions to any rule, it was essentially dictated that a writer would be entitled to 5 percent of the *net profits* (sometimes called *net proceeds, project net proceeds,* or some other variant) derived from the exploitation of the motion picture. The 5 percent would be contingent upon the writer being accorded *sole writing credit.* If the writer received *shared writing credit,* the writer's share of net proceeds would instead be reduced to 2.5 percent. If the writer ultimately did not receive any writing credit (i.e., the script was rewritten so substantially that the WGA determined that credit should be awarded to some other writer or writers), the writer would not receive any such contingent compensation.

Talent representatives will often seek to narrow the contract language to provide that in the event the writer shares credit, her 5 percent would be reducible only by third-party writers contractually entitled to receive contingent compensation, to a floor of 2.5 percent. In other words, if the studio hires a *script doctor* to polish the screenplay, and the studio's deal with such script doctor does not include a back end, the representatives for the primary writer will argue that the 5 percent should not be reduced, since the studio is not "out of pocket" more than the original 5 percent. The studio, of course, will argue that 5 percent is not deserved, since the first writer's efforts were not sufficient to secure a *green light.* Whether the studio or the talent will prevail on this issue is a matter of bargaining power and negotiating skill. In any event, it is important to note that a "net profit" participation will not necessarily generate additional payments to the writer, even in cases where the film is a box office hit. This is because "net profits" is a contractually defined term, which often bears little resemblance to the layman's understanding of such term. Studio definitions typically provide for numerous fees and deductions that can make net proceeds difficult to achieve.

While the 5 percent rule (writers receiving sole screenplay credit are accorded 5 percent of the project net proceeds) is still largely in effect, in early 1999, amid much fanfare, Sony Pictures announced that it would accord certain writers a *gross participation,* rather than a net participation. While the intricacies of studio profit definitions are discussed in chapter 10, it can be said with relative certainty that a gross participation, no matter how defined, is immensely preferable (from the talent perspective) to a net participation. Under Sony's formula, certain high-level, established writers that have sold screenplays *on spec* for prices exceeding $1 million or have been engaged to write screenplays for guaranteed fees in excess of $750,000 would be entitled to receive 2 percent of the studio's gross revenues after the deduction of very specific costs and expenses (1 percent for shared credit). It was expected that other studios would feel compelled to match Sony's deal. To date, some studios have, while other studios offer a variation of Sony's formula, and still others have chosen not to modify their existing practices at all.

A category falling in between "net proceeds" and a true "gross" participation is AGR, i.e., a percentage of the "adjusted gross receipts." AGR is a broad category that varies definitionally from studio to studio and even within a studio from deal to deal. In most cases, the distinguishing factor about AGR versus net proceeds is that a reduced *distribution fee* is charged by the studio. Many studios have established set parameters for defining a writer's back end depending on her level of up-front compensation. Consequently, in many cases the writer's representative simply needs to request that the studio grant the writer the "best" definition (whether it is net proceeds, AGR, or something better) available to a writer of that stature. Chapter 10 explains the concept of profit participation in greater detail.

Production Bonuses

Another item falling within the category of contingent compensation is the *production bonus* (i.e., a bonus paid if and when the movie gets made). The production bonus is sometimes called the credit bonus, because, like a profit participation, the production bonus is tied to credit. Thus, if the movie is produced, and the writer is accorded sole credit, the writer will be paid an additional bonus, usually at the time the final credits are determined by the WGA. If the writer is accorded shared credit, rather than sole credit, her production bonus will usually be reduced by 50 percent. Sometimes, the writer representative will request that the shared bonus be reduced only by amounts paid to other writers sharing credit, but in no event should the reduction exceed 50 percent. This would be advantageous if the subsequent writer does not have a production bonus guaranteed in her contract or if the bonus is low. If the writer is not accorded any credit, in most cases she will not be entitled to any portion of the negotiated production bonus.

Writer representatives or the *trades* will often report that a writer was paid, for example, $300,000 against $500,000. What this typically means is that the writer was guaranteed a writing fee of $300,000 (although sometimes the optional steps are included in the figure, so that the studio actually has to order the optional steps for the entire $300,000 to materialize) against a potential total compensation of $500,000 if certain events occur, most importantly, that the movie is produced and the writer receives the requisite credit. That additional $200,000 is typically the production bonus.

In order for the writer to receive the bonus as soon as possible, writer representatives will often request that in the event that no subsequent writers are hired to work on the script prior to the start of *principal photography,* the studio advance an amount equal to the shared credit bonus to the writer upon commencement of principal photography. The rationale is this: The arbitration process heavily favors the initial writer. In other words, it is very difficult (but possible) for the initial writer creating material to be awarded less than sole credit and virtually impossible for such writer to receive no credit—i.e., the first writer will almost always be accorded shared credit at a minimum, unless the script has been completely and substantially rewritten. Since the writer is all but guaranteed to receive credit in such circumstances, studios will typically agree to advance an amount equal to the shared credit bonus at the start of principal photography, since at that point the picture is actually going forward and should be completed absent extremely exigent circumstances. Even if a dispute regarding credit subsequently arises requiring an arbitration, the dispute is likely to affect only whether the writer is accorded sole or shared credit (the advance being fully earned in either case). Without an explicit agreement by the studio to advance a portion of the credit bonus, the writer must wait until final credits are determined, which can be months after conclusion of principal photography.

Sample contract language dealing with the advance of the shared bonus may read as follows: "In the event that no other writer is engaged to render writing services on this project prior to the start of principal photography,

Writer will be paid fifty percent (50 percent) of the production bonus referenced herein as an advance. Such sum shall be payable no later than ten (10) days following commencement of principal photography. In the event that Writer receives sole credit, the balance of Writer's production bonus will be payable at such time as final credits are determined. In the event that Writer is not accorded any writing credit on this project, Writer will return such advance within ten (10) days of final credit determination."

As mentioned in the provision above, the writer is contractually obligated to return the advance if the production bonus is not ultimately warranted. Accordingly, studios will tend to limit this provision to instances in which it is all but assured that the writer will be accorded shared credit at a minimum, as they do not want to find themselves in a position where they must attempt to collect money from an individual (no matter how affluent such individual may be).

Award Bonuses

In order for a writer to improve her deal, the writer representative will often look for creative ways to "sweeten the pot." One such method is to request that the writer be paid a bonus in the event that the writer wins, or is even nominated for, a particular award, such as a Writers Guild Award, Golden Globe Award, or even an Academy Award. It is difficult for a studio or producer to refuse a modest bonus in the event the film wins an Oscar for best screenplay, as such an award will undoubtedly contribute to an increase in the picture's revenues. The dollar amount of such a bonus is negotiable, in most cases escalating with the level of prestige of a particular award (with a win typically being more valuable than a nomination). In some cases, a request for an award bonus is not appropriate, and it should be noted that such provisions do not appear in the majority of writer deals. Rather, these bonuses are more typically found in A-level actor and director deals.

Box Office Bonuses

Another type of bonus that studios sometimes grant is a bonus that is payable if and when the picture generates a certain amount of money in its initial theatrical release, either worldwide or in North America alone. A typical provision might state that "at such time, if ever, as the domestic (i.e., United States and Canada) box office receipts, as reported in *Daily Variety* or a similarly reliable publication, reach $30 million, Writer will receive a bonus of $20,000." A box office bonus might be granted in an instance where a writer agrees to work below her quote, such as in connection with a low-budget film. A savvy agent or attorney will argue that if the alleged low-budget picture grosses as much or more than a higher-budgeted picture, the studio will be sitting on greater profits (as costs were lower) and, therefore, should grant *deferred compensation* to the writer, payable at such points in time as the picture is heavily *in the black.* It is common for box office bonuses to be paid at more than one point. For example, the writer might be granted $20,000 at $30 million, an additional $20,000 at $40 million, and an additional $50,000 at $50 million. Such bonuses are often preferable to a traditional profit participation, as the money breaks are more easily verifiable and not likely to be affected by the actual profitability of a film.

In some cases, a writer's representative may ask that these bonuses be paid if worldwide box office receipts reach a level that is twice the level (of domestic box office revenues) that would require payment of a bonus. For example, a bonus might be payable at the earlier of such time (if ever) as domestic box office receipts reach $50 million or such time as worldwide box office receipts reach $100 million. A bonus that is structured in this manner will benefit the writer with respect to films that "outperform" expectations overseas (or underperform in the domestic territories). However, if the studio's projections indicate that a film is likely to attract larger audiences overseas, the studio might insist on a higher multiple and two to one (for example, the bonus might be payable at $50 million in domestic gross or $120 million in overseas gross).

Credit (On Screen and in Paid Advertising)

It should be noted that, with respect to projects falling within WGA jurisdiction, credits are not subject to studio discretion (as they were prior to the formation of the WGA). If that were still the case, studios might be tempted to cut writers out of the credit process for various reasons. In instances where a writing deal is not subject to the terms and conditions of the WGA, more precise language needs to be negotiated regarding credits. For example, a contract might state that "in the event that 75 percent or more of the final script has been written by Writer, Writer will be accorded sole screenplay credit." In addition, there might appear further language providing for an arbitration mechanism in the event the writer and hiring entity do not agree on the form of final writing credits, or language stating that the parties agree that credit will be determined "in accordance with the WGA credit manual."

Accordingly, if a writer's employment agreement falls under WGA purview, essentially, all aspects of the writer's credit will be determined by WGA regulations. The WGA Agreement provides a mechanism for the determination of all writing credits, including "Written by," "Screenplay by," and "Story by." The WGA Agreement further provides for an arbitration (among the studio and all writers participating in all versions of the screenplay) in the event that there is a dispute relating to credit.

A "Written by" credit generally signifies that the writer has created both the story and the screenplay. In instances where a different writer or writers were responsible for the underlying story, a separate "Story by" credit will follow a "Screenplay by" credit, signaling that the writer or writers of the screenplay did not create the plot entirely on their own. Consider the following example: Jack and Jill pitch a story to Universal. Stanley and Jill end up writing the screenplay. Final screen credits may read: "Screenplay by Stanley and Jill; Story by Jill and Jack."

The WGA requires that the writer's screen credit must be accorded in the same size and style of type as that of any other non-cast individual accorded credit on the project, such as the director or producer. The words "Written by," "Story by," or "Screenplay by" must be at least one-half the size of type used for the name of the writer(s). The WGA also ties writers' credits in *paid advertising* (such as magazine print ads, billboards, *one-sheets,* and radio ads that the producer or distributor has paid for) to that of the director and producer of the film. In other words, if the studio credits the director or producer in such ads, it will be required to accord credit to the writer as well. The WGA Agreement provides that in advertising, names of the individual writers given credit must be in the same size and style of type as that used for the director or producer, whichever is larger.

If the agreement does not fall within WGA jurisdiction, key items that will need to be addressed include:

★ **Placement.** The writer should receive on-screen credit on a *separate card* in the *main titles.* If writing credit is shared, it is likely that the card will have to be shared.

★ **Paid Advertising.** The writer should have her credit included in paid advertising wherever the director or producer receives credit. It's best for a writer to tie her credit to the director's, because (like the WGA) the Directors Guild of America (DGA) comprehensively governs the inclusion of the director's credit in paid advertising, while there is no union in place to date that governs producing credits. Even if a studio agrees to include the writer's credit in all paid advertising in which the director's credit appears, the studio will typically exclude award, nomination, or congratulatory ads, arguing that the studio should not be required to credit the writer in ads purchased by the studio in order to congratulate the director on winning an award. While logic supports the exclusion of such award and congratulatory ads, the savvy writer's representative will insist that the exclusion be specifically limited to award/nomination ads "in which only the honoree is mentioned." In other words, if a congratulatory ad (congratulating the director) also happens to mention that the film was "executive produced by Tom Hanks," the writer's agent will argue that such an ad must include the writer's name as well. Although the ad in question is indeed a congratulatory ad, it is one that mentions individuals other than the honoree.

★ **Size of Credit.** The writer's credit should be the same size and type as other individual credits, including such aspects as boldness, height, width, and thickness.

★ **Merchandise.** In addition to items of paid advertising, the writer should be credited on any item of merchandise that contains the film's *billing block* (i.e., the credit banner that appears at the bottom of most posters and print-ads promoting a film), such as a soundtrack cover or videocassette and DVD packaging.

Separation of Rights

Under U.S. copyright law, the creator of an original written work is entitled to certain proprietary rights as the author. However, that is not the case when a writer is hired to write a script and works under the direction and control of her employer. In such cases, the writer's work product is classified as a work-for-hire, which is defined under the 1976 Copyright Act as either:

★ A work prepared by an employee within the scope of her employment; or

★ A work specifically ordered or commissioned for use as a contribution to a collective work as a part of a motion picture or other audiovisual work.

When a script is considered a work-for-hire, the employer is deemed to be the "author" for copyright purposes and can control when and how the project is exploited, if at all. As a result, many unproduced scripts sit gathering dust in studio libraries.

In an attempt to recapture some of the rights ordinarily reserved to authors under the Copyright Act, the WGA "separates out" a certain group of rights that would otherwise be owned by the writer's employer and instead grants them to the writer (assuming certain conditions are met). While the Agreement does not actually divide the copyright itself (the Copyright Act provides that the copyright is not divisible), the parties to the WGA Agreement contractually agree that certain rights in the screenplay (described below) will be retained by the writer.

Qualifying for Separated Rights

Entitlement to Separated Rights is subject to WGA determination. In order to qualify for such rights, a writer's work must meet certain criteria, similar to those criteria required for copyright entitlement. The initial criterion is that the work constitutes an original story or original story and screenplay (i.e., it is not based on material previously published or produced). If a writer is assigned material to work from, such as a book or a play, the writer is unlikely to qualify for Separated Rights, unless she creates a "substantially new and different story" (i.e., there is no substantial similarity between the new and the underlying material).

The second and final criterion is that the writer must also receive sole "Story by," "Written by," or "Screenplay by" credit on the motion picture. If the writer meets both criteria, she will qualify for separated rights.

The writer receiving Separated Rights will be entitled to the following:

Reserved Rights (Book Publication/Live Stage). The writer will retain the right to publish a book based on the script subject to a *holdback period.* Nevertheless, the producer can publish a *novelization* of the film for marketing purposes, to be released in conjunction with the release of the film, provided that the writer is given the first opportunity to write the novelization. Even if the writer chooses not to participate in the novelization, she will be entitled to a WGA-mandated minimum fee for the right to publish. The writer will also maintain the right to produce a live stage version of the material (again, after expiration of a holdback period) if the producer has not already exploited the rights. If the producer or studio wants to exploit these rights, it must pay the writer a WGA-prescribed fee.

Sequel Payments. A writer qualifying for separated rights will also be entitled to receive royalties in the event that additional productions (such as theatrical sequels, television movies, and television series) are created using principal characters from the original production. Generally, writers will try to negotiate for payments in excess of those required by the WGA Agreement. A standard negotiated sequel payment for a theatrical film is 50 percent of the writer's fixed compensation under the original contract. In addition, the writer may be entitled to receive a "Based on the Character Created by" credit in connection with a theatrical sequel and can negotiate to receive a similar credit on other sequels.

Right of Reacquisition. The qualified writer will have the right, under very limited circumstances, to reacquire ownership of her work if certain conditions are met. In instances where the writer's work remains unproduced (in any medium) for a period of five years, the writer will have a twenty-four-month period to repurchase the material from the studio, provided that the studio is no longer actively developing the property. In order to reacquire the material, the writer must repay the script purchase price or writing fee she previously received from the studio. In addition, the writer must ensure that any remaining literary costs, such as bonuses to other writers or rights holders that may become due (plus interest), are borne by any entity that ultimately produces the work. The right of reacquisition is similar to (but generally more onerous for the writer than) the right of "turnaround," which is discussed below.

Mandatory Rewrite. The qualified writer must also be given the opportunity to write the first rewrite of the script at no less than WGA minimum. If the producer/studio wants to replace the writer, she must first be given the opportunity to meet with a senior production executive who has read the script to discuss the writer's continued involvement.

Perks

While the perks of a writer will rarely compare to those of a "star" actor or director, writer representatives will nonetheless try to secure the following basic perks.

First-Class Air Travel, Hotels, and Expenses

Under terms of the WGA Agreement, in the event that a writer is required to travel to a *distant location* (which is considered by the WGA to be at least 150 miles from the writer's principal residence) to perform writing services, the producer must provide round-trip transportation (by air, if appropriate), accommodations, and expenses. The WGA requires that all such travel and accommodations be first class. In instances of non-WGA employment, these terms must be specifically negotiated, and thus, depending on the writer's leverage, such travel may or may not be first class. The writer will also want to ensure that the producer pays for hotel accommodations and living expenses (covering meals, taxis, tips, etc.). Higher-level writers will typically receive extra plane tickets for their companions and larger expense allowances.

Office/Secretary/Parking

If the writer is performing services at the studio, she will often request a parking space, use of an office to work in, as well as the help of an assistant/secretary. Whether the writer will receive these perks is clearly dependent on her status in the entertainment industry, as well as the particular circumstances surrounding her employment.

Blu-Ray/DVD/Soundtrack Copies

It is common for the studio to contractually promise that the writer will receive one DVD and/or one Blu-Ray copy of the finished film "at such time, if ever, as such become commercially available." Believe it or not, studios will rarely grant more than one copy (contractually), and most studios do not include this language until it is specifically requested by the writer's representative. The writer may also request a copy of the soundtrack album, if applicable.

Premieres and Expenses

The writer or her representatives will likely request that she receive an invitation to all celebrity premieres (or even film festivals at which the film is exhibited). The distributor will usually grant a request for an invitation (for the writer and one guest), but may or may not agree to reimburse the writer for travel and related expenses incurred in connection with the writer's attendance, depending on the budget of the film and the clout of the writer.

Research Expenses

If research is required, the writer's representative will typically request either a lump sum to cover research expenses or reimbursement for actual, verifiable expenses.

Turnaround/Reversion Subject to a Lien

"Turnaround" refers to the right of an individual to take partial control over a project or a script on a temporary basis. It is a contractual right that must be specifically negotiated. It is by no means an automatic right, nor is it granted to writers by the WGA Agreement.

The way turnaround generally works in the entertainment industry is as follows: A studio or producer engages a writer to write a script or acquires an existing script. Sometime later, the studio or producer passes on the project—in other words, the studio determines that it will not produce the project and, therefore, ceases all development activity and abandons the project. At this point, unless a right of turnaround has been granted, it is likely that the script or other literary material will languish on the shelves of the studio warehouse. Alternatively, if turnaround has been granted, the writer or producer may have the ability to resurrect the project if she can find another buyer willing to take it over.

Turnaround is most often granted to writers or producers (as opposed to actors or directors). As mentioned above, this right is conferred for a limited period of time—most often, eighteen months. During this eighteen-month period, the producer or writer is free to "shop" the project to other production entities or financiers. If the producer or writer is successful in "setting up" the project at a competing company, the first studio will agree to relinquish all rights to the project, subject to the requirements set forth in the turnaround agreement. First and foremost is the requirement that the newfound buyer reimburse the first studio for all its costs in developing the project. These costs will include literary acquisitions, writer fees, producer fees—essentially all costs incurred by the studio through the date it abandoned the project. In most cases, interest is added on as well.

Another common requirement imposed by studios when granting turnaround is a 5 percent net profit participation in the project (payable by the acquiring studio/production company) should the project ever see the light of day. If such profits materialize, they will be paid to the original studio. Another key provision contained in most turnaround agreements is known as a "changed elements" clause. This clause dictates that if a material element of the project changes during the turnaround period but prior to its acquisition by another studio, the initial studio or producer will retain the ability to resume development of the project (as if it never "passed"). These changes are defined in the agreement and include a change in the director, principal cast, and a material change in the script or budget.

It should be noted that, in most cases, the writer's negotiation is limited to a request for a turnaround right. If the studio agrees, it will send its standard turnaround agreement to the writer for signature, and in most instances, such document will be signed as is. Notwithstanding the above, turnaround provisions can be difficult to interpret, and a skilled attorney can protect the writer's interests in important ways.

Finally, it is important to note the distinction between turnaround rights in an entire project versus turnaround to a script only. Here's an example:

Showtime Networks develops a limited series entitled *Mothers-in-Law*. The network engages five writers to script a half-hour episode each. The network abandons the project, and Writer X wants turnaround. Showtime is unwilling to part with the rights to the entire anthology, partly because Showtime is uncomfortable granting Writer X rights to scripts written by other writers. Instead, Showtime grants Writer X a right of turnaround to her script only. Writer X can then try to set this up as a television special or one-act play, or simply rework the plot and use it in an unrelated television series.

It should be evident that most producers and writers will prefer turnaround in the entire project. However, in instances where a studio is unwilling to part with all of its rights in the project, it is still possible that the studio will grant the writer turnaround rights in such writer's script only. This might be important to a writer, because the writer could then rework her script for potential use in connection with another project. Conversely, a studio might want to hold on to certain underlying rights in a project and, at the same time, be willing to part with the rights to a single script relating to the project.

What happens after expiration of the turnaround period? If the producer or writer with turnaround rights has been unsuccessful in breathing new life into the project, the first studio or producer will retain its rights, and the project will remain in limbo (until such time as the studio decides to exploit that project in some way, including a potential sale of the property to a producer some time in the future). At times, however, upon the writer's request, the studio may agree to extend the turnaround period.

Consider the following example: New Line Cinema develops a film entitled *The Truth about Cats and Dogs*. New Line passes on the project. Fortunately, the writer negotiated for turnaround. Twentieth Century Fox becomes interested in the project and agrees to reimburse New Line for New Line's development costs, but doesn't want to pay any interest charges. As a favor to the picture's director, New Line agrees to waive interest. Fox goes on to produce the film, which is quite successful. New Line receives 5 percent of Fox's project net proceeds (per the turnaround agreement).

Another example: New Line develops *Dumb and Dumber*. New Line passes. The producers shop the project to other studios. During this time, Jim Carrey agrees to star in the picture (an element that did not previously exist). New Line explains to the producers that it (New Line) is contractually entitled to reacquire the project and continue development, if it so chooses, due to this "changed element" (i.e., Jim Carrey's interest). New Line decides to produce the film, which goes on to become New Line's highest-grossing movie until *Austin Powers* is released years later.

Reversion

Unlike turnaround, the right of reversion is permanent. A writer with considerable leverage can negotiate for a reversionary interest. Even if the writer does not possess enormous clout, a particular writer may be unwilling to part with her work product unless she knows that the work will revert in the event that the project is not produced.

If reversion is granted, then once the studio passes on the project, the rights in and to the writer's work (including the copyright) will actually revert to the writer. This is very different from a right of turnaround, in that the writer will have complete control and ownership of the material, subject to one important proviso: The studio will continue to have a financial stake in the property. The precise amount of this stake is subject to negotiation, but it will most likely be equal to the studio's development costs (plus interest). This financial stake is known as a "lien." It should be noted that the studio's lien does not affect the writer's ownership interest. In other words, the writer has no duty to exploit the property or to attempt to realize any profits. The writer can simply choose to keep the property in her filing cabinet. The studio's lien merely grants the studio the right to collect funds in an amount equal to its financial interest when and if the writer exploits the property and realizes any proceeds.

Miscellaneous

Beyond the broad strokes of any writing deal, there are issues that may not be specifically discussed by the agent and business affairs executive. Nonetheless, provisions relating to such matters will be found in many writing contracts. Accordingly, dealmakers should become familiar with these concepts.

Certificates of Authorship

A certificate of authorship (or "C of A," as it is sometimes referred to by industry insiders) is a document created by lawyers that is meant to serve as a shortcut to securing appropriate copyright ownership in a script or other work. The document is typically two to three pages in length, and a sample is included in appendix A.

The need for the document arises primarily when a studio is anxious for a writer to begin working, but has not concluded negotiations relating to the long-form agreement. The long-form contract will convey all requisite rights to the studio/producer (thereby rendering the certificate of authorship redundant). However, a fully negotiated agreement can easily take weeks to complete.

Consequently, studio lawyers devised the certificate of authorship as a shortcut. It purports to grant to the studio/employer all necessary rights, but is amazingly brief and requires little negotiation. The idea is that if the writer signs this certificate, the employing studio or producer has sufficiently protected its rights and can authorize the writer to commence work. The studio will frequently register the C of A with the U.S. Copyright Office. Many studios will agree to begin paying the writer in the absence of a signed contract if she executes the C of A. The certificate is not designed to replace a contract, and negotiations over contract language typically continue.

The most important provision contained in the certificate of authorship is the work-for-hire clause. Essentially, the writer must acknowledge that his work constitutes a work-for-hire as such term is defined by the U.S. Copyright Act. Accordingly, the studio (or producer) will be deemed the "author" of the work and should be able to freely exploit (or refrain from exploiting) the work, subject to any rights specifically reserved to the writer by contract, copyright law, or by the WGA Agreement.

Other elements of the certificate of authorship include certain representations by the writer as to the originality and non-defamatory nature of the work, as well as an acknowledgment that in the event of a dispute, the writer will be limited to seeking monetary damages and cannot obtain injunctive relief (i.e., the right to seek a court order halting or delaying production or release of the film).

Whether a C of A, in the absence of a signed agreement, sufficiently protects the studio's interests is a question subject to some uncertainty. This precise issue has seldom been litigated, and when it has, there have usually been some unique circumstances that helped sway the court or the jury. Some experienced writer representatives will not allow their clients to sign the C of A if any material deal issues are outstanding, knowing that once the C of A is signed, the writer will be left with little leverage. In any event, the requirement that a C of A be executed initially (with a full contract to follow) is a practice that is not likely to change in the near future.

Pension, Health, and Welfare Contributions

In addition to writing fees, WGA members are entitled to certain health benefits and contributions to their pension fund. Article 17 of the WGA Agreement requires that producers contribute an amount equal to 6 percent of the writer's gross compensation for writing services (excluding travel and other expenses) to the WGA pension plan. In addition, producers are required to pay 8.5 percent of the writer's gross compensation to a health fund.

Merchandising Royalties

Merchandising refers to the manufacture and sale of items of merchandise (e.g., mugs, t-shirts, hats, toys) relating to the motion picture in question. The studio/producer will retain the sole right to sell merchandise based on the literary material it owns. Notwithstanding the foregoing, the WGA Agreement provides that if a studio or producer sells an object that is first physically described in the writer's material, and such a description is unique and original, the writer will be entitled to a payment in the amount of 5 percent of the gross monies remitted by the manufacturer for the sale of such merchandise. This payment is not dependent on the writer's entitlement to separation of rights. If the deal falls outside WGA jurisdiction, the writer may still be able to negotiate for this payment.

Remakes/Sequels

The WGA writer is typically entitled to an additional payment if a remake based on her original script is produced. Many older films have recently been remade. The motion picture *Bedazzled* (with Liz Hurley and Brendan Fraser), for example, was a remake of an earlier version (with the same title) released in the 1960s that starred Dudley Moore. Many studio contracts attempt to tie the writer's right to receive passive payments for remakes to her entitlement to separation of rights. The WGA Agreement, however, does not make this distinction. Thus, regardless of whether the writer qualifies for separated rights, a credited writer will be entitled to a payment if the subsequent version of her film is written under WGA auspices. Such writer may even be entitled to writing credit on the remake. Most writer representatives request a passive remake payment well above WGA scale, customarily in an amount equal to 33.33 percent of the writing fee paid to the writer under the original deal. Non-guild writers frequently demand a similar commitment.

Similarly, a writer would typically request and receive a passive sequel payment (akin to a royalty) equal to 50 percent of the writing fee paid under the original agreement.

First Opportunity to Write Subsequent Productions

The writer will often request that the studio engage her to write the screenplay or teleplay for any subsequent productions (sequels, remakes, pilots) based on her initial screenplay, given that she originated the story. While this is not something that the WGA guarantees to writers (regardless of whether they qualify for separated rights), many studios will nonetheless agree to allow the writer to participate in the creation of subsequent productions under certain circumstances. For example, the writer's employment agreement may include the following language:

> If, within seven years after the initial theatrical release of the Picture, Producer elects to commission a script for a theatrical sequel or theatrical remake of the Picture, and provided Writer receives sole writing credit on the Picture, and is then active as a Writer in the entertainment industry, and is available, Producer shall negotiate with Writer in good faith for Writer's services on the screenplay for such production upon terms no less favorable than those herein. If the parties fail to agree within thirty days, or Writer is unavailable or elects not to write, Producer will have no further obligation other than the payment of royalties, if any, to which Writer may be entitled.

If the writer and studio reach an agreement in connection with the subsequent production, so that the writer actually renders writing services, she will typically not be entitled to the passive payments referred to above, as her negotiated writing fee on the subsequent production will be deemed to compensate her fully. If, however, the writer chooses not to perform services or otherwise does not reach an agreement with the studio, she will be entitled to the passive payments described above in lieu of direct compensation for actual services.

Residuals

The WGA Agreement mandates minimum payments to writers in the event that a feature film based on their screenplay is exploited in "supplemental" markets (i.e., other than in movie theaters), whether in the United States or abroad. These markets include free television, basic and pay cable, as well as DVDs, videocassettes, pay-per-view, and in-flight entertainment. Accordingly, distributors must pay residuals to the Guild on behalf of the writers, pursuant to formulas set forth in Article 65 of the WGA Agreement.

Errors and Omissions Insurance

One final point worth mentioning briefly relates to errors and omissions insurance (commonly referred to as E & O insurance). All distributors and most production companies carry such policies. These policies are designed to protect the distributor or other insured entity against financial losses resulting from lawsuits or other claims that arise due to error, omission, or negligence in regard to the insured's duty to verify that the copyright to a motion picture is clear. Such policies usually require that the insurance company defend all insured parties and pay the costs of litigation, irrespective of whether any particular claim is frivolous or unfounded.

Here's an example: Warner Bros. releases a *Batman* film, and an English professor in Wyoming claims that he submitted a substantially identical script to a Warner Bros. script reader two years prior to such release. Even if such claim is ultimately determined to be without merit, there will be costs associated with defending and investigating such claim. Legal expenses, for example, must be paid no matter who wins in court. By securing E & O insurance, the distributor or producer ensures that the insurance company will pay any settlement or judgment against the distributor, up to the limits of liability stated in the policy and after payment of the applicable deductible.

Why is this important, or even relevant, to writers? The sharp agent or attorney will insist that his writer/client be named as an additional insured on the studio's E & O policy. Most studios readily agree to this request. This is important (to the writer), because if a copyright claim or lawsuit is initiated, the plaintiff will typically name the studio, the producers, the writer, and maybe even the director as defendants. In such cases, the writer will be comforted by the knowledge that the studio is contractually required to defend the

writer (assuming that the lawsuit is covered under the applicable E & O policy). While most major studios might undertake such a defense on the writer's
behalf without a contractual obligation, it is crucial for the writer to negotiate
for such coverage before any claims arise.

Annotation Guides

Studios and producers will usually include language in the writer agreement
requiring writers of true stories to annotate (i.e., substantiate the source of)
every nonfictionalized line of the script. For example, if an item of information came from a newspaper article, the writer would need to specify the name
of such article and where it appeared.

Deal Point Summary:
FEATURE WRITER AGREEMENTS

1. Contingencies (i.e., Conditions Precedent)
- Creative Meeting
- Acquisition of Underlying Material or Rights
- Signature of Third Party Agreements Relating to the Project

2. Compensation and Services
- Negotiating the Money
- Guaranteed Writing Steps versus Optional Writing Steps
- Reading and Writing Periods
- Payment Schedule
- Rewrites versus Original Screenplays

3. Contingent Compensation (i.e., Back End)
- Share of Net Proceeds or Adjusted Gross Receipts
- Production Bonus
- Award Bonus(es)
- Box Office Bonuses

4. Credit

5. Separation of Rights
- Reserved Rights
- Sequels
- Mandatory Rewrite/Creative Meeting
- Right of Reacquisition

6. Perks
- Travel and Expenses
- Office/Secretary/Parking
- Videocassette/DVD
- Premiere and Festival Invitations/Expenses
- Research Expenses

7. Turnaround/Reversion Subject to a Lien

8. Miscellaneous
- Certificates of Authorship
- Pension, Health, and Welfare Contributions
- Merchandising Royalties
- Remakes
- First Opportunity to Write Subsequent Productions
- Residuals (Television and Supplemental Markets)
- Errors and Omissions (E & O) Insurance
- Annotation Guide

TELEVISION WRITER/PRODUCER AGREEMENTS

*W*hile many consider film to be a director's medium, most agree that television is a writer's medium. In television, particularly series television, the writer is "king." Successful television series creators often take on the expanded role of *showrunner* on the shows that they create, supervising all other writers and overseeing all aspects of production, from casting to editing. These showrunners serve as the chief executives of the production, reporting only to the studio financing the series and to the network that is airing the show. They are usually credited as executive producers, which is considered the highest level credit available in television.

THE ECONOMICS OF TELEVISION

In order to better understand the mechanics of a television writer/producer deal, it is useful to review the economic model that underlies the television business.

Unlike the motion picture industry, where the consumer directly contributes to the studios' profits by purchasing a theater admission ticket, most television series generate revenue through the sale of commercial advertising time. It is the advertisers (i.e., manufacturers and service providers who purchase air time on the network during particular programs) that contribute the bulk of the network's revenues. Clearly, the more popular shows attracting the most sought-after viewers (i.e., viewers falling between the ages of eighteen and thirty-four) will garner higher prices for the typical eight minutes of available ad time within each half hour of programming. Thus, the most entertaining shows, achieving the highest television ratings, will generally be the most lucrative to their owners.

Historically, studios (rather than networks) have financed the production of television series. In accordance with this business model, studios license, or rent, series episodes to networks (for initial exhibition in the United States), but retain ownership of the programs. In fact, until the 1990s, networks were prohibited by FCC (Federal Communications Commission) regulations from taking an ownership interest in the programs they aired. These rules have been relaxed, and many series today are co-owned by networks and studios, while others are wholly owned by either the studio or the network. In some cases, networks have entered into the business of producing and owning, rather than merely licensing, television programs by merging with studios (i.e., Disney/ABC) or setting up independent companies that produce television (such as NBC Studios or CBS Productions). In some instances, networks enter into a partnership arrangement with one or more studios in order to jointly produce programming. However, since in almost all cases the network continues to operate as a separate entity from the studio, the historical economic model for producing and licensing programming has largely remained in effect.

Studios, therefore, continue to produce series, spending enormous sums of money that are not recouped until years later, if ever. This is because networks typically pay only a fraction of the series budget as a *license fee* for their right to air the program. Clearly, if the networks paid 100 percent of the costs associated with producing programming, they would insist on owning the shows outright. A network will usually pay 50 to 60 percent of the applicable budget in exchange for the right to air each episode up to two times per season (i.e., an initial broadcast plus a repeat exhibition). Companies in the business of series television production enter into this type of arrangement (risking millions of dollars in capital expenditures) because the ownership of a *successful* television series can yield enormous profits. **Syndication** sales of *Seinfeld* reruns, for instance, have generated $2 billion to date. This sum is above and beyond the license fee paid by NBC for its right to exhibit episodes.

The following example illustrates the most typical financial relationship between studios and networks.

NBC licenses *ER* from Warner Bros. Under the terms of the license agreement, NBC is permitted to air each episode of *ER* twice. NBC also has the exclusive right to order additional seasons of the series, for up to five years. Moreover, Warner Bros. is prohibited from authorizing anyone else in the United States to air any episodes (new or old) of the series for at least four years from NBC's initial exhibition of the first episode (assuming that the show has not been cancelled by the network earlier). After four years, Warner Bros. might be able to sell previously aired episodes of *ER* to local stations (such as WPIX in NY, which might air the show weekday afternoons at 3 P.M.), as well as to cable stations (such as USA, which might air the series on weekends). Of course, once new episodes of the series are no longer in production, Warner Bros. can continue to exploit the show and may derive revenues from video sales, foreign television exhibition, as well as continued U.S. broadcast on stations ranging from Nick at Nite to KCOP in Los Angeles.

It is interesting to note that, in most cases, until such time as a sufficient number of episodes of a series are produced to enable sales in supplemental markets (beyond the initial network license), the studio is losing money on its series. This is known as "deficit financing," because the studio must finance the difference between the cost of each episode and the amount of the network license fee. As mentioned above, this difference, or deficit, can be as high as 50 percent of the cost of the episode. In addition, the studio bears the risk of any particular episode going over budget.

One megahit, such as *Seinfeld, Friends,* or *Everybody Loves Raymond,* however, can offset losses from as many as nine or ten failed series. This is because local television stations in almost all cities throughout the United States will pay studios/distributors for the right to air repeats of successful series. Sales to such local stations are known as "domestic syndication sales." *I Love Lucy,* for example, is still generating sales more than forty years after series production ended. In addition to domestic sales, the owners of television programming are free to sell episodes to foreign exhibitors. While some North American television series do not appeal to foreign audiences, shows such as *Dallas, Dynasty,* and even *Beverly Hills, 90210* have proven to be very successful in countries ranging from New Zealand to Israel.

A general rule of thumb is that a minimum of one hundred episodes must exist in order to realize the potential of syndication revenues. This is because most local stations air such programs every weekday (sometimes twice per day) and require a sufficient number of episodes. Consequently, three seasons of a series such as Castle Rock's *The Single Guy*—which did not reach the hundred-episode mark—will not generate much interest among buyers. Studios producing successful series have become more creative in their dealmaking and sometimes sell syndication rights to programs prior to reaching one hundred episodes. This is possible in instances where a network has committed to licensing additional episodes. Thus, if only sixty or seventy have been produced to date, but the studio has a firm order from a network to license additional episodes, the studio may enter into syndication negotiations at an earlier point in order to realize the resulting cash infusion.

Airing a successful series can be a lucrative endeavor for the network as well, as it typically negotiates to pay a fixed license fee for at least four seasons. Consequently, if a series begins to attract large audiences (particularly in the desired demographic), the network is usually able to extract higher rates for commercial time, so that advertising dollars will exceed the network's cost in airing the program. Networks generally sell their advertising time once per year (in late spring/early summer) at what is commonly knows as the **upfronts** or "upfront market."

With the declining revenue stream from traditional advertising, networks have blatantly increased their reliance on product placement. DVR use is approaching 30 percent in U.S. households, and the current economic recession has forced companies to dramatically trim their advertising budgets. In the traditional "product placement" arrangement, a particular product (e.g., a Ford SUV or a can of Mountain Dew) will visibly appear onscreen for a negotiated duration, or will be mentioned by a host or cast member within the body of the episode. A recent episode of *Desperate Housewives* mentioned a character's new Lexus hybrid, and also depicted a character holding a Sprint shopping bag. Reality programs such as *American Idol* and *Survivor* have relied on product placement for years. It's hard not to miss the Coca-Cola logo on each of the drinking glasses placed in front of the *American Idol* judges. Similarly, when contestants on *Survivor* win a reward challenge, the prize is typically Coors beer or McDonald's french fries rather than a non-branded item. Many experts believe that branded entertainment will continue to increase in the near future, which actually resembles the early days (or "golden years") of television, when programs sometimes included a sponsor's name in the title (such as "Procter and Gamble presents *The Flintstones*").

Cable Networks

As stated, the economic model for the broadcast networks (i.e., CBS, ABC, NBC, UPN, WB, FOX) is a relatively simple one—the network achieves profitability if advertising sales exceed the license fee paid to the studio. In the case of most cable networks, such as USA, TNT, Cartoon Network, or ESPN, revenue is derived from two sources: (1) advertisers, and (2) consumers (i.e., subscribers who pay a monthly fee to their cable or satellite company). A portion of this "subscription revenue" is paid to the cable networks carried on such satellite or cable services. Pay cable networks, such as Showtime and HBO, do not sell advertising time and, therefore, derive the lion's share of their revenue from subscribers.

License Fee Renegotiations

Since most license agreements between networks and studios normally span four to six years (with the network retaining an option to order each applicable batch of episodes on a season-by-season basis), there will frequently come a time when a studio producing a successful series can extract a considerably higher license fee from the network (with the network sometimes covering the entire cost of production or even paying a premium). For example, it was reported that NBC began paying more than $10 million per episode for its right to exhibit *ER* beginning with the fifth season, just after the four-year term of NBC's initial agreement expired. If a network and studio cannot reach an agreement relating to the network's continued license of a series upon expiration of a license agreement, the studio is then free to sell subsequent episodes to a competing network (subject to any matching rights or rights of refusal held by the initial network). This was the case with *Buffy The Vampire Slayer* (produced by Twentieth Century Fox Television), which recently moved from the WB network to UPN after a highly publicized failed renegotiation.

It is under this backdrop of large capital investments and the potential for huge profits that studios negotiate pilot/series writing agreements with television writers.

MAKING THE DEAL

Many successful television writers are signed by studios or networks to multi-year *overall deals,* in which the writer is paid a large annual fee and, in return, is expected to "develop" (i.e., come up with ideas for) potential television series. These deals raise several unique issues, but in order to understand the mechanics of an overall deal, it is helpful to first walk through a typical writer/executive producer deal for a pilot/series. These are sometimes referred to within the industry as "one-shot" or *one-off* deals, because they encompass the writing of a single *pilot* script and, therefore, will yield, at best, one possible series (excluding potential spin-offs, as described later in this chapter).

As most in the TV business know, the great majority of pilot scripts do not get produced. Of those that do, only a handful make it to series. Thus, in order for a studio to generate a single megahit like *M*A*S*H,* it must make dozens of pilot-writing deals, in the hope that one such pilot script will yield a successful series.

In television, unlike film, the writer's continued involvement in a series project is often desired. Accordingly, the television writing deal generally requires the negotiation of not only the fee payable to the writer for her pilot script, but various additional provisions relating to the writer's role in the event that the pilot is produced and ordered to series.

It is important to note that, in most cases, the pilot writing fee is the only portion of the writer's potential compensation that is guaranteed. All other negotiated deal terms will materialize only in those rare instances when a pilot is ordered to production. Even then, if the pilot does not proceed to series, or if the series is ordered but is cancelled early in its run, many of the deal points will become moot.

Nevertheless, when a script works and yields a multiyear series, the writer's representatives will want to ensure that the creator is protected and not only shares in the riches, but retains some control over the creative process. Thus, savvy agents and attorneys will fight tooth and nail for each and every one of the provisions discussed in this chapter.

Pilot Writing Fee

The first item of negotiation is typically the pilot script writing fee. The current WGA Agreement prescribes that *scale* (union minimum) for a thirty-minute pilot script is roughly $38,000 and approximately $52,000 for a sixty-minute script. It should be noted that most U.S. television series (excluding reality series, such as *Survivor*) are produced under the auspices of the WGA, as all of the major broadcast networks are signatory to the WGA Agreement. However, as discussed in previous chapters, the WGA Agreement merely establishes minimums, not maximums. Thus, an A-level television writer (i.e., one who has already created at least one successful series) might be paid as much as $250,000 or more to write a half-hour pilot script.

In determining the amount that a writer will be paid for writing a pilot script, the writer's quote will be extremely important. Since most pilots do not proceed to series, there are plenty of writers in the marketplace who are hired at least once each television season to write pilot scripts. When (and if) the applicable network passes on a writer's project, such writer will typically re-enter the marketplace, trying to improve her quote when entering into new pilot writing deals.

Of course, every writer has a first deal, and most television executives have been faced with the task of making deals for writers with no applicable quotes. An unpublished novelist with absolutely no television or film-writing credits would probably not receive a fee in excess of scale her first time out. Conversely, a writer with extensive feature film quotes, television movie quotes, or miniseries quotes (but lacking experience in the area of pilot script writing) might, nevertheless, secure a salary considerably in excess of WGA scale, as studios will generally acknowledge that such prior experience is relevant, at least to a modest degree. Often, a writer being engaged to script her first pilot will have most recently been employed as a staff writer on an existing television series. After gaining experience writing on a series for several seasons, many staff writers will secure pilot deals for themselves. In fact, the success of a show often rubs off on many individuals associated with that show. A writer coming off of a season or two of *Friends,* for example, was not only likely to "get a deal," but her compensation was likely to be well above scale.

Pilot Writing Steps

Unlike a feature writing agreement, little time is spent negotiating the number of writing steps that will be required in a particular pilot writing deal. This is because pilot writing compensation customarily covers a story, a first draft, two revisions, and a polish. The standard payment schedule for a pilot writing fee is 30 percent upon delivery of the story, 40 percent upon delivery of the first draft, and 10 percent upon delivery of each of the sets of revisions and the polish.

Pilot-Producing Services

The next item of negotiation concerns the nature of the writer's services (if any) in the event that the script is well received and the pilot is ordered to production. In many cases, the producer will guarantee the writer employment as an executive producer of the pilot episode at a negotiated fee (see below). The writer's executive producer services, in connection with such pilot production, will usually include overseeing casting, participating in budget discussions, consulting on the selection of the various department heads (such as the set designer, the costume designer, and the casting director), as well as serving as the "point person" for the network and studio. Many of these functions are similar to those of a director on a motion picture. Such services will, in almost all cases, be required to be rendered by the writer on an exclusive, full-time, in-person basis.

There are instances, however, when the studio will not agree to employ the writer as an executive producer. For example, if the pilot writer is not a proven showrunner (i.e., someone with experience running the day-to-day operations of a television series), or at least someone with a track record as a series producer, the studio may be unwilling to guarantee an executive producer role. In such cases, the studio might agree to attach the writer to the project as a supervising producer (or some more junior role), so that the studio will have the benefit of the writer's creative vision, while still being able to bring on a more experienced showrunner. Of course, the writer's precise credit and defined function in connection with the pilot is ultimately a result of negotiation between the studio and the writer, dependent upon such factors as the writer's clout and prior experience.

It should be noted, however, that even when the studio does agree to attach the writer to the pilot as a producer, it will usually condition such attachment on the writer receiving writing credit on the pilot and "Created by" credit on the series. Since it is unlikely that the WGA will have made a final credit determination by the time production of a pilot commences, the studio may include language in the writer's contract stating that: "if the pilot writer is substantially rewritten prior to pilot production" or "if the pilot ordered is not based (or substantially based) on the writer's script," then the studio will not have the obligation to engage that writer on the pilot (but may still have the option to do so).

The studio relies on this language in situations where a second writer reworks the original script so substantially, and improves it so dramatically in the view of the studio or network, that the studio wishes to go forward with a pilot and/or series only if the second writer serves as showrunner. In such cases, the studio tries to ensure that it will have no continuing obligation to the original writer (other than the possible payment of royalties), even if the final script still maintains some connection to the first writer's concept.

Pilot-Producing Fee

The negotiated fee paid to a writer for her executive producer services is not governed by the WGA per se. However, if the writer is expected to continue writing during pilot production (as she likely will be during series production), her compensation must not fall below $5,000 per week. This rate is referred to by the WGA as the pay rate for "Writers Employed in an Additional Capacity" (i.e., writers employed as writer/producers). The writer's pilot-producing fee is almost always in addition to, and separate from, the pilot-scriptwriting fee. For example, a writer being paid $50,000 for a pilot script might be paid an additional $35,000 to produce the pilot.

In determining an appropriate producing fee for a writer, studios will again examine the writer's quote (from previous pilot deals), but will often also consider whether any of the writer's previous scripts were produced—in other words, whether the writer's pilot-producing quote was actually earned (through rendering services on an actual pilot) or was merely superficial, a dollar figure that was negotiated, but never earned. In addition, hard-to-quantify variables, such as the "heat" surrounding such writer, the degree of interest in the pitch on the part of the studio (i.e., is it a pitch that just squeaked in because the studio desperately needed a cop show, or did the creative executive absolutely fall in love with the idea?), and whether a bidding situation exists (i.e., two or more studios vying for the same writer), will also play an important role in any negotiation. The identity of the particular studio or network involved in the transaction may also be relevant (certain writers might deem NBC more desirable than UPN, for example), as will such entity's general economic condition.

Series Services

The next issue to be addressed is the nature and extent of the writer's services in the event the pilot is "picked up" by the network (i.e., series episodes are ordered).

It is in the studio's interest to have the option, but not the obligation, to engage the writer as a producer on the series for as many seasons as possible. At the same time, it is in the writer's interest to have the right, but not the obligation, to serve as producer on the series for as many seasons as she chooses.

Lock

A studio will usually agree to "lock" the writer/creator to the series for at least one year, and in many cases, two years. This means that if the series is produced, the writer will be guaranteed employment as a producer on a pay-or-play basis for a minimum number of seasons (as negotiated). High-end writer/producers, such as Steven Bochco or Dick Wolfe, might be guaranteed an executive producer fee and credit for the "life" (i.e., duration) of the series. Interestingly enough, some writers will not want to commit to render services on a series in excess of two years. This is because the writer may want to create the show, shepherd it as showrunner for two seasons, and then, once it is up and running, entrust it to the able hands of some senior writers on the show, so that she can then move on to create another series. Of course, there are some series creators that prefer never to leave their first show. Lorne Michaels, for example, has been the executive producer of *Saturday Night Live* for over twenty years.

A writer's attachment or lock to the series will generally be subject (per the standard studio contract) to the writer's default, disability, or death, or an event of force majeure—as is the case with most entertainment agreements. In addition, the writer's attachment as a producer or consultant is frequently conditioned on the writer receiving sole "Written by" credit on the pilot and sole

"Created by" credit on the series (both of which are governed by the WGA), although studios will occasionally agree to lock the writer even if she is accorded shared "Written by" credit on the pilot. The studio's rationale is clear: If the produced pilot bears so little resemblance to the original writer's script that she is not accorded credit by the WGA, the studio should not be required to pay the writer an episodic producing fee for one or more full seasons.

Series Role

If the studio agrees to attach the writer as executive producer on the pilot, it will most likely agree to attach the writer in the same capacity during the initial season of the series. In those instances in which the writer is unable to secure executive producer status on the pilot, and instead is guaranteed a more junior position such as supervising producer, it is likely that the writer will remain in this capacity during the first season of the series. However, such writer may be able to negotiate for a more elevated credit and status (such as co-executive producer) in the second and subsequent seasons.

Exclusivity

The requisite series-producing services will usually be rendered on an exclusive basis (i.e., the studio will not permit the writer to work on writing projects for others during pre-production and production periods). During post-production, however, the studio will typically agree to allow the writer to render services on a "first-priority," rather than an exclusive, basis. Accordingly, such writer would be permitted to work on outside projects during this period, provided that these third-party services do not interfere with the writer's series work, which, contractually, must be the writer's first priority. Consulting services, if applicable, are generally rendered on a nonexclusive basis.

Series-Producing Fee

Usually, the writer's episodic producing fee (i.e., the fee payable to the writer upon rendering producing services on each series episode) is lower than her pilot-producing fee. This is generally the case because the producing services required in connection with a pilot are more extensive than those relating to a single series episode. For example, the casting process starts at ground zero on the pilot. All of the available roles must be cast at this stage, with most of the selected actors continuing to render series services, so that casting duties for episodes beyond the pilot will be minimal. In addition, shooting a pilot generally takes longer than shooting a subsequent episode. For example, a pilot shoot for a one-hour drama might be scheduled for fifteen days, while each series episode may be slated for just eight days. This is the case because sets will already exist and locations will already have been secured. In addition, studios frequently provide funds for a larger crew once series production begins, since such episodes are almost certain to air, unlike most pilots. Finally, as there will generally be a larger production staff on board by the time a pilot is ordered to series, the creator/producer can delegate some duties to his staff, which he will be unable to do during production of the pilot. Set forth here is an example illustrating some of the fees that are typically paid to series creators:

Joe Smith writes a pilot script for Century Films. Century agrees that if the pilot is produced, Joe will serve as supervising producer on the pilot at a fee of $35,000. In addition, if a series based on such pilot is produced, Joe will be granted a one-year lock (as supervising producer) at a fee of $20,000 per episode. Moreover, Century will have the option to engage Joe in connection with the second season as co-executive producer, at a fee of $22,500.

Consulting Services

Usually, the writer of a pilot script will be guaranteed the opportunity to render consulting services on the series once that writer is no longer rendering exclusive executive-producing services. Such services will typically be rendered on a nonexclusive basis, so that the writer can maintain some (albeit limited) involvement in the series and receive a fee, yet still retain the ability to work on outside projects.

It is customary for the studio to agree to lock the writer as a consultant on a *one-for-one basis* (i.e., for the same number of years that the writer rendered full-time producing services). For example, if the writer was locked to the series for two years as executive producer, and the studio persuaded the writer to come back in the same exclusive capacity for a third season, after which either the writer or the studio decided to move on, the writer would thereafter be locked to the series as a nonexclusive consultant for three additional years (assuming the series is still in production), at a prenegotiated consulting fee.

Consulting Fee

Most writers' representatives will request that the first season's consulting fee equal one-half of the writer's most recent executive-producer fee on the series. While some studios agree to these terms, many others prefer to lock in a specific (lower) sum, usually ranging from $7,500 per episode to as much as $15,000 per episode. Many studios will negotiate for a fixed consulting fee, regardless of the number of seasons, while the writer's representatives will likely request that, at a minimum, the consulting fee be increased by 5 percent from season to season. Ultimately, the precise amount of any writer's consulting fee will be determined through negotiation between the respective parties.

Series Sales Bonus

In addition to series-producing fees, the savvy writer representative will request a *series sales bonus* (i.e., a sum of money payable as a bonus if and when the network orders series episodes based on the pilot). Statistically, a series order is a rare occurrence, as several hurdles must be overcome in order for a pilot script to ultimately generate episodes securing a slot on a network's fall or mid-season schedule.

Studios may not initially offer to pay a series sales bonus, but will usually agree to a modest sum if so requested by the writer's agent or attorney. While the dollar amount of a series sales bonus will vary and is subject to negotiation, it is fairly standard today for a series sales bonus of $25,000 to be granted in the event the writer receives sole "Written by" credit on the pilot and sole "Created by" credit on the series, reducible to $12,500 if the writer receives shared credit.

Studios will frequently insist that the sales bonus be paid only if a minimum of twelve episodes is ordered by the network. In most cases in which a network orders a series, it will order at least six episodes, and sometimes as many as thirteen. The writer will likely argue that regardless of the number of episodes ordered, the fact that the pilot "made it" to series is enough to justify payment of the bonus. The compromise frequently reached is that the bonus will be based on an order of twelve episodes and prorated down if fewer than twelve are ordered, *provided that* a minimum of six episodes is produced. Thus, if a network produces only three episodes on a trial basis, but orders no more beyond the three, the sales bonus will not be payable. As long as six or more episodes are produced, however, some portion of the sales bonus will be payable. Some writer representatives will be successful in extracting a commitment on the part of the studio to prorate the bonus upwards (in the event that the network's order exceeds twelve episodes), so that, for example, if the network orders fifteen episodes (rather than twelve), the series sales bonus payable to the writer will be increased accordingly.

Royalty

The WGA Agreement requires that the writer or writers accorded "Created by" credit on a series receive a *royalty* (or payment) for each episode of the series that is produced beyond the pilot. The current WGA-required royalty for network prime-time programming is approximately $1,000 per episode. Subject to this minimum, the actual amount of the royalty payable to the series creator is negotiable.

Some writers can secure an episodic royalty as high as $5,000 per episode for "sole credit." Such writers can conceivably write a pilot script that spawns a successful series, never render any series services, and yet still be paid over $110,000 per television season in royalties (when more than twenty-two episodes are produced). The negotiated royalty will usually be reduced by 50 percent in the event that the writer is accorded shared "Created by" credit. Some lawyers and agents, however, are able to negotiate that the royalty will only be reducible by *actual dollar amounts paid by the studio* to other writers receiving credit, to a floor (or minimum) of 50 percent of the sole-credit royalty. This is beneficial to the writer in cases where the studio hires a lower-level writer to rework the first writer's script and negotiates a deal granting such writer only $1,000 per episode if such writer receives shared credit. In such an instance, the first writer's royalty would be reduced from $5,000 per episode to $4,000—rather than to $2,500. Savvy writer representatives will request that the episodic royalty increase each successive season (typically, by 5 percent).

Many agents request that the writer's episodic royalty be paid not once, but twice, in accordance with a *100/5* (pronounced "one hundred over five") formula. The second royalty payment, however, will be paid only if a particular episode is rebroadcast, as a rerun, several times. The 100/5 formula provides that the writer will be paid one-fifth of her episodic royalty upon rebroadcast of any particular episode (i.e., when it is first rerun), up to a maximum of five such re-airings. Thus, the writer would be paid a total of 200 percent of her episodic royalty (100 percent upon production or first exhibition of the episode and another 100 percent spread over the first five re-airings of such episode). The writer would not be entitled to additional royalties after the sixth exhibition of each applicable episode (unless otherwise mandated by the WGA Agreement).

Studios producing television for broadcast networks will generally agree to such request on the condition that the additional 100 percent of the writer's royalty will be deemed a prepayment, to the maximum extent allowable, of any WGA-mandated royalties that might otherwise become due and payable upon subsequent repeat broadcasts. As the WGA does not allow its members to waive their right to receive residuals, it is possible that additional residual payments might become due if the episode continues to air for many years. In any event, the writer benefits in that her royalty payments are accelerated under the 100/5 formula. It should be noted, however, that most cable networks refuse the writer's request for 100/5, as these cable broadcasters tend to re-air episodes almost immediately after their initial broadcast. Granting the 100/5 request would almost certainly trigger the full royalty payment within the first exhibition year for such cable networks. Accordingly, most cable television producers deny this request on the grounds that the resulting cost would be too cumbersome.

Profit Participation

As mentioned above, the writer's profit participation in a television project is generally more significant than that of a feature film and is more likely to generate payment to the writer for two reasons. First, a television writer can normally negotiate for *points* (i.e., a percentage of the profits) in excess of five (percent), while motion picture writers can rarely do better. Moreover, not only can the number of points exceed five, but the contractual terms setting forth the calculation of such points may be more favorable in television deals. Second, an enormously successful series may generate so much cash relative to its costs that, regardless of the precise definition of the project's "net proceeds," it is extremely likely to generate some payment.

It is, therefore, imperative for a writer's representative to take great care in negotiating the definition of project proceeds in the writer's contract. Chapter 10 explains various types of participations (adjusted gross, gross, net), as well as the most common areas of negotiation in connection with such back-end deals. A top-level showrunner/creator will often be able to negotiate for 15 percent or more of the adjusted gross, or for up to 50 percent of the net (reducible by net participations granted to third parties). If a project survives the uphill battle toward syndication, these profits may indeed materialize. Although far from a household name, Larry David (who cocreated the hit series *Seinfeld*) was listed as number two on *Forbes* magazine's list of highest-paid entertainers in 1998, ahead of Steven Spielberg and Oprah Winfrey. This was largely due to David's profit participation on *Seinfeld*.

Credit

As with other WGA-governed agreements, there is little need to negotiate credit provisions, as the WGA determines the form of most writing credits. Typically, the writer or writers sharing "Written by" or "Story by" credit on the pilot will be accorded a "Created by" credit on the series. This is the credit that is typically tied to royalty provisions. If one writer originated the story and characters and is accorded "Story by" credit while a different writer is ultimately awarded "Teleplay by" credit, it is the "story" writer that will (in most cases) be entitled to the "Created by" credit. "Written by" is designed to encompass both "Story by" and "Teleplay by," so that if a single individual or team of individuals originated both the story and teleplay, the appropriate credit will be "Written by" (and there will not be a story or teleplay credit). The "Created by" credit will appear on screen in connection with each episode exhibited after the pilot. It is possible to see a "Created by" credit even on a pilot episode, in instances where the pilot is produced within a sufficient amount of time prior to its broadcast (so that the "Created by" credit has already been determined by the Guild). The WGA, however, does not require the producer to accord "Created by" credit until the second episode (i.e., first episode after the pilot).

Producer Credit

Although the WGA governs the above pilot and series writing credits (including the "Created by" credit), it does *not* govern producing credits. Hence, the terms and conditions relating to the writer's "Executive Producer," "Supervising Producer," or even "Consultant" credit need to be specifically addressed by contract. The writer will usually request that her "Executive Producer" or other producing credit (if applicable) appear in the main titles, on screen, on a separate card, in a size of type not smaller than that of any other individual, non-cast credit (such as the director's credit). If the writer renders consulting services in later seasons, the studio will sometimes refuse to commit to a main title consulting credit, promising only that such credit will appear, at a minimum, in the end titles. Some writers, however, have been able to negotiate for a main title guarantee. In addition, some writers choose to negotiate for a credit varying slightly from the traditional, such as that of "Executive Consultant."

Logo Credit

In recent years, a number of established writers have requested "logo" credits (which will typically appear in the end titles) in addition to their producer credits. Many television viewers are familiar with these types of credits. One example is David Kelley's ubiquitous rocking chair, which tips over after the end-title credits. Essentially, the writer's production company is allocated a few seconds of screen time at the conclusion of all end-title credits. Some networks have policies precluding the granting of more than a certain number of such logo credits. The studio producing the series (e.g., Paramount Television) will almost always insist on a logo, and at times, the star of the series might request one as well. Sometimes, there is more than one production company, and possibly a distributor, that are each guaranteed a logo credit. Studios granting logo credits will normally insert language in the contract stating that the granting of such credit, as well as its form and placement, will be "subject to network approval," since the network typically reserves final approval rights over credits.

Perks

As is the case with most production agreements, the writer will typically negotiate for some basic "perks," including (1) first-class travel if the studio or network requires the writer to travel; (2) first-class accommodations; (3) a per diem; and (4) ground transportation to and from airports, hotels, and sets. In addition, a writer will often request that an exclusive office and assistant be provided by the studio during all periods in which she is expected to render exclusive services. Finally, a reserved parking space is considered a bit of a status symbol in Hollywood and is requested by most series creators.

Guaranteed Script Assignments

Writers will often request that they be contractually guaranteed the right to write a minimum number of series episodic scripts. This essentially amounts to a money guarantee, as the studio is ultimately free to decide not to use (or even order) these scripts, but would nevertheless be obligated to pay for them. The studio will typically guarantee the writer one script in the first season (since only six episodes may be ordered) and two in each subsequent season in which the writer continues to render exclusive services.

Certain top-level television creators (think David Kelley) may not bother requesting this provision, as they know that the studio is likely to prefer that such individual write as many scripts as possible. The creator, therefore, knows that he will be free to write as many (or as few) episodic scripts as he wishes.

Episodic scripts (excluding only the pilot) are generally paid at WGA scale, which is currently roughly $25,000 for a half-hour episodic script and $40,000 for a one-hour script, and thus require little negotiation. Even the highest-level writer/producers are seldom paid more for the scripts they write during production of a series.

Subsequent Productions

The writer will often request a "right of first negotiation" to write and produce any subsequent productions based on the original series, such as spin-offs (discussed below), theatrical motion pictures, television movies, and Internet productions. In addition, the writer may request "passive payments" or royalties in the event such productions ultimately reach fruition without the writer's involvement.

A *spin-off* is a separate television series that is based on (or spun off) an existing series. There are two categories of spin-offs: generic spin-offs and planted-spin-offs. The appropriate royalty for the original series creator will usually vary, depending on which type of spin-off is produced. A "generic spin-off" is one in which one or more central characters in the new series were characters in the original series. An example is the short-lived *The Ropers,* a spin-off of *Three's Company,* or *Angel,* which derived from *Buffy The Vampire Slayer.* A "planted spin-off" refers to a series in which the central character or characters were introduced (or "planted") into a story line of an existing series with the express purpose of creating a new series that includes such characters. A well-known example is the *Melrose Place* series, in which several of the lead actors appeared in two or three episodes of *Beverly Hills, 90210* just prior to the launch of *Melrose*. Studios typically insist on paying a series creator (i.e., the writer that created the original series) a lesser royalty on the production of episodes of a planted spin-off.

The studio will try to impose certain limitations on the writer's ability to be "attached" to subsequent productions. For instance, the studio will attempt to limit the *first negotiation* right to television series spin-offs, arguing that theatrical productions or even TV movies require the expertise of a different type of writer. One of the most contentious elements of this negotiation relates to some studios' insistence that the writer be tied to series spin-offs only if such spin-off is developed while the writer is still serving as executive producer of the original series. The studio's logic is that, if the series creator has since moved on to other projects and the studio decides to develop a spin-off, the then-current executive producer of the original series should have the opportunity to create the spin-off, since this individual is now more intricately involved in the series. Moreover, it may be the current showrunner (and not the original creator) that has persuaded the studio to develop a spin-off. Alternatively, there are times when a series destined for cancellation is substantially reworked and "saved" by a replacement showrunner. Conversely, any series creator will argue that she alone created the characters that have spawned not only a successful series, but the possibility of a spin-off.

In situations where the writer/creator succeeds in securing a right of first negotiation to write and produce subsequent television productions, the writer's representative will usually request that the financial terms of the writer's initial agreement serve as a financial floor (or minimum) for any subsequent negotiation. Studios will generally agree to this request, on the theory that if the initial series was successful enough to generate a spin-off, the creator's stature in the television industry will have been elevated to a sufficient degree, such that she should receive no less than her prior fee when engaged to render services on the spin-off.

Once the terms governing the writer's attachment to subsequent productions have been negotiated, the studio and writer must set forth the amounts of royalties, if any, to be paid to the writer in the event that such productions are exploited without the writer's direct involvement. The writer's contract (in connection with her initial series/pilot) will usually set forth the amount of royalties, or passive payments, to be remitted to the writer in the event that good-faith negotiations fail to yield an agreement relating to the writer's services in connection with a subsequent production. Most commonly, studios will agree to the following: if a remake or generic spin-off of the series is produced, and the writer is not engaged to render writing or producing services thereon, the writer will receive a passive royalty equal to 50 percent of her royalty on the original series (upon production of each episode), as well as a profit participation on the generic spin-off or remake equal to 50 percent of her profit participation on the original series. If a planted spin-off is produced, the original writer (if not engaged) will, in most cases, be entitled to a royalty and profit participation equal to one-third of her negotiated episodic royalty and profit participation on the original series. Some studios refuse to pay more than 25 percent of such applicable amounts (rather than one-third) in connection with planted spin-offs.

Separated Rights

A writer receiving "Created by" credit on a series will typically be entitled to separated rights, which is a WGA-defined bundle of rights that are reserved to writers who create original material. While such rights can be sold or otherwise transferred to a studio or producer, they will not automatically be granted to the studio/producer merely because such studio/producer employs the writer.

The writer's separated rights include dramatic stage rights (the right to create, produce, or authorize production of a play based on his original work), theatrical rights (the right to authorize production of theatrical films based on the material), publication rights, merchandising rights (the right to sell merchandise based on the material), radio rights, and interactive rights.

As mentioned above, the employing studio/producer can negotiate to acquire some or all of these additional rights (apart from television rights, which were already contracted for). In order to do so, however, the studio must pay no less than the WGA-established minimum rates for each such set of rights. One exception to the obligation of studios/producers to pay minimum rates for the acquisition of separated rights is if the studio, at the time it initially hired the writer, paid a pilot-writing fee to such writer that was equal to, or in excess of, what the WGA calls the *upset price.* The upset price is a number significantly above the WGA minimum pilot fee and is established by the WGA. The WGA Agreement provides that if a writer has been paid not less than the applicable upset price, a studio is free to negotiate with the writer for the acquisition of separated rights, without regard to the WGA rates relating to such rights.

Turnaround

As discussed in chapter 3, some writers are able to negotiate for a turnaround provision in their deals. A turnaround right will allow the writer to attempt to set up her television project elsewhere if the employing studio does not elect to produce the project.

Miscellaneous

Television writing agreements typically address the following additional issues:

Pension/Health Fund

When negotiating a writing agreement that falls within the jurisdiction of the WGA, the writer's agent or attorney will usually request that the producer confirm its obligation to make required "fringe" payments to the WGA's health, pension, and welfare funds. Studios will generally agree to acknowledge this obligation in the writer's employment agreement.

E & O Insurance

As is the case when employed to write feature film scripts, television writers typically request to be named as additional insureds under the applicable errors and omissions (E & O) insurance policy. Studios typically agree, as their insurance policies are designed to cover errors and omissions attributable to writers that they employ.

DVD/Blu-Ray

Finally, most writers insist on the inclusion of a provision in their employment contract promising them a copy of the pilot and each series episode on both DVD and Blu-Ray. Again, while studios generally refuse to provide writers with more than one copy of the series, they will, as a matter of course, insert language in the agreement stating that the writer will be entitled to receive a single copy of each episode on DVD and Blu-Ray at such time, if ever, as such become commercially available.

Character Payments

It is worth noting that under the terms of the WGA Agreement, writers who create characters within existing series are entitled to certain royalties in each subsequent episode in which such characters appear, so that, for instance, if a writer credited with episode 134 of *Frasier* originates an "Uncle Leon," and such character appears in future episodes, the writer will receive a royalty for each future episode in which the "Uncle Leon" character appears.

WRITERS ON STAFF

Once a pilot is picked up by the network, the studio will hire a staff of writers to assist in the writing and production of the series. These writers will work under the direction of the showrunner. Depending on the seniority of the writer, the deal may require little negotiation (e.g., a "staff writer" might be hired at WGA scale and grant the studio options to employ such writer for up to three full seasons) or somewhat more negotiation (a writer hired as co-executive producer at $30,000 per episode with a two-year lock and elevation to executive producer credit in the second year). Since writers on staff are brought on after the pilot has already been produced, many of the issues that must be negotiated for show creators (e.g., sales bonus, royalties, and profits) are not relevant. It should be noted that, as discussed earlier in this chapter, if a staff writer creates a new character in any episode she writes, the WGA requires that such writer be paid a "character payment" for each subsequent episode in which that character appears. This payment is currently $405 per series episode. For writers hired to work on new or existing series, the following are the bullet points for any negotiation:

★ **Compensation** (whether weekly or episodic). While staff writers or story editors may be paid scale, senior-level writer/producers can earn as much as $50,000 per episode.

★ **Lock.** Is the writer guaranteed the full season or just a limited number of episodes with the studio's option to extend?

★ **Number of Options.** Can the studio require the writer to return for any additional seasons, and if so, how many?

★ **Credit.** Normally, the studio will agree to elevate the credit in successive seasons, so that a season-one executive story editor will be a co-producer if that writer returns in season two.

★ **Date of Option Exercise.** While broadcast networks operate on (more or less) the same schedule, cable networks do not. In recent years, an increasing number of cable networks have entered the series production business. Because a cable series may be produced during a different part of the calendar year (than the typical network series), the cable writer will want to ensure that the option exercise date for her next season is early enough so that if the option is not exercised, the writer will have the opportunity to find work on a network series without losing an entire season due to these differing schedules.

★ **Guaranteed Scripts.** The writer will often request the right to write (and be paid for) a minimum number of scripts during each season in which she is employed. It is customary for writers to be paid scale for any episode they write, in addition to their negotiated episodic producing fee. It should be noted that "staff writers" (as such term is used by the WGA, connoting the most junior writers on a television series writing staff) are rarely paid more than Writers Guild minimum for each week in which they render services, without any additional "producing" component in their fee.

The TV Writer/Producer Hierarchy

The current hierarchy among television writers, both in terms of credit and compensation, from most junior to most senior is as follows:

* ★ Staff Writer
* ★ Story Editor
* ★ Executive Story Editor
* ★ Co-producer
* ★ Producer
* ★ Consulting Producer[1]
* ★ Supervising Producer
* ★ Co-Executive Producer
* ★ Executive Producer

OVERALL DEALS

When a studio or network signs a writer to a *term deal*, or overall deal, the studio/network pays a lump sum to the writer during the term of the deal (typically one to two years with possible options for one or more additional years). In return, the writer's television writing and producing services are exclusive to the employing studio/network, and the writer cannot accept employment elsewhere. In addition, the writer will usually be required to write a minimum number of pilot scripts during the term for consideration by the studio or network.

The overall deal also governs the terms of the writer's services in the event that any of the scripts written during the term are ordered to production as pilots. Such provisions mirror those described above with respect to discrete writer/producer deals. Accordingly, the overall deal will provide for pilot and series producing fees, royalties, profit participations, series sales bonuses, etc., in much the same manner as previously discussed in this chapter.

Overall deals are most often reserved to the upper echelon of television writers, who can secure millions of dollars by agreeing to work exclusively for a

---

[1]The title "consulting producer" does not exist in all television series. At times, this credit is reserved for experienced writers hired on a part-time basis to assist with the writing or creation of plot lines for a series.

particular studio. At times, studios will enter into overall deals with mid-tier writers as well, although the dollars paid in connection with such deals will be substantially lower.

During the recent writer's strike, several studios availed themselves of the opportunity to terminate certain overall deals that the studios determined to be unproductive or too expensive. Most overall deals include a provision stating that if an event of "force majeure" (see Appendix B, "The Lingo") continues beyond a certain period of time (e.g., eight weeks), then the studio has the option to terminate the deal. During the recent WGA strike, which lasted for one hundred days, almost all studios instructed their legal departments to analyze the language in such contracts so that the executives could then determine whether they should terminate some of these expensive term deals. Once the strike ended, the economy had already started to decline, and studios have been more selective about renewing existing term deals and entering into fresh ones. The steady increase in successful reality shows has also made it more difficult for writers below the highest echelon to secure such lucrative arrangements. As somewhat of a counter-balance, many networks and studios have entered into overall deals with reality television producers.

Deal Point Summary:
TELEVISION WRITER/PRODUCER AGREEMENTS

1. Pilot Writing Fee

2. Pilot Services

3. Pilot Producing Fee

4. Series Services
- Guarantee/Lock
  - Producing
  - Consulting
- Exclusivity
- Series Producing Fee

5. Consulting Services

6. Series Sales Bonus

7. Episodic Royalties

8. Profit Participation

9. Credit
- "Written by"
- "Created by"
- "Executive Producer"
- Logo

10. Perks

11. Guaranteed Script Assignments

12. Subsequent Productions

13. Separation of Rights

14. Turnaround

15. Writers on Staff

16. Overall Deals

17. Miscellaneous
- Pension/Health
- E & O Insurance
- VHS/DVD
- Character Payments

FEATURE FILM

and

TELEVISION DIRECTOR

AGREEMENTS

*A*s with writers and actors, directors hired on studio films are governed by the terms of a collective bargaining agreement—the Directors Guild of America (DGA) Basic Agreement. The DGA Agreement comprehensively regulates many elements of a director's engagement on motion picture projects and in other media. The DGA Agreement covers not only theatrical films, but also television programs, documentaries, industrial films, educational films, commercials, and even music videos. There are currently more than twelve thousand members in the DGA, which include not only directors, but assistant directors (ADs), stage managers, and unit production managers (UPMs). Of course, not all directors are DGA members (and thus protected by the terms of the DGA Agreement), nor do all productions fall within DGA jurisdiction. Such nonunion deals will require added attention.

THE DEAL: FEATURE DIRECTING

A director employed on a feature film can spend as much as a full year working on the film, when one factors in development, pre-production, production, and post-production/editing. However, the director's services may not need to be rendered on an exclusive basis during all of these periods. When negotiating a director deal on a feature film, the following key issues should be addressed.

Development Services

During the development stage of a project (i.e., prior to such time as the film is "green-lit"), the director is typically expected to participate in *development activities* such as attending story meetings, supervising the writing of the screenplay, and participating in casting, budgeting, location scouting, or other activities related to the project. Whether the director's services will be rendered on an exclusive or nonexclusive basis during such development periods is a matter of negotiation. As the director may not be compensated for her development services (as discussed below), she is likely to prefer to be nonexclusive during this period. Conversely, the studio will usually prefer that the director spend all of her time working on the studio's project. The parties may ultimately compromise. For instance, a director may be permitted to render nonexclusive services if she agrees that such services will be in "first priority" or "high priority" or, at a minimum, that no outside services will interfere (or "materially interfere") with the director's expected services.

Pre-Production Services

During "formal" *pre-production* (typically, the period commencing eight weeks before the scheduled start date of principal photography), the studio will normally require that a director's services be rendered on an exclusive basis. During this period, casting and budgeting are finalized, set designs are completed, and script changes are (hopefully) kept to a minimum. In addition, rehearsal periods are often scheduled. An official "green light" from the studio (i.e., a commitment to produce the film) typically precedes the start of formal pre-production.

Principal Photography Services

Most studios require that the director be available to render directing services on an exclusive basis throughout the entire period of principal photography. Studio contracts are often worded in this way, as opposed to merely listing the required dates in which the director needs to render services. Thus, if a picture is still shooting after the anticipated end date, the director will be required to continue working on the film. Clearly, production cannot continue without the director's involvement. However, there may be instances where a high-level director will only accept a directing assignment if she is assured that she will be released by a specific date (for instance, if the director wishes to commit to another film scheduled to begin production). Studios will strongly resist granting a *stop date* to a director. Although a film may have, for example, a scheduled period of principal photography lasting twelve weeks, a studio might be reluctant to agree to a stop date occurring even after a total of fifteen weeks, since various unforeseen events might arise that can delay a production (such as an actor injury or illness, or even inclement weather).

Notwithstanding the fact that studios are loathe to grant stop dates (not only to directors, but to actors and producers as well), a studio will occasionally acquiesce in order to secure the services of a particular director. In such instances, if film production has not been completed by the stop date, the studio will need to schedule the remaining portion of production around the availability of the director.

Production Requirements

Most studio director contracts contain the following requirements:

Length

First-draft agreements normally state that the picture, as delivered by the director, must have a running time of "not less than 95 minutes and not more than 110 minutes." This is the optimal running time for a motion picture, as it enables theatre owners to exhibit the film numerous times each day. Since directors prefer maximum flexibility, their representatives are usually able to modify this language, expanding the range to "not less than 90 minutes nor more than 120 minutes." Notwithstanding these contractual requirements, studios in many cases approve cuts with longer running times, which is one reason that some of today's moviegoers complain that the art of brevity has been irretrievably lost.

Budget

Studio contracts generally state that "the picture shall be produced and delivered in accordance with the approved budget—subject only to changes approved by the studio, in writing." The studio hopes to minimize the risk of budget overruns, such as those that occurred during the shoot of Jim Cameron's *Titanic*. Directors often request language limiting this provision to situations within the control of the director. Such request is designed to exclude costs resulting from the demands of a star, for example (if such demands were met not by the director, but by the producer or studio), as well as costs resulting from added scenes requested by the studio.

One area of negotiation that can be crucial to a director's deal is the determination of what costs are considered part of the budget and what costs (if any) are outside of the budget. For example, if a major studio employs a producer that remains under the terms of an exclusive term deal at a third-party studio, the studio producing the film will typically need to repay a portion of that producer's overhead to the third-party studio. Such costs will normally be budgeted as a cost of the picture. Another example relates to tax incentives offered by many city municipalities, state governments, and foreign countries. If a studio receives a rebate as a result of shooting the film in the U.K., for example, the parties to a director agreement need to ascertain whether such costs will serve to reduce the film's budget.

Screenplay Conformity

Studios frequently include language requiring that the picture conform to the "approved shooting script." This requirement is designed to minimize the risk that the director will deviate significantly from the approved screenplay (which might result in the delivery of a film very different from the one contemplated by the studio executives).

Rating

Director contracts almost always contain a ratings requirement along these lines: "The Picture shall qualify for an *MPAA* rating of no more restrictive than [R, PG-13, etc.], unless otherwise approved in writing by the studio." Obviously, the director may not be able to predict the rating imposed on the film by the Motion Picture Association of America. Nonetheless, this is an important provision for the studio, as films geared towards male teens, for example, might generate less money when carrying an R rating. Similarly, the common wisdom in the industry dictates that an NC-17 rating significantly hinders a film's box office performance. Director representatives will attempt to limit the scope of this language by inserting the words "to the extent within Director's control" or "Director shall use 'reasonable' or 'best' efforts" to secure the necessary rating (which might include delivering additional cuts that conform to changes imposed by the MPAA).

Of course, there are sometimes major disagreements between the studio and the director as to what rating the film should attempt to qualify for. For example, the prevailing wisdom at many studios is that a PG-13 rating is preferable to an "R" because more teenagers can purchase tickets on their own (this is despite the fact that one of the highest grossing films of 2008, *The Dark Knight,* was rated "R"). The director, on the other hand, may believe that his vision for the film can only be realized with the more graphic violence that an "R" rating denotes.

Cover Shots

Cover shots refer to alternate scenes and dialogue used to "cover" scenes (such as those containing nudity or profanity) initially shot for the film's theatrical release. These cover shots are inserted into the network television, airline, or other versions of the picture, which may require a more conservative version. Disney's recent film, *Pearl Harbor,* required cover shots for the Japanese version, not because of raciness, but in order to scale back the appearance of the Japanese as villains. Studios generally include contractual language requiring the director to furnish requisite cover shots. In order to protect herself from any claim of breach, the director (through her attorney) will usually request that this contractual requirement be limited to covering scenes specified in a written memo generated by the studio.

Post-Production

Unlike actors, the director's services do not end when the camera is turned off. Rather, the director is required to deliver one or more *cuts* (edited versions) of the film to her employer. The director must, therefore, supervise the editing and mixing of the film. At times, reshoots are required after the conclusion of principal photography. The director's fee (discussed below) is typically deemed to include compensation for all such post-production services.

Compensation

A director's aggregate compensation can be structured in a variety of ways and may include a development fee, a profit participation, and bonus(es).

Development Fee

Studios will sometimes agree to pay a *development fee* to a director, which is designed to compensate the director for services rendered during development periods. A development fee is important in that it is quite possibly the only money that the director will actually receive in connection with any given project, since the "guaranteed" fee described in the next subheading is payable only if the movie is produced. It has previously been noted that within the studio system, most development projects do not graduate to the production stage. Accordingly, the "guaranteed" directing fee may not materialize.

When a development fee is paid, it is almost always in the form of an advance against the directing fee (as opposed to a sum in addition to the directing fee). The standard amount of the development fee in most studio deals is $25,000, which is usually payable one-half upon commencement of services and one-half upon the earlier of (1) *abandonment* of the project (i.e., the studio formally "passing" on the project, declaring that it will not be produced), or (2) the studio formally electing to proceed to production.

In some cases, a development fee is not paid, and the director must assume the risk that the project will not proceed to production. Studios seldom pay development fees to directors in connection with made-for-network television movies, for example. When engaged on these types of projects, a director may spend considerable time on a project without receiving compensation.

Finally, it should be noted that there are instances in which a director is hired at a very late stage in the development period, when the film might be only days or weeks away from being greenlit. Under such circumstances, most studios argue that the payment of a development fee is inappropriate.

A final example of an instance in which a development fee might not be payable to a director is if the director has also been engaged as a writer on the project. In such cases, the studio believes that paying the director or writer a development fee is inappropriate since the primary function of the development fee is to compensate the director for his or her time and effort in supervising development of a screenplay.

Guaranteed Fee

The DGA prescribes minimum compensation requirements for "high-budget" theatrical films (defined by the DGA as films with budgets in excess of $1,500,000). Most studio films fall into this category. Directors of such films, per the current DGA Agreement, cannot be paid less than roughly $157,000 for directing services on the picture. This amount is slightly lower for DGA-covered films with budgets falling below $1.5 million (i.e., $83,688 for films budgeted below $500,000 and $112,411 for films with budgets over $500,000 but under $1,500,000). Like the WGA, the DGA sets minimum weekly and daily rates for directors (currently $12,106 per week for high-budget films). Accordingly, the minimum fee set forth above will increase for films with longer production periods.

Subject to the above-described minimums, producers/studios and directors will negotiate the nature and amount of the director's compensation package based on factors that include the director's quote, the box office performance of that director's last film, the critical success of any films directed by her (including award nominations or wins), the budget of the film in question, as well as other factors that may come into play in any particular negotiation.

If a director is hired to work on a non–DGA-governed film, the DGA minimums can serve as guidelines when negotiating the director's fee.

The director's directing fee (exclusive of bonuses or profit participations) is often referred to as the guaranteed, or fixed, compensation, although it is not actually guaranteed unless and until the director is made "pay-or-play," as discussed later in this chapter.

Studios and producers typically impose the following payment schedule for the director's fixed compensation:

★ 20 percent of the guaranteed fee payable in weekly installments during the eight-week period immediately preceding principal photography (i.e., during pre-production)

★ 60 percent of the guaranteed fee in equal weekly installments over the period of principal photography

★ 10 percent upon completion of the director's last cut of the film

★ 10 percent upon delivery to the studio/producer of the *answer print*

This payment schedule is commonly referred to by industry insiders as a *20/60/10/10* payment plan and is seldom modified through negotiation.

Consider the following scenario: Joe Director is paid a $25,000 development fee against a directing fee of $300,000. If the project goes forward, Joe will receive a total of $300,000 (not $325,000), payable as follows: $12,500 when the deal is closed (development services would begin), $12,500 when the studio formally decides to go ahead with production, and $275,000 pursuant to a 20/60/10/10 formula. In other words, the $300,000 directing fee is inclusive of the $25,000 development fee.

Contingent Compensation

Like writers, most directors are able to negotiate for participation in the studio's net proceeds (as such term is defined in the director's contract). Unlike writers, however, there is a greater degree of variation as to the type of back-end compensation that a director might receive. First-time directors may receive a token 5 percent of net profits; more experienced directors might negotiate for 10 percent of net or even a percentage of adjusted gross (please see chapter 10 for a more detailed explanation of these concepts). The most successful directors, such as Spielberg and Scorcese, might secure a *first dollar gross* participation.

The nature and percentage of a director's back-end participation may, in some cases, be dictated by her front-end compensation. In other words, certain studios may offer a set back-end deal (for instance, 7.5 percent of net proceeds) to all directors paid less than $500,000 on a picture. Other times, the director's points will be determined entirely by negotiation, in which case numerous factors will come into play. These include many of the same factors influencing the director's fixed compensation, such as the director's quote, the heat surrounding the director, the budget of the film, the customary parameters of the applicable producer and/or distributor, and whether the director agreed to accept a lower up-front fee in return for a greater back-end.

It should be noted that *hyphenate* directors (i.e., directors serving in a dual capacity such as a writer-director, actor-director, or producer-director) might have greater success in extracting a more meaningful back-end participation in a motion picture. Examples of hyphenates are John Hughes and Spike Lee, who often write the screenplays for the films they direct; Steven Spielberg, who sometimes produces as well as directs, and Woody Allen, who often serves as lead actor and writer, as well as director.

Bonuses

Directors sometimes negotiate for the payment of additional sums as bonuses upon the occurrence of certain defined events. These bonuses are similar to the ones discussed in chapter 3 ("Feature Writer Employment Deals") and may include box office bonuses payable when and if a film achieves certain levels of box office receipts or award bonuses payable upon the director's winning (or being nominated for) certain awards, such as DGA Awards, Golden Globe Awards, or Academy Awards.

Advances

A final element of compensation that a director might negotiate for is the payment of an advance, i.e., the studio would agree to advance a certain portion of the director's anticipated profit participation at a predetermined point in time. An advance is valuable to the recipient in that she benefits from use of the funds prior to the time such amounts are actually owed (sometimes as early as one to two years before the studio's obligation to pay would otherwise materialize).

Example: A director is paid $400,000 (inclusive of a $25,000 development fee) plus 10 percent of the adjusted gross receipts (AGR) of the film. The studio might agree to advance $200,000 of such AGR at such time as the film is first released on video and DVD. When monies are first payable under the director's AGR participation, $200,000 would be subtracted, as it would have already been advanced at an earlier point and is fully recoupable from the director's percentage of AGR. An advance differs from a bonus in that it is deemed to be a prepayment of a sum that the director is likely to receive at a later date, while a bonus is generally not deducted from compensation otherwise owed to the director.

Pay-or-Play

As discussed in previous chapters, the following question often arises in Hollywood negotiations: At what point in time, if ever, is the director's (or producer's, actor's, etc.) fixed compensation guaranteed? This issue is particularly important for directors, since, unlike actors, the director is often hired during the development stage of the project, before a determination is made as to whether the project will proceed to production.

When a director becomes pay-or-play, her directing fee is guaranteed (subject to very limited exceptions) regardless of whether she actually directs the film. Thus, if the studio decides to halt production of the film, or replace the director, it must nevertheless remit the director's fee in its entirety. The term "pay-or-play" derives from the fact that the director either gets to "play" (i.e., direct the picture) or, alternatively, be "paid." The term is a bit of a misnomer, since if the director gets to "play," she will also, obviously, be "paid." The relevant negotiation therefore involves determining the point in time, if ever, that the director becomes "pay-or-play."

The most common exceptions to the studio's commitment to pay a director, even after such director is deemed "pay-or-play," include (1) a breach of the contract by the director, (2) the director's death or a disability preventing her from rendering or completing services, and (3) acts of force majeure that affect the picture's production. If any of the foregoing scenarios arise, the studio will generally be able to terminate the director's services without owing additional compensation.

As discussed in chapter 3, there is a concept known as "pay-and-play," which studios rarely commit to. If a director is hired on a pay-and-play basis, the studio cannot fulfill its obligation to the director merely by paying her fee. Rather, the studio must allow the director to actually direct the film. The studio's only alternative (absent exigent circumstances, such as the director's default or disability) is to refrain from producing the film. It is highly unusual for directors to secure a pay-and-play commitment, so the experienced director's representative will focus on ensuring that the contract clearly delineates the events that must take place in order for the director to reach the point of pay-*or*-play, after which the studio will be obligated to pay the entire director's fee regardless of whether the movie is actually completed or whether the director is replaced (again, subject to several contractual exclusions, such as a material breach by the director).

Studios will usually agree that if the director has not been terminated during the development stage (at which point the director would commonly be paid her full development fee and nothing more), then the director will be deemed pay-or-play when *all* of the following events occur:

1. The studio has approved the final screenplay
2. The studio has approved the final budget
3. The studio has engaged the producer on a pay-or-play basis
4. The studio has engaged the principal cast on a pay-or-play basis
5. The studio has set a firm start date for beginning principal photography

In most instances, the studio does not anticipate replacing the director. However, the studio will attempt to ensure that it will not be obligated to pay the director's directing fee unless the picture is certain to reach the production stage. Once the studio sets a start date and hires the principal cast members on a pay-or-play basis, it will be fairly confident that the movie will be made.

In the course of negotiations, a director may be able to whittle away at some of the requirements listed above. For instance, the studio may agree to modify condition 4 above by limiting it to the employment of one or two principal cast members (i.e., the condition will be satisfied if at least one or two cast members have been hired, rather than the entire cast). Additionally, the studio may waive the condition relating to the hiring of a producer, or at least agree to specify the type of producer that must be hired.

Of course, even after the conditions referred to above have occurred, the studio may nevertheless exercise its right to terminate the director (so long as the director was not made pay-*and*-play). However, unless such director is fired for "cause"—a defined set of circumstances encompassing material breach, disability, death, or unforeseen circumstances such as wars or strikes— the studio will be obligated to pay the director's entire fixed compensation.

Vesting of Contingent Compensation

A discussion of pay-or-play begs the following question: If a director is "pay-or-played off a film," will the director be entitled to any portion of the negotiated contingent compensation? From the director's perspective, she was fired from the project without cause and prevented from rendering services. In extreme situations, the director's termination may have occurred halfway through production, and the studio might even be planning to use some of the footage directed by the director who was subsequently replaced.

The studio's initial position is likely to be that a director that is terminated at any point prior to the completion of all services on the picture will not be entitled to her back-end participation, and that payment of the fixed compensation will satisfy the entirety of the studio's obligation. The studio might argue that even if it could not "pin" the director's termination on any sort of breach by the director, and that the director's termination can only be attributed to "creative differences," the bottom line is that the studio believed it needed to take the drastic (and expensive) measure of replacing a director in order to improve the quality of the movie and that, therefore, any payment beyond the guaranteed director's fee is inappropriate.

Often, however, both parties agree to a schedule in which the negotiated contingent compensation will be payable. This is referred to as a *vesting schedule*. There are various ways to structure such a schedule, and studios will almost always refuse to entertain a vesting schedule at all unless the director was replaced *after* principal photography began.

Three common methods of vesting contingent compensation are the following:

- ★ The contingent compensation shall vest in the manner that the fixed compensation is payable (i.e., the 20-60-10-10 formula). Note that in this scenario, the director would be entitled to some portion of the contingent compensation even if she was terminated prior to the start of principal photography.
- ★ The contingent compensation vests in the same ratio as the number of weeks the director worked during principal photography compares to the total number of weeks of principal photography, so that if the director worked two out of ten weeks, the director would be entitled to 20 percent of her contingent compensation.
- ★ The contingent compensation vests in the same ratio that the number of linear feet of film (contained in the final, released picture) directed by the director compares to the total number of linear feet contained in the completed film. For example, if the released picture consists of 10,000 feet of film, 3,000 of which were shot by the first director, that director would be entitled to 30 percent of her contingent compensation.

Credit

Many aspects of the director's credit, including placement, minimum size, and paid advertising requirements, are governed by the DGA. However, as the DGA merely provides minimum requirements, there is room for negotiation in the area of credits. Moreover, as noted above, not all films fall within the jurisdiction of the DGA. On non-DGA films, all elements of credit must be specifically negotiated.

"Directed By" Credit

Per the DGA, the "Directed by" credit must be the final credit appearing on screen in the main titles. If there are no main titles (in other words, all credits follow the picture), the "Directed by" credit must be the first such post-picture credit. If the film is not subject to the terms of the DGA, placement must be specifically negotiated. However, most non-DGA films tend to follow the practice of placing the "Directed by" credit last among main title credits or first within the end title credits.

Other key issues relating to the director's on-screen credit, aside from placement, include (1) its appearance on a separate card (i.e., no other credit to appear on screen at the same moment); (2) boldness, color, and width; and (3) size of type (the DGA agreement requires that the director's credit not be smaller than 50 percent of the size of type used for the film's title. Some directors can successfully negotiate for a 75 percent size tie to the title).

The DGA also prescribes guidelines for the inclusion of the director's credit in items of advertising (whether print ads, billboards, radio ads, or one-sheets). Directors employed under DGA jurisdiction may attempt to negotiate improvements in this area beyond the DGA's minimum requirements, while non-DGA directors will need to specifically negotiate the types of advertisements that will carry their credit. One common request made by directors' representatives during credit negotiations is that their client be credited in all forms of advertisements in which any other individual is credited, regardless of whether such ad constitutes a DGA-regulated advertisement. If the studio agrees, it will usually exclude cast credits (so that a poster, for example, can mention the stars of the film without triggering the director's credit), as well as award, nomination, and congratulatory ads (so that an ad taken out in the *Hollywood Reporter* congratulating one of the producers will not need to include a credit to the director). Talent representatives sometimes get quite technical and request that the contractual provisions limiting the studio's credit obligations within award and nomination ads specify that these are "award, nomination, or congratulatory ads *in which only the honoree is mentioned*" (so that if an ad congratulating the writer *also* credits one of the producers, the director would need to be credited as well).

Possessory Credit

Many directors are accorded a credit separate from, and in addition to, the "Directed by" credit. This credit is commonly referred to as the "Film by" or *possessory credit* and appears in one of two forms: "A Film By [Name of Director]" or "A [Name of Director] Film." This credit is not governed by the DGA Agreement, so that directors desiring such credit must negotiate all aspects of its appearance on screen and in paid ads, if such credit is guaranteed at all. While first-time directors rarely secure a possessory credit, studios grant these credits quite freely to experienced directors.

It should be noted that in the recent negotiations between the Writers Guild and motion picture producers, many writers objected to the granting of possessory credits to directors. These writers felt that such credits diminished their own contribution to the authorship of films. As a result, motion picture producers who are signatory to the WGA and DGA agreements have agreed to enter into discussions with the DGA in the hope of arriving at specific guidelines regarding the granting of possessory credits to directors.

Logo Credit

The highest echelon of directors will usually seek a logo credit (see discussion in connection with producer agreements) in addition to their "directed by" and possessory credits. Even if the studio acquiesces, a negotiation will ensue as to whether the logo is onscreen only (or also in paid ads), whether it is tied in placement to the distributor's logo, and whether it will appear in the main titles before the picture or elsewhere.

Cuts and Previews

Many people are familiar with the term "*final cut,*" which is, essentially, the ability, or power, to dictate final changes to a motion picture. In most instances, the entity financing the motion picture (e.g., the studio, independent producer, or distributor) will have final cut. What this means is that, although the director may turn in a cut or version of the picture that she finds satisfactory, the studio may, nevertheless, have the ability to tinker with that version and re-edit it to the point of making material changes, such as changing the ending.

Only the upper echelon of film directors, such as the late Stanley Kubrick, are able to secure the right of final cut. If a director is granted final cut, the studio will have only two choices: to release the film exactly as it was turned in by the director or to shelve the picture (which it would be loathe to do, after having spent tens of millions of dollars).

Many film directors view their movies as "works of art," and therefore might agree to forego certain financial remuneration in return for the right of final cut. Giving up the final cut, however, is generally not a viable option for the major studios, and accordingly, this right continues to be granted to a very limited number of elite directors. Independent producers are sometimes a bit more flexible in this regard, but even independent producers typically feel that their own right of final cut is crucial in order to protect their investment. Accordingly, they may be unwilling to take the risk that a director will sacrifice a film's commercial elements for the sake of "art."

While final cut may not be available in most instances, what is negotiable is the number of cuts the studio will grant the director (before being able to make its own changes), as well as the number of *previews* (test screenings) that the director will be guaranteed, so that the director might benefit from an audience's response.

It should be noted that "final cut" does not necessarily mean final cut for all forms of media. The most common form of final cut (which in and of itself is fairly uncommon) refers to final cut for the domestic theatrical version and possibly the home video version of the film. Studios often resist granting final cut for theatrical versions in foreign territories and for non-theatrical media such as television and airlines.

The DGA requires producers to grant a minimum of one cut and one preview to feature film directors. First-time directors will rarely succeed in gaining more than the DGA minimum. Customarily, directors with some experience will be able to secure two cuts and two previews. Studios will occasionally grant three cuts to high-end directors. Beyond that, the elusive "final" cut is generally available only to the most renowned directors.

On the occasions where the studios grant more than one cut and preview, they frequently attach certain conditions to the grant of the second or subsequent cuts. For instance, studios might condition the director's second cut on the film being completed at or below the approved budget and schedule. In addition, a studio might attempt to make all cuts beyond the first subject to the studio's post-production schedule and anticipated release date. In other words, the studio might be able to withhold its second cut or preview in the event that the picture's release date was moved ahead. All of these conditions are subject to negotiation and may or may not appear in the final draft of the director's agreement.

Approval Rights

The director has sometimes been analogized to the CEO of a corporation (the film taking on the role of "corporation"), with the studio serving as board of directors. In her capacity as CEO, the director is the chief on-set decision maker with respect to issues ranging from casting, set design, lighting, and even the tone and demeanor of the actors in any particular scene. Often, however, many of these decisions are subject to the studio's (or "board of directors'") veto power.

Because the director will be held responsible, at least by the press, for the ultimate quality of the picture, most directors fight hard for a contractual right of approval over all major creative elements relating to the film. Directors often seek approval over the principal cast, key crew members, final screenplay, budget, music, locations, schedule, and even the marketing campaign and *release pattern* (i.e., in which cities will the movie be first exhibited, on how many screens, and how will it subsequently be rolled out, or extended, to other cities nationwide and overseas?).

Novice directors may be unable to secure more than a right of consultation with respect to some or all of the above areas. More experienced directors, however, are likely to be able to secure a right of approval over most, but not necessarily all, of the elements described above. Studios are often reluctant to grant approval rights with respect to final budgets, release patterns, and marketing campaigns. In most instances in which directors are granted approval rights, the studio, nevertheless, reserves the right to make the final decision in the event of a disagreement between the director and the studio. In addition, studios often attempt to limit a director's approval over the selection of key crew members by subjecting the terms of such hires to budgetary requirements.

Right of First Negotiation

Most directors will request a right of first negotiation, or first opportunity, to be engaged as a director in connection with any subsequent production, such as a prequel, sequel, re-make, or theatrical spin-off of the motion picture. The director may want to leave all of her options open, and will be unlikely to commit to direct a sequel in advance, but may want the security of knowing that the option of directing a sequel or remake is available to her. It should be noted, however, that studios will sometimes require that a novice director grant to the studio an option (i.e., the right, but not the obligation) to require the director to direct a second picture, such as a sequel, at a pre-negotiated price (which the studio hopes will be lower than the director's future market rate). Such a provision is commonly referred to as a "second picture option." Relatively unknown actors (especially when cast in a leading or prominent role in a motion picture) are sometimes required to grant second picture options as well, particularly if the first film is considered likely to spawn a sequel.

Most studios and producers will agree to grant the director a right of first negotiation with respect to directing subsequent productions, subject to certain limitations. For instance, the studio will typically limit the right of first negotiation to subsequent *theatrical* productions, thereby excluding television or even straight-to-video productions, as well as Internet or other types of productions. In addition, a studio will attempt to limit the term of a first negotiation right in two ways: First, it may try to set an "outside" expiration date on the right itself. In other words, the studios will typically require that the subsequent production occur within five or seven years of the release of the first picture in order for the director's right of first negotiation to remain in effect. Second, the studio may set a time limit on the actual negotiations for each subsequent production (typically ten to thirty business days) so that, if an agreement on financial and other terms is not concluded within such preestablished time frame, the studio will be free to employ a different director.

At the request of the director's representatives, studios sometimes agree that any offer to engage the director on a subsequent theatrical production (whether a prequel, sequel, or remake) will be on terms no less favorable than that of the director's engagement on the current motion picture. In other words, if the director was paid $500,000 for the first picture, the studio would be obligated to offer a minimum of $500,000 for services in connection with such prequel, sequel, or remake. Such a provision is designed to ensure that, if and when the studio makes an offer of employment to the director on a subsequent production, such offer will not be illusory and will be made in good faith.

Within the general parameters described above, the specifics of any particular director's right of first opportunity will vary, depending in large part on the relative leverage and negotiating skills of the respective parties.

Turnaround

The concept of "turnaround" has been discussed previously in chapter 3. Directors will sometimes seek the right to remain "attached" to a project in turnaround (i.e., to retain the right to direct the picture if it is ultimately produced) if the employing studio abandons the project and allows it to be shopped elsewhere. Such attachment affords protection to the director, ensuring that if the motion picture does in fact get made (albeit at another studio), the director will continue to have the opportunity to remain involved.

At times, a director will not be satisfied with mere "attachment" to the project and will request the actual right of turnaround (i.e., the right to shop the project to competing studios). While this right is more commonly afforded to producers, there may be instances in which the director will be granted the sole turnaround right, or one that is shared with other parties involved with the project, such as the producer(s) or writer(s). As with many issues, the director's leverage in a particular negotiation will impact whether she secures a right of turnaround.

Insurance

As is the case with writers, directors typically seek assurances from the studio or producer that the general liability and E & O (errors and omissions) insurance policies relating to the motion picture will cover the director. Studios generally agree to such coverage as a matter of course.

Travel, Expenses, and Perks

The DGA agreement requires that studios provide directors with first-class travel, accommodations, and a minimum *per diem* (currently in the range of $75) while the director renders services on location. Some directors can successfully negotiate to receive amounts substantially in excess of DGA scale. Other matters that are addressed in such negotiations include the use of a rental car (as well as the size and quality of such rental car), additional plane tickets for the director's use (for family members, companions, etc.), the size and type of trailer made available for the director's use on location, and payment or reimbursement for an exclusive or nonexclusive assistant. Directors working on nonunion productions must negotiate for these or similar provisions. As with many other issues, the nature and extent of the director's perks will be attributable in large part to the film's budget and to the director's stature. A-list directors, for example, often receive star trailers, luxury hotel suites, and chauffeured town cars while rendering services on location.

Premieres/Festivals

Most directors will request contractual language guaranteeing that the studio will invite the director to all premieres of the motion picture (as well as all festivals in which the motion picture is exhibited), and that the studio will provide the director (and a guest) with travel, hotel accommodations, per diem, and ground transportation in the event such premiere or festival is held more than fifty miles from the director's residence. Studios may attempt to limit this right to a single premiere, or to one east-coast and one west-coast premiere, so that if additional premieres are held, including overseas, the studio would not be contractually obligated to invite the director or to pay for her expenses. In practice, most studios believe it to be advantageous for the director to attend premieres, as the director's absence might lead to speculation (by the media) that the film was plagued with problems.

DVD/Soundtrack Album/Blu-Ray

Directors usually request a complimentary copy of the film on DVD and on Blu-Ray and, increasingly, a copy of the motion picture's soundtrack. The studio will usually accommodate this request, provided that such products are actually manufactured and made commercially available.

Pension, Health, and Welfare

DGA-governed studio contracts typically provide that the studio will make all required pension, health, and welfare (PH&W) contributions to the Directors Guild of America, if applicable. Such payments can increase the studio's costs by as much as 13 percent of the applicable minimum director fee, and talent attorneys generally insist that such obligations on the part of the studio be specified in writing.

TELEVISION DIRECTORS

Television director deals are often quite formulaic and uncomplicated. Nonetheless, a few brief points are worth mentioning.

Made-for-Television Movies

Negotiations involving the engagement of directors in connection with made-for-television movies are nearly identical to those involving feature films. The primary difference relates to the definition of the back-end profits, if applicable. Chapter 10 describes the basic elements of a television net profits definition.

Episodic Television

Directors employed to direct episodic television (excluding television pilots, as discussed below) rarely involve any meaningful negotiation. This is primarily because the accepted practice in the television business is to pay DGA minimum to directors of episodic television. DGA minimum for a half-hour network prime-time filmed show is currently approximately $20,000. DGA scale for a one-hour filmed episode is roughly $35,000. Occasionally, deal points unrelated to the director's compensation do arise. A director being booked months in advance, for instance, may request a "pilot out" or "feature out." In other words, the director would like the ability to opt out of the directing assignment (upon providing the employer with sufficient advance notice) in the event that a more lucrative assignment arises, such as a pilot or a feature film. Some studios will agree to such "out" if the director provides sufficient notice (most commonly, four weeks); however, there are times when a studio will refuse such a request on the grounds that it can potentially cause too much disruption. Another potential element of negotiation relates to the director's travel and expenses. While most programs that film in New York or Los Angeles will utilize local directors in order to avoid inflating the budget, there are many instances in which a director may be required to travel to a distant location. In such instances, travel and expense provisions must be negotiated, subject to the DGA's minimum requirements.

As almost all television series are produced under the auspices of the DGA, credit and most remaining terms (other than those discussed above) will generally be addressed by the DGA Agreement.

Television Pilots

Unlike directors engaged to direct episodes of existing series, the employment of pilot directors typically involves a good deal of negotiation. First, there is not an accepted practice of paying DGA minimum for such services. Pilot directors on a half-hour program can be paid anywhere from approximately $50,000 to as much as $250,000. The reason pilot directors are paid considerably more than they would be to direct subsequent episodes is that the director's contribution to the pilot is highly valued, and usually, an established TV director is hired for one pilot. The pilot episode establishes the look and feel of the series as a whole, and the artistic elements brought to fruition by the director will be significant. In addition, a television director will generally be required to render services over a longer period of time in connection with a pilot, as a pilot's shooting schedule can be as much as twice as long as that of a subsequent episode.

In addition to the director's initial compensation, a pilot director will, in many cases, be offered a back-end (i.e., profit participation) in connection with the series—generally in the range of 2.5 to 5 percent of net. As discussed earlier, television net profits can be extremely lucrative if the series succeeds. Consequently, a fair amount of time is sometimes spent negotiating the terms of the director's profit participation.

Another important element found in most pilot director agreements is an episodic royalty. Pilot directors are frequently able to secure a contractual provision guaranteeing payment of a royalty upon production of each series episode beyond the pilot. While directors' royalties generally fall below the range of writer/creator royalties, many directors of prime-time network pilots can obtain a royalty in the range of $1,500 to $2,500 per episode (the amount will be somewhat lower for alternative programming, such as for basic cable or a late-night series).

While credit and many remaining terms concerning pilot services will generally be covered under the DGA Agreement, issues relating to travel/expenses (again, subject to DGA minimum requirements), length of services, and exclusivity will need to be addressed separately.

Deal Point Summary:
DIRECTOR AGREEMENTS

1. Services
- Development Services
- Pre-Production
- Principal Photography
- Post-Production

2. Compensation
- Development Fee
- Guaranteed Compensation
- Contingent Compensation
- Bonuses and/or Advances

3. Pay-or-Play

4. Vesting of Contingent Compensation

5. Credit (On-Screen and Paid Ads)
- "Directed By"
- Possessory Credit

6. Cuts and Previews

7. Approval Rights

8. First Negotiation/Subsequent Productions

9. Turnaround

10. Insurance

11. Travel, Expenses, and Perks

12. Premieres/Festivals

13. VHS/DVD/Soundtrack

14. Pension, Health, and Welfare Contributions

15. Television Directors
- Type of Production
  - Made-for-Television Movies
  - Episodic Television
  - Pilots
- Compensation
- Credit

FILM PRODUCERS

$\mathcal{M}$ost films released today list a variety of producing credits, including "Line Producer," "Producer," "Executive Producer," "Co-Executive Producer," "Produced by," "Co-Producer," "Associate Producer," and others. One reason for this proliferation of producing credits is that there is no studio-recognized union governing the engagement of producers in Hollywood, as there are for writers, actors, and directors. (The Producers Guild of America, not a traditional union but more of a trade organization, is discussed in chapter 1.) As a result, studios are able to bestow "producer" credits at their discretion. Because the employment of producers is not regulated by a union, every aspect of a producer's deal is subject to negotiation, limited only by certain parameters established through custom and practice. While there is a professional organization known as the Producers Guild, it functions solely as a trade association, and its pronouncements and suggested practices are not legally binding on the part of studios.

It should be noted that in many of the remaining chapters of this book, as well as in many contracts relating to the employment of individuals on motion pictures, the terms "studio" and "producer" are used interchangeably, as the studio is deemed to be the entity creating or producing the film. As this chapter discusses individual film producers (who are themselves hired by studios), the term "producer" in this chapter will refer only to such non-studio employees who are hired to render producing services on a motion picture, rather than to the studio itself.

SERVICES: THE PRODUCER'S ROLE

Unlike "writer" or "director," the "producer" title does not intrinsically convey a specific function. As mentioned earlier, there are many different types of producers. Most productions, for example, employ at least one "line producer," whether such individual is referred to by that title or not. The line producer generally serves as the hands-on manager of the production, preparing budgets, securing locations, negotiating leases, and supervising the accounting staff, among other functions.

Other individuals may have earned their producer status by serving as the personal manager to one of the stars, or even the film's writer. The star of a motion picture might demand a producing credit for himself. Such credits are sometimes referred to as "vanity" credits. Similarly, a particularly powerful director or star might be able to secure a producer credit for someone in his entourage. In each of the foregoing cases, the studios will seldom require full-time actual services from such producer. The executive producer title, for example, was traditionally bestowed on individuals who helped secure financing for a motion picture, although this is no longer necessarily (or even primarily) the case. Some production companies today accord executive producer credit to their own employees, usually the creative executive responsible for championing the project during its development stage.

During the development stage of a motion picture project, the producer will be expected to supervise the screenwriter or writers, attend story meetings, and suggest potential directors and cast. During pre-production and principal photography of the picture, the producer may be called upon to ensure that the production runs smoothly, potentially even easing tensions (to the extent such tensions arise) between the studio executive and the director, or among cast members. Finally, during post-production periods, the producer will generally assist in the editing process and supervise looping, dubbing, and reshoots.

Many independent producers (those that find independent financing for their films outside the studio system) and production attorneys utilize a production checklist (a form of which is included in appendix A) to ensure that all necessary rights, agreements, and other elements pertaining to the production and distribution of a motion picture are in order and properly documented.

MAKING THE DEAL

This chapter will discuss motion picture producers in the conventional sense—those directly responsible for the production of the film, reporting to the financing studio, and generally receiving the "Produced by" credit.

Production Requirements

Most studio producer contracts require the producer, like the director, to adhere to the following standard production guidelines in connection with the film:

Picture Length

The producer's contract will generally state that the completed picture must have a running time of "not less than 95 minutes and not more than 110 minutes." Through negotiation, the studio may agree to modify this language to expand the range of permissible picture length. While the studio will ultimately sign off on the precise running time, it is the producer's job to work with the editor to ensure that a desirable running time is achieved.

Budget

Studio contracts generally require that "the picture shall be produced and delivered in accordance with the approved budget—subject only to changes approved by the studio, in writing." The producer is expected to pay close attention to costs and to anticipate problems in this area.

As unlikely as it may seem, the definition of "approved budget" in this context sometimes involves lengthy negotiations. This is because the producer's ability to deliver a film within the budgeted cost is not always simple, especially when certain increased costs result from factors beyond the producer's control. Such factors may include currency fluctuations (e.g., a U.S. film shooting in Mexico, Canada, or the U.K.), film lab delays, or even third-party breaches such as the star of the picture failing to show up for work on a particular day. These issues become even more important in instances where a producer is subject to an *overbudget penalty* or when a producer is entitled to an *underbudget bonus*.

Screenplay Conformity

Studios frequently include language in the producer's contract requiring that the picture conform to the approved shooting script. This requirement is designed to minimize the risk that the final version of the film will deviate significantly from the approved screenplay.

Rating

Studios will typically specify a particular rating requirement in the producer's agreement, which will vary depending on the type of film. For example, producers of animated children's movies might be required to deliver a film qualifying for a "G" rating. Ultimately, the Motion Picture Association of America (MPAA) serves as final arbiter of the rating. Nevertheless, the producer is expected to use his best efforts to ensure that the film will qualify for the desired rating.

With the increasing popularity of the PG-13 rating, studios are more reluctant than ever to release "R"-rated movies if such a rating can be avoided. Even horror films, which were traditionally released with an "R" rating in the past, are now sometimes brought to market with a PG-13. Studios are loath to limit the potential audience for a film in this climate of increased costs. The average studio film now costs $70 million to produce and $35 million to market. While some viewers prefer the adult content that an R-rated film offers, most studio executives believe that the chances for commercial success will be increased if the most explicit scenes in the film can be modified or deleted in order to qualify for PG-13. Not surprisingly, many producers and most directors want the freedom to deliver a picture that conforms to their creative vision, regardless of the rating placed on the film by the MPAA. Consequently, the requirement to deliver a film with a rating no more restrictive than that designated by the studio is often a contentious point.

Cover Shots

Cover shots refer to alternate scenes and dialogue used to "cover" scenes (such as those containing nudity or profanity) initially shot for the film's theatrical release. These "cover shots" are inserted into the network television, airline, or other version of the picture. Studios generally include contractual language requiring the producer to deliver the requisite cover shots.

End Credits

Studio agreements sometimes impose limits on the length of the end credits (i.e., credits appearing at the end of the film), often insisting that the running time of such credits cannot exceed three minutes.

Compensation

Like directors, a producer's aggregate compensation can be structured in a variety of ways and may include a number of different components.

Development Fee

When a producer becomes "attached to" a project (either because he partici-pated in the pitch, is the manager of the writer or one of the actors, was brought in by the studio, or for some other reason), he may be able to negoti-ate for payment of a development fee as an advance against his negotiated producing fee. The development fee is intended to compensate the producer for services rendered during development periods. This fee is important in that it is quite possibly the only money that the producer will actually receive. As previously mentioned, many projects are developed; few are produced. Some successful producers, known colloquially as "pitch-meisters," can eke out a relatively good living by simply setting up pitches all over town and col-lecting their development fees, with years passing before any one project actu-ally goes forward.

In instances where a development fee is paid, most studios customarily pay $25,000, although the amount of the development fee can range from $10,000 to $60,000, depending on the project. The development fee is typically payable half upon commencement of services and half upon the earlier of (1) abandon-ment of the project or (2) the studio electing to proceed to production.

Guaranteed Fee (a.k.a. Producing Fee)

Since there is no union-prescribed minimum producing fee, studios are free to pay as low a fee as they are able to negotiate (subject, of course, to the federal minimum wage statute!). As in other above-the-line negotiations, the produc-er's fee will be influenced by such factors as his quote, the box office perfor-mance of the producer's last film, the critical success of any films with which he was associated, the nature of the services that he will be expected to pro-vide, the budget of the film, as well as, in the case of the personal manager, the industry stature of his particular client.

Those receiving "vanity credits" (producing credits given to one or more actors involved in the film) are seldom entitled to a producing fee, as the actor's performing fee will be deemed by the studio to include compensation for any services rendered in the capacity of producer.

The producer's producing fee, less the development fee, is typically paid in accordance with the schedule used to pay directors—in other words, the 20/60/10/10 schedule described in chapter 5. First-time producers can earn fees ranging from $50,000 (for low-budget pictures) to $250,000, while high-level producers such as Jerry Bruckheimer can secure fees in excess of $1 mil-lion per picture, with a significant back-end participation.

Pay-or-Play

When negotiating his deals, a producer will want to contractually identify the point in time in which he becomes pay-or-play (i.e., the point at which his producing fee is guaranteed, subject only to events of default, disability, death, and force majeure).

The issue of pay-or-play can impact credit as well. Many studios take the position that the pay-or-play obligation relates to compensation only, so that if a producer is "pay-or-played off the picture" (i.e., terminated without cause), the studio is relieved of its obligation to accord credit to such producer. Producers obviously resist this interpretation and attempt to secure a commitment by the studio to include their name on-screen as well as in print advertisements relating to the film, even if they are terminated early. Studios and producers, therefore, frequently negotiate heavily with respect to specifying the point in time, if any, at which the studio must commit to crediting the producer on the film (provided the film is actually released), regardless of whether the producer is subsequently pay-or-played off the picture. Unlike the determination of credits for writers and directors, the according of producer credits is governed only by the producer's contract, with no recourse to union arbitration.

Negotiations surrounding the issue of early pay-or-play termination and its impact on the producer's credit can be particularly heated in instances where the producer pitched the project to the studio. In such cases, the producer is likely to argue (quite forcefully) that he has earned a producer credit simply by bringing the project in to the studio. Thus, even if the studio makes drastic changes to the project, so that the film that is ultimately exhibited is radically different from the producer's initial vision, the producer is likely to feel that he should be paid (as well as credited) as a reward for discovering the project, regardless of whether he was permitted to render actual services.

Contingent Compensation

Depending on the type of producer being engaged, and the factors underlying such producer's employment, the back end of the producer's deal can be as varied as the front end. Studios are, of course, under no obligation to give out points (i.e., a percentage of the film's profits) to producers, and certain categories of producers (such as co-producers and associate producers) will rarely secure any meaningful contingent compensation. True producers, however (of the type discussed herein—those rendering actual services as the chief production executive), will often be successful in negotiating for some form of profit participation.

Established producers (those who have delivered a string of hits to the studios) often receive a percentage of a film's adjusted gross receipts (AGR), which is more significant than a percentage of net proceeds, in that the fees and expenses charged against revenues are substantially lower when calculating AGR. For the highest-level producers, of course, the sky is the limit. Like A-level actors, these producers can secure *first dollar gross* (although the percentage a producer will obtain will rarely exceed 5 percent). One form of profit participation commonly granted to film producers, when supported by their quotes, is a participation of "50 percent of 100 percent of the project net proceeds, reducible by all third-party participations to a floor of 25 percent." What this means is that the producer's percentage of net proceeds will fall within the range of 25 percent to as much as 50 percent. If the studio accords net proceeds to other individuals, such as to the writer or director, these will be subtracted from the producer's share, until the studio has doled out 25 or more "points" to such individuals. At that point, the producer hits his floor or 25 percent, so that additional points granted by the studio will not be deducted from the producer's share. Although the foregoing is based on a "net" definition (as opposed to gross or adjusted gross), the producer benefits by receiving a large percentage (25 to 50 percent). Some producers with this type of back-end will request a right of approval over the granting of profit participations to third parties, to the extent that such grants reduce their own stake. Studios usually deny this request, but sometimes grant a right of consultation (rather than approval).

It should be noted that independent producers that secure partial financing for a film will usually be able to negotiate for a profit participation above and beyond the norm, with the distributor deducting limited verifiable expenses and a distribution fee well below its standard charge from all revenues received by such distributor.

Like directors, producers may be able to secure other forms of contingent compensation, such as box office bonuses, award bonus advances, and deferments. Ultimately, the form and amount of a producer's contingent compensation can vary widely and will depend in large part on his stature and recent filmography. The budget of the film may also play a role in the negotiation.

Vesting of Contingent Compensation

The issue of vesting of contingent compensation (i.e., determining the point in time in which the producer's contingent compensation is deemed fully or partially earned) becomes important in the event that the producer does not complete services or is terminated prior to final delivery of the answer print. While no revenue will be generated if the film remains unproduced, the issue materializes in the event that the producer is no longer involved with the project at the time of release.

Most producers argue that they should be entitled to the full amount of their contingent compensation unless they were terminated for cause, such as a material breach of the agreement. The studio's initial position is likely to be that a producer who is terminated at any point prior to completing all services on the picture should not be entitled to any portion of his back-end participation, and that payment of the fixed compensation will satisfy the entirety of the studio's obligation. The studio might argue that if it was necessary (in its opinion, at least) to replace the producer in order to help shepherd the film toward production or completion, that fact alone warrants the withholding of anything beyond the producer's fixed fee.

Frequently, negotiations over this issue result in a compromise, in the form of a vesting schedule that will dictate the points in time at which portions of the compensation will be deemed "earned" and, therefore, payable. If the studio agrees to grant a vesting schedule, such schedule will typically provide that the contingent compensation will vest in the same percentages that the producer's fixed compensation is payable—i.e., the 20-60-10-10 formula.

Credit

As mentioned previously, unlike the credits of writers, directors, and actors, the form of a producer's credit is not influenced by the provisions of any collective bargaining agreement. Consequently, all elements relating to the producer's credit (such as position on screen, size of type, separate versus shared card, and paid advertisement requirements) must be specifically negotiated.

In television, the preferred producing credit is "Executive Producer." In film, the "Produced by" credit is believed to be superior, as it typically signifies the most senior, creative, hands-on producer on the production. Producers such as Walter Parkes and Kathleen Kennedy typically receive the "Produced by" credit. The "Executive Producer" credit in film can signify a variety of functions. Some production companies, such as New Line Cinema, accord this credit to their own employees. At such companies, the president of production may receive an "Executive Producer" credit on virtually every film it releases. In other cases, the "Executive Producer" credit is assigned to a financial backer of the film. At times, a well-respected producer or director who assisted in the development of the property or in getting it green-lit or financed, and thereafter had only limited involvement with the film, may be accorded this type of credit.

The "Associate Producer" or "Co-Producer" credit is normally relegated to one or more junior members of the production staff. These individuals presumably aspire to graduate to a "Produced by" credit later in their career.

While there may be several "Executive Producer," "Co-Executive Producer," and even "Producer" credits on a film, there is typically only one "Produced by" credit per movie, its singularity making it more desirable.

Placement (On Screen)

In most films, the single "Produced by" credit immediately precedes the "Written by" credit, which precedes the "Directed by" credit in the main titles. If all of the film's credits appear at the end of the film, the order will be reversed (so that the "Directed by" credit is first). Lower-level producers (such as associate producers) may not be guaranteed a main-title credit. Others may be guaranteed a main title credit "with placement at the studio's discretion." Fortunately for these producers, most studios adhere to industry practice when formulating on-screen credits. Consequently, most producer credits above the associate or co-producer level will usually appear in roughly the same location on screen (i.e., after the presentation and possessory credits, and after the film's title and cast credits, but prior to the writer, director, and source material credits).

Separate Card

Most producers will request that their screen credit appear on a separate card (i.e., no other credits to appear on screen at the same time that the producer's credit appears). While studios will rarely list a producer's credit alongside the credit of other talent (such as that of an actor) or even combine two forms of producing credits (such as placing a "Producer" credit alongside an "Executive Producer" credit), the studio will be free to do so unless otherwise provided in the producer's agreement. Studios are inclined to combine identical credits on a card, so that, for instance, three co-executive producers will share a card. While some producers will be successful in securing a main-title, separate-card credit, others will be forced to share a card. At times, the producer may be able to limit the number of credits appearing on his card, so that his credit provision might read: "main titles, on a card shared with no more than one other individual." In instances where a producer is not guaranteed a separate card, his representatives may be able to secure a commitment by the studio to list their client's name first within a shared card (i.e., above the names of any other producers credited on such card). As alluded to above, the "Produced by" credit will almost always appear on a separate card, adjacent to the "Written by" credit.

Some producers will request an additional form of credit protection—i.e., a request that no other individual receive the same credit. For instance, if Joe Smith is an executive producer, Joe might request that no other individual receive an "Executive Producer" credit on the film. Studios are generally reluctant to restrict their ability to accord credits in this manner. However, depending upon the leverage wielded by a particular producer, studios will sometimes acquiesce.

Size

Producers generally request that the size (including width, boldness, etc.) of their credit match that of any other individual's credit, such as that of other producers, principal cast members, and the director. Studios sometimes exclude cast credits when granting this request. In other words, the producer's contract will provide that "the size of type used to accord credit to Producer shall be no smaller than that used to accord credit to any other non-cast individual." Such language leaves open the option to highlight the credits of the film's stars by utilizing a larger size of type or boldness. Some producers will request a credit "tie" to the size of type used in connection with the title of the film (i.e., 100 percent of the size of type used for the title, or 75 percent of such size of type). Again, depending on the producer's leverage, the studio may agree to some form of size tie to the picture's title.

Presentation/Production Credit/Logo Credit

The top tier of producers are able to secure a "presentation" credit, similar to the director's possessory credit. This credit takes the form of "a Kopelson presentation" or "in association with Kopelson Productions" or even "An Arnold Kopelson Production." If a presentation credit is agreed to by the studio, all of the above elements (including size, placement, and position) must be addressed vis-a-vis this credit. Sometimes, a studio will agree to tie the size of the presentation credit to that of the director's possessory credit. Whether the producer's logo (which may be "animated"), in addition to the name of his company, will appear is also a matter of negotiation.

Paid Advertising

Once the provisions relating to screen credit are negotiated, the parties generally proceed to negotiate terms relating to the inclusion of the producer's credit in advertising materials relating to the film. Some producers may secure a guarantee that they will be credited in all ads containing a billing block. Other producers might secure a tie to the director or to other producers on the film (i.e., a guarantee that their credit will appear in all advertisements in which the director or any other producer is credited, excluding congratulatory ads). Still others may be promised credit not only on advertisements, but on the DVD and Blu-Ray packaging and other merchandise, as well as on the soundtrack album (not only as producer of the film, but at times as a producer of the album itself).

Approval Rights

Producers often seek approval rights over creative elements of the picture, such as the principal cast, key crew members, the final screenplay, the budget, music, locations, the shooting schedule, and even the marketing campaign and release pattern.

Inexperienced producers may be unable to secure more than a right of consultation with respect to some or all of the above categories. More experienced producers might receive a right of approval over most, but not necessarily all, of the elements described above.

Studios are often most reluctant to grant approval rights with respect to final budgets, release patterns, and marketing campaigns. In most instances in which producers are granted approval rights, the studio will, nevertheless, reserve the right to make the final decision in the event of a disagreement between the producer and the studio. In addition, studios often attempt to limit a producer's approval over the selection of key crew members by subjecting the terms of such hires to budgetary requirements, which are imposed by the studio.

First Negotiation (a.k.a. First Opportunity)

Producers frequently request the right to be attached as producers on subsequent productions (such as prequels, sequels, or remakes) based on the initial film. This right can be particularly lucrative in instances when a film generates successful sequels, such as *Twilight* or *Harry Potter*. Studios will, in many cases, agree to grant to the producer a right of first negotiation in connection with subsequent productions. This right bestows a commitment on the part of the studio to enter into good-faith negotiations regarding the engagement of such producer on these future projects. Many times, at the request of the producer's representatives, the studio will also agree to set the financial parameters of the initial engagement as a floor for any subsequent agreement. In other words, if the producer's fee was $250,000, the studio would be obligated to offer a minimum of $250,000 in connection with any future services.

As with directors, studios will often attempt to impose the following conditions on the producer's attachment to subsequent projects:

★ **Budget.** In many cases, studios will condition the producer's right of first negotiation on the producer having adhered to the budget of the first picture. In other words, the producer's attachment to any sequel, remake, or other production will be contingent on the first picture being produced at or below the cost specified in the final approved budget. Producers can usually negotiate for some form of budgetary cushion (i.e., that the right of attachment will remain intact if the picture does not exceed its budget by more than 5 or 10 percent).

★ The applicable subsequent production must be produced within a set period of time—typically, five to seven years from the date of the agreement or, more commonly, from the date of release of the first picture. Top-level producers might be able to negotiate for the removal of this restriction, which is useful in instances where a studio produces a remake almost a generation later than the initial film's release, albeit during the producer's lifetime.

★ The producer must be active in motion picture production at the time the subsequent production is put into place.

Within the general parameters described above, the specifics of any particular producer's right of first negotiation will vary, depending in large part on the relative leverage and negotiating skills of the respective parties.

Turnaround

Many producers request that turnaround rights to the film project be granted to them, particularly in instances where the producer pitched the project to the studio or acquired certain rights to the project that were ultimately assigned to the studio. Powerful producers are often granted such rights with little objection from other participants in the film (such as the writer), as the ability to interest a competing studio in the project is often in direct proportion to the stature of the producer. In many cases, a right of turnaround will be granted. Exceptions include instances where the producer was assigned to the project by the studio or became involved through a relationship with a cast member, the writer, or the director. Some studios grant turnaround only to producers who "came into the studio with rights" (e.g., when the producer has acquired an option on the underlying book). In some cases, the producer's turnaround rights will be shared with the writer of the work.

The standard studio turnaround language provides for a term of eighteen months. If the producer is not successful in situating the project with another studio within such time frame, the rights will permanently reside with the studio (subject to WGA requirements) unless the studio subsequently agrees to relinquish its rights. In addition, most studio turnaround clauses require the producer to resubmit the project to the original studio in the event that the project acquires any "changed elements"—such as a new director becoming part of the package or a material change having been made to the script.

Insurance

As is the case with writers and directors, producers typically seek assurances from the applicable studio that they will be covered under the terms of the studio's general liability and E & O insurance policies relating to the motion picture. Studios generally agree to such coverage as a matter of course.

Travel and Expenses

Producers typically request that any expenses incurred by the producer in connection with the motion picture be reimbursed by the studio. In addition, the producer will usually request travel and living expenses if services are required on location (outside the producer's home city). While there is not a guild agreement requiring a particular class of flight service, it is typical for major studios to agree to first-class travel, first-class hotel accommodations, and a weekly living allowance to cover meals, taxis, and incidentals. Such weekly expense allowances can range from $1,000 per week, at the low end, to as much as $5,000 per week for high-end producers. Most often, the contract will provide for differing amounts of money, depending on the actual locale in which the producer's services are required. For example, the studio might agree to cover $2,500 per week in cities such as New York, Paris, and London; $2,250 per week in other major cities; and $1,750 per week in all other locations. Other matters that are addressed in such negotiations include the furnishing of a rental car (and the size of such rental car), additional plane tickets or even private jet travel for the producer's use (for family members, companions, etc.), and payment for an exclusive or nonexclusive assistant. Major studios typically agree to provide at least one additional first-class plane ticket in instances where the producer is required to remain at a distant location in excess of fourteen days. Ultimately, the level of travel and expenses to which a producer will be entitled is a matter of negotiation with consideration to the picture's budget.

Premieres/Festivals

Most producers request contractual language guaranteeing that the studio will invite the producer to all premieres of the motion picture (as well as all festivals in which the motion picture is exhibited), and that the studio will provide the producer (and a guest) with travel, hotel accommodations, per diem, and ground transportation in the event such premiere or festival is held more than fifty miles from the director's residence. Studios may try to limit this right to a single premiere, or to one east-coast and one west-coast premiere, so that if additional premieres are held, including some that take place overseas, the studio would not be contractually obligated to invite the producer or to pay for his expenses. In addition, many studios initially insist on providing travel and expenses only if the premiere is held more than one hundred miles from the producer's home, although the studios frequently agree to reduce the mileage requirement to a distance of seventy-five miles. Some producers also request invitations, travel, and expenses to each audience preview of the film. Whether the studio accommodates such a request is a matter of negotiation.

DVD/Blu-Ray

Finally, producers usually request (and studios generally agree) that a complimentary copy of the film on DVD or Blu-Ray will be provided to the producer at such time as those products become commercially available.

Deal Point Summary:
PRODUCER AGREEMENTS

1. Producing Services
- Development/Pre-Production
- Production (Principal Photography)
- Post-Production

2. Compensation
- Development Fee
- Guaranteed Compensation
- Contingent Compensation

3. Pay-or-Play

4. Vesting of Contingent Compensation

5. Credit
- On Screen
- Paid Ads
- Logo/Production Company Credit

6. Approval Rights

7. First Negotiation/Subsequent Productions

8. Turnaround

9. Insurance

10. Travel and Expenses

11. Premieres/Festivals

12. VHS/DVD

FEATURE ACTOR
AGREEMENTS

*L*ike screenwriters, actors are protect-
ed by a union, the Screen Actors Guild (SAG). In fact, as discussed in chapter
1, there are three key actors' unions: SAG, Actors' Equity Association (Equity),
and the American Federation of Television and Radio Artists (AFTRA). SAG
governs "filmed" motion pictures and television and digital programs; Equity
generally governs live performances, such as stage productions; and AFTRA
covers most "taped" programs, as well as certain digital programs. SAG, which
is the largest of these unions, not only sets out minimum fee requirements for
filmed pictures, but also comprehensively regulates actors' working conditions,
travel, and residuals. Of course, as is the case with writers, not all actors are
SAG members, nor are all production companies guild signatories. In addition, when principal photography occurs in foreign locations, outside SAG's
jurisdiction, even guild signatory companies may be exempt from SAG's
requirements (although SAG's strict enforcement of "Global Rule One" aims
to prevent this). Moreover, unlike writers, high-level actors often negotiate for

many perks and benefits above and beyond those required under the SAG Agreement.

NEGOTIATING THE DEAL

Actor agreements can vary dramatically from deal to deal, and often are the most onerous to negotiate. What follows is a discussion of the essential terms included in many feature-length motion picture actor agreements.

Contingencies/Conditions Precedent

As with other talent agreements, the producer's obligations may not be contractually binding unless and until certain conditions are met. For the most part, unlike with writer deals, these conditions are fairly basic and include such formalities as obtaining appropriate work visas (if applicable), providing pertinent tax documents, and executing the agreement. Another common condition precedent is that the actor must qualify for insurance at normal premiums. For most actors, this is not a problem. However, for some with reputed substance abuse problems (such as Robert Downey, Jr.) or serious health issues, this condition may be a barrier. The savvy actor representative will address this issue by requesting that the producer include language that will give the actor the right to pay any excess insurance premium required out of his or her own pocket in order to qualify.

Compensation

Once again, the first deal point to be discussed is compensation. In recent years, star actors have negotiated enormous salaries plus significant back-end compensation packages.

The following factors will be relevant to the negotiation:

SAG Minimums

As mentioned above, the SAG Agreement sets out minimum fees, although for seasoned actors, these fees are often surpassed. Of course, the stars of most big-budget pictures will earn hefty salaries, as will many members of the supporting cast. However, the majority of players working on a SAG production will receive SAG minimum or SAG minimum plus a 10 percent agent's fee. SAG specifies several different categories of minimums, depending on the budget of the film and the nature of the services required. For example, under SAG's modified low-budget agreement, if a film is made for less than $500,000, the producer can pay the actor half-scale. Please contact the Screen Actors Guild for a list of SAG minimum fees.

The Actor's Quote

As with writer deals, the producer or studio will consider the fees that the actor has earned for similar work in the (preferably) recent past. Quotes may be given on a per-picture basis (if the actor worked the *run of the picture*) or on a per-week basis, depending on the nature of the services in question. Quotes are usually used as a floor for negotiations, subject to the other factors discussed herein.

Heat (or Lack Thereof)

The actor may have earned little money on his most recent film, but might have won a prestigious award (such as an Academy Award or Golden Globe) for his work on that project. For example, Hilary Swank may have been paid little more than scale for her acting services in the low-budget film, *Boys Don't Cry*. However, after attracting critical acclaim and winning an Academy Award, her fee undoubtedly rose significantly. Similarly, an actor with a successful television career, but little feature experience, may nonetheless garner a large fee because of his television success. For example, according to the trades, following James Gandolfini's enormous success on the praised HBO show, *The Sopranos,* his already-successful film career flourished, and his acting fee skyrocketed. On the other hand, an actor whose last few films were flops may be forced to accept a fee below his quote. Of course, some actors who are no longer hot in the United States might still have "foreign value" (i.e., popularity overseas) and collect very high fees from foreign producers or distributors (unfortunately, such projects are often B films).

The Nature of the Particular Assignment

Many actors are willing to forgo enormous salaries in order to work with a talented director or producer whom they admire. For example, actors eager to work with directors like Woody Allen or Spike Lee will often accept significantly less than their current quote, or even SAG minimum, to participate in these directors' low-budget films. In some cases, an actor will accept a lower up-front fee with a significant back-end deal in lieu of greater fixed compensation. In any event, the budget of the film will often play a key role in determining compensation (at least up-front salaries). For example, if the film is budgeted at $10 million, it would not be possible for the producer to pay Tom Cruise his current quote, at least not up front.

The Role

The size of the role and length of the work period will usually be significant considerations. For example, if the actor is cast as one of the lead roles and is required to work the full schedule of principal photography, his fee will be greater than if the actor was merely making a cameo appearance (which only required one or two days of work). Similarly, supporting cast and bit-part players will typically receive a lower fee than principal cast members.

Escrow

When negotiating with independent producers, foreign producers, or financially unstable entities, a talent representative might request that the entire amount of the actor's compensation be placed in escrow prior to the commencement of services or, if travel is required, prior to the actor boarding the plane. In other words, the actor's representative will want the producer to place the actor's full fee in a bank, which would release the money to the actor in accordance with the terms of the actor's employment contract. Entering into an escrow agreement provides added security to the actor, as it ensures that the producer is "good for the money." An actor will not want to travel to Bulgaria to render acting services, for example, only to discover that the producer cannot pay the actor's salary. While opening an escrow account usually represents an added cost to the producer, most producers will acquiesce if they believe that the actor will otherwise refuse the role.

Payment Schedule

Acting fees are typically paid in equal weekly installments over the actor's scheduled period of principal photography, one week in arrears. In other words, if an actor receives $100,000 for ten weeks of work, he will be paid $10,000 per week, commencing with his second week of services. In some cases, depending on the situation, an actor may negotiate to be paid a larger portion of his compensation up front or to be paid the entire sum upon completion. For example, an actor may wish to postpone payment in order to realize a tax benefit or for other personal reasons.

Contingent Compensation

The vast majority of motion picture actors receive a fixed salary only and are not entitled to participate in the profits of the film. However, those who have reached a certain level of recognition may be able to obtain, in addition to their fixed compensation, some form of contingent compensation, particularly when they are working on low-budget films for less than their usual salaries. In fact, many producers are able to attract top talent (who they otherwise would not be able to afford) to their project by offering the actor a favorable back-end deal in lieu of higher up-front fees. If the actor believes in the project, he may be willing to gamble on the project's success. For example, Tom Hanks reportedly agreed to a reduction of his guaranteed up-front compensation for a greater back-end participation for his acting services in the film *Forrest Gump*. Even lesser-known actors may receive some form of profit participation for their work in a low-budget film.

Net Profits, Adjusted Gross Receipts (AGR), and First-Dollar Gross

Unlike screenwriters, who routinely receive a token 5 percent of net profits, an actor rarely receives a net participation. This is generally the case because, once an actor reaches the level of success at which he is offered a back end, he will usually be able to negotiate for a more meaningful participation than net points, such as a first-dollar gross or *adjusted gross participation*.

While studios rarely grant true gross participations to talent (i.e., a percentage of revenue received by the studio with no deductions of any kind), some of Hollywood's A-list stars (such as Julia Roberts, Tom Cruise, Mel Gibson, and Jim Carrey) are generally able to secure something very close to a true first-dollar gross participation. Thus, references to first-dollar gross in the context of talent deals signify that the actor will receive a share of the producer's or studio's receipts less certain limited "off-the-top" deductions, such as taxes, trade dues, and guild fringe payments. Depending on the contractual definition set forth in the agreement, it may also permit the deduction of limited distribution costs. A variation of first-dollar gross is a "first-dollar gross at breakeven" participation, in which the negative cost (i.e., the cost of making the film) is recouped before the actor's participation kicks in. Major stars, such as Hugh Jackman and Angelina Jolie, typically receive up to 10 to 20 percent of the first-dollar gross.

In most cases where the actor is entitled to first-dollar gross, the actor's up-front fee will be deemed an advance against his back-end, i.e., applied against his gross profit participation. For example, if Tom Cruise is promised $20 million against 10 percent of the gross, this would mean that he is guaranteed a salary of $20 million regardless of the film's box office success. However, if the studio takes in more than $200 million dollars (i.e., the point at which Tom's 10 percent of the producer's gross is earned out), Tom would be entitled to receive an additional ten cents of each dollar earned by the studio beyond the $200 million point. If the studio does not earn more than $200 million, Tom would not receive any compensation in excess of his $20 million.

Another variation of the gross participation is an "adjusted gross participation." The principal difference between a gross and adjusted gross participation is that in an adjusted gross definition, a distribution fee (usually ranging from 10 to 25 percent) is generally levied against the gross revenues in addition to the off-the-top deductions.

The negotiation of profit participations has become increasingly complex, as both studios and talent representatives use computer models to construct algorithms that attempt to predict a film's performance. As with most deal points, the greater the actor's leverage (and sometimes, the more sophisticated his representation), the more favorable his participation definition is likely to be. Profit definitions are discussed in greater detail in chapter 10.

Deferments

A *deferment* is a payment that is delayed until the occurrence of some defined event. Actors working for salaries below their quotes will frequently ask for "deferred compensation." For example, an actor may request that a certain sum be paid to him in the event that the foreign or North American distribution rights to the film are sold. The actor might ask for a percentage of such sale or the payment of a flat sum at that time. The agent or manager's justification for such payment is that the client has taken less money up front in order to help the movie get made. Accordingly, if the producer subsequently receives $5 million, for example, for the foreign distribution rights (and the film only cost $2 million to produce), the actor might argue that he should receive additional compensation. Studios and producers rarely agree to grant deferments to actors being compensated at their market rate. However, the payment of deferments is not uncommon among independent producers hoping to attract marquee talent to low-budget projects.

Box Office Bonuses

Actor representatives will sometimes request that bonuses be paid if and when the picture generates a certain amount of money in its initial theatrical release, either worldwide or in North America alone. A typical provision would provide that such a bonus be payable "at such time, if ever, as domestic (U.S. and Canada) box office receipts, as reported in *Daily Variety*, reach fifty million dollars." Studios rarely agree to base such bonuses on worldwide receipts, more commonly tying them to domestic box office performance. If the studio does agree, the worldwide receipts will typically need to be double the domestic receipts in order for a bonus to kick in. Generally, an actor will request box office bonuses when he is working for less than his typical fee. The rationale is that the actor has invested himself or herself in the picture and, therefore, should participate in the film's success. As mentioned before, these types of bonuses are often preferable to a traditional back-end, because the money breaks (i.e., the points at which additional monies are payable) are easily verifiable and are not distorted by complex studio definitions. It is also possible to request that box office bonuses be payable against (i.e., as an advance against) some other type of back-end participation.

Award Bonuses

An actor may attempt to sweeten his deal with a provision for award bonuses payable in the event that the actor is nominated for or wins an Academy Award, a Golden Globe, or even a SAG Award. Of course, such bonus provisions are most appropriate if the role is particularly challenging or intense and the film is considered to be a possible Oscar contender. As mentioned earlier, it is difficult for a studio or producer to argue against an award bonus, as even a nomination is likely to bring added recognition (and box office revenues) to the film. Although, like most issues, the amount of these bonuses is negotiable and varies depending on the actor's stature, a typical nomination bonus might be in the range of $50,000 to $75,000, with an additional $75,000 to $100,000 payable in the event of a win.

Loan-Out Companies

A *loan-out* corporation is a corporation that is generally wholly owned by a single individual, such as an actor, who renders services on behalf of the corporation. The corporation, rather than the actor, contracts with the studio or producer to "lend" the employee's services (in this case, acting services) to the studio or producer. The studio remits the acting compensation to the loan-out corporation, and the loan-out, in turn, distributes this money to the actor (its "employee") in the form of salary or dividends. The terms of the actor agreement are not affected by the use of a loan-out corporation, although the paperwork will look slightly different. Working actors (typically earning at least $250,000 per year) and other talent, such as writers and directors, will often form loan-out corporations in order to take advantage of certain tax benefits, pension and health benefits, and the liability limitations that the loan-out offers. Studios will generally agree to pay an actor through his corporation, provided the actor executes an *inducement agreement.* Such an agreement basically states that the actor acknowledges the terms of his loan-out's agreement and that, in the event of a breach by the corporation, the actor can be sued directly. Many actors formed LLCs (limited liability corporations) rather than corporations in the 90s. However, due to the complexities of the tax code (which are too lengthy to discuss here), most studios prefer to contract with corporate entities and to discourage the formation of LLCs. Actors and other talent contemplating incorporating are advised to consult with business managers or accountants specializing in this area to discuss the costs and benefits involved.

Start Date

Actors generally try to secure as firm a start date as possible. This is important to the actor, as he does not want to lose out on other roles while waiting for production to begin. A more precise schedule ensures that the actor can fit in other projects. Also, since actors essentially sell their time, actor representatives are often successful in requiring producers to commence payment on the scheduled start date even if the project is delayed (for reasons other than force majeure or other excused contingencies) and, if necessary, pay *overages* (i.e., a prorated additional fee) if the overall work period (including the nonworking hold days) exceeds the period contemplated in the initial deal.

Conversely, the producer will try to build into the deal as large a slide on the start date as possible, as there are many variables that can potentially hold up a start date, such as weather, availability of talent, etc. Typically, the most specific start date the producer or studio will commit to is an "on or about" date, which is usually defined in the employment contract as between one and two weeks on either side of the specified date.

Employment Period

Another item that must be negotiated is the number of weeks of work required of the performer in exchange for the negotiated fee, often called the "guaranteed period" or employment period. The actor's representative will usually try to limit the number of paid weeks and free weeks that the actor will work. The concept of *free weeks* or free days refers to services that are not technically paid for and, as such, is primarily utilized to inflate the actor's quote. For example, if an actor was paid $100,000 for ten weeks plus two free weeks, his quote would be $10,000 per week. However, if he were paid $100,000 for twelve weeks, his weekly quote would only be $8,333. This is important in calculating the point at which overages kick in (i.e., when the actor will be entitled to additional compensation above and beyond what was guaranteed for his services). The "overage compensation rate" is typically calculated by dividing the fixed compensation by the number of work days. The resulting figure represents the daily rate for any such additional services. For example, if an actor was employed for five weeks at $50,000 and was required to work five weeks plus two days, based on a five-day work week, he would receive $54,000 for his services, as his daily overage rate would be $2,000 per day.

Another issue commonly addressed when negotiating the employment period is the number of free post-production days and pre-production/rehearsal days (i.e., days for which no compensation accrues) that will be included. In most cases, the actor will grant a minimum of two free post days, unless the actor is working for scale, in which case the actor must receive the SAG daily rate. Per the SAG agreement, all nonconsecutive days of service, unless negotiated otherwise, will be subject to the actor's *professional availability.* Some representatives will ask for a stop date if the actor has other professional or even personal commitments on fixed dates. Studios are reluctant to give an end date in most cases, since there is always some degree of uncertainty as to whether principal photography will run over schedule. In most cases, and per the SAG agreement, the actor must be exclusive to the producer "until completion of all services required in connection with principal photography," as long as such principal photography services are consecutive. Under the current SAG agreement, a *Schedule F* deal allows the studio to buy out overtime from actors earning at least $65,000 (i.e., overtime is prepaid and no additional sums are due if the actor works beyond a specified number of hours).

Publicity Services

In most cases, an actor's guaranteed compensation is deemed to include not only acting services, but all requisite publicity and promotional services, such as attending press junkets, giving interviews, posing for still photos, making promotional films and trailers, and the producer's right to use behind-the-scenes footage and clips from the film on the Internet, as well as in DVD bonus materials. The producer or studio will usually provide first-class travel and expenses if any publicity services need to be rendered outside the actor's place of residence. Publicity and promotional services occurring after production is complete will be subject to the actor's then-preexisting contractual professional commitments or professional availability. Some actors will also request that such services be subject to their "reasonable approval," so that they will not, for example, be required to appear on a talk show with a host they dislike.

Pay-or-Play Language

Studios generally hire actors on a pay-or-play basis, giving the studio the right to terminate the actor for any reason without cause (for example, if the director and the actor are not getting along or the studio is just not happy with the actor's services). The actor will want the pay-or-play language included in the contract in order to ensure that he will be paid if replaced or if the movie never gets made. For example, Steven Spielberg's proposed film, *Memoirs of a Geisha* (which was to be based on the bestselling book of the same title), was slated to shoot several years prior to its actual production date (i.e., the film was scheduled to shoot but was delayed). Some actors hired to render services on the film had pay-or-play deals, and thus, when the contractually specified start date came and went, these actors began receiving their guaranteed compensation as if they were rendering services. Such provisions typically provide that "if at any time producer elects not to require actor's services, the producer's obligations shall be fully performed by payment of the fixed compensation" provided in the agreement. Usually, producers and studios won't make pay-or-play offers unless they are quite sure that the project will proceed to production. Top-level actors, however, usually won't consider an offer unless it is pay-or-play.

Working Conditions and Guild Applicability

It is important to identify which guild agreement, if any, applies to a given production, since the actors' working conditions can be greatly affected. The SAG Agreement, where applicable, comprehensively regulates working conditions for actors. For example, the SAG Agreement requires a minimum turnaround time (i.e., the time from when the actor is dismissed from the set at the end of the day until the time he or she must return to work) of twelve hours. The SAG Agreement permits the producer to reduce the rest period to eleven hours on any two nonconsecutive days in a work week if the production is at an overnight location. If the producer needs the actor to return to the set without a full twelve-hour break, the producer may require the actor to do so one time only, provided that the producer pays the actor a *forced call* penalty fee (currently in the range of $800). The producer may not violate the turnaround requirement by recalling the actor early more than once without the actor's consent. Even if the actor agrees to return to work early, the producer still must pay the penalty. If services are rendered outside the United States, the SAG Agreement will not generally apply, unless the parties specifically agree (by contract) to be governed by its terms.

The SAG Agreement also provides that its member actors receive meal periods of at least thirty minutes within six hours of commencing services, and roughly every six hours thereafter. SAG enforces these rules by imposing monetary penalties known as *meal penalties* upon producers who violate such provisions. SAG further stipulates that when a performer uses his own clothes at the request of a producer, the producer must pay a set cleaning allowance to such performer. If the wardrobe is damaged during production, the performer must be reimbursed for its cost. Non-guild productions are not bound by these requirements, and hence, the actor representative will want to specify the working conditions in the contract.

Engagement of Minors

A "minor" is someone who has not yet reached the age of majority (eighteen years old in most states). The Screen Actors Guild excludes from its definition of minor those who have satisfied the compulsory education laws of the state, married individuals, members of the armed forces, and those who are otherwise legally emancipated by court order. Child actors such as Macaulay Culkin and Drew Barrymore have petitioned the court to be legally emancipated in order to gain independence from their parents. The parents (or legal guardians) of emancipated children are, likewise, released from guardian responsibilities. Both California and New York labor laws as well as the SAG Agreement impose restrictions in connection with the employment of minors. These regulations limit child actors' work hours and require that minors receive a certain minimum number of hours of schooling per day. In addition, a minor may not participate in work activities that are deemed hazardous or involve a health or safety risk. Many state regulations, including those of New York and California, require the child and the production to each obtain proper work permits specifying the employment.

It should be noted that under basic contract law, a minor may disaffirm (i.e., reject the terms contained in) a signed contract. California and New York laws, however, provide an exception for child entertainers. Such minors cannot disaffirm an employment contract if it has been deemed fair and been approved by a court of law prior to the minor's execution of the agreement. California law also mandates that a certain percentage of a child actor's earnings be placed in a trust fund established for the benefit of the minor. The power to disaffirm a contract and the need for a blocked trust account, however, do not typically apply to a minor who is emancipated (i.e., married, enlisted in the armed forces, or otherwise deemed an adult by the courts), as emancipated minors have the right to enter into binding agreements as well as the right to be sued. It is important to note, however, that labor-code work rules and school rules (if the emancipated minor has not graduated high school) will still apply to emancipated minors.

SAG Pension, Health, and Welfare

If a production falls within SAG purview, the producer will be required to pay SAG pension, health, and welfare benefits on behalf of the actors, which amount to roughly 15 percent of each actor's minimum requisite salary. SAG performers working in Canada or in other non-SAG jurisdictions must specifically negotiate for such contributions.

Credit

Unlike the WGA Agreement, the SAG Agreement does not comprehensively regulate credits. The Agreement merely requires that the entire cast receive credit in films with fifty or fewer performers. If there are more than fifty actors, at least fifty must receive credit. However, the SAG Agreement does not specify which actors must receive credit, nor does it regulate the placement, size, or nature of such credits. Accordingly, the actor or the actor's representative must negotiate many issues relating to credit including the following:

Placement

Actors typically request that their on-screen credit appear in the main titles (as opposed to the end titles, since most filmgoers leave the theater by then), on a separate (or individual) card. In some cases, the director or studio may decide (usually for aesthetic reasons) that the film will not have main titles, in which case all credits will appear at the end of the film. Producers typically refuse to grant separate card credit to actors with smaller roles. These actors are often accorded credit on a shared cared, i.e., shared with actors with similar-sized roles. If the role is very minor, it is unlikely that the actor will be guaranteed a credit other than in the end titles. Savvy representatives of actors receiving shared cards will ask that their client's name appear first on the shared card and that the number of individuals credited on the card be limited to a total of two. Name actors, such as Julia Roberts and Brad Pitt, will typically receive their credit "above the title," i.e., prior to the card containing the title of the film.

Position

In most cases, first or second position among cast credits is the most desirable. If there are many stars in a film (as is typical in many Robert Altman films, for example) and the first two or three positions have already been taken, many agents or managers will demand that their client receive the "and [actor's name] as [character name]" or "with [actor's name]" card, which usually appears at the end of the credit sequence, to bring added distinction to the client (as opposed to settling for fifth or sixth position). Some directors may opt to have the credits appear in alphabetical order.

Size

A star actor might request that the size of his credit be no smaller than 100 percent of the size of the title of the film. Depending on the stature of the actor in question, in certain circumstances, this request may be granted. In addition, most actors will request that their credit be no less than the size of type of any other actor's credit, including the height, width, boldness, and duration on screen. This request is rarely denied by the producer or studio, as it is rare that screen credits (other than for above-the-title stars) will appear in different sizes or types. However, the producer will often carve out one or two exceptions. For example, the contractual language may stipulate that the size and type of the particular actor's credit will be equal to that of all other cast members, excluding the lead actor in the film.

Paid Advertising

Some people mistakenly believe that the term "paid advertising" means that the actor will receive a fee every time his name appears in an ad. Rather, paid advertising refers to ads taken out and paid for by the producer or distributor of the film, generally for promotional and publicity purposes. Paid ads include movie posters ("one-sheets"), billboards, print ads in magazines or newspapers, radio spots, and television spots. The majority of actors appearing in a film will be guaranteed screen credit, but not paid advertising credit. If the actor is of a high enough stature, he will likely receive credit "in the billing block portion" of paid ads. High-level stars may also request the following:

Artwork Title Credit
Star actors will not only receive credit in the billing block, but will usually receive credit in the artwork portion of one-sheets and other paid ads.

Likeness Parity/Inclusion
The savvy agent or manager will request *likeness parity* or, depending on the stature of his client, likeness inclusion. Likeness parity requires the producer to include the actor's likeness (i.e., image) in any ad in which any other actor's likeness or photo appears, usually in substantially the same size. Likeness inclusion obligates the producer to include such actor's likeness in paid advertising regardless of whether anyone else's likeness appears therein.

Audio Parity
Seasoned agents might also request audio parity, i.e., if another actor's name is mentioned in an audio ad, on radio or television, the name of the actor in question must also be mentioned.

Excluded Ads
Often a producer will agree to credit an actor in paid advertising "subject to its customary exclusions." Such exclusions may include billboard ads, other outdoor advertising, and print ads smaller than a specified size. In many cases, the exclusions are so broad that the producer's credit commitment is rendered meaningless. As a result, actor representatives will often ask to be credited in "excluded ads" when any other actor is credited in such ads, with a reasonable exception for congratulatory or nomination ads naming only the lauded individual.

DVD, Videocassette, and CD Packaging
The actor may also request that his name appear in the billing block portion of videocassette, DVD, and CD packaging. This request will generally be granted by the producer to those actors prominent enough to secure billing block credit.

Nudity

The SAG Agreement requires that before an actor or double performs nude scenes or sex scenes (including simulated sex), he must sign a "nudity waiver" granting his written consent to perform such acts. The waiver must describe the extent of nudity or physical contact required. If consent is subsequently withdrawn by the actor, a double may be used. The SAG Agreement also mandates that during the filming of sex or nude scenes, the set must be closed to all parties other than essential cast and crew and prohibits the taking of still photographs during the filming of such scenes without the actor's prior written consent. If the acting services do not fall under the jurisdiction of SAG, the actor or his representatives will likely request that the above restrictions be included in the actor's deal. It is important to note that SAG does not cover the use of nude scenes in trailers or in music videos. Accordingly, some seasoned talent representatives will attempt to prohibit all uses of nude or sex-scene footage other than as embodied in the completed picture (sometimes even requesting evidence of destruction of the negatives) and forbid the use of doubles without the actor's prior approval. Additionally, an actor representative may request that the actor be given the opportunity to view *dailies* that contain the actor's nude appearance.

Dressing Facility

On location, A-list actors will usually be granted a first-class single trailer for the artist's exclusive use. Actors generally prefer a stand-alone trailer to multiunit trailers, in which two or more actors are each allocated a section. Such multiunit trailers are often called *double-bangers* (two-unit trailers) or triple-bangers (three-unit trailers). Some movie stars own their own custom-built trailers, which they lease out to the studio or producer for such star's own use during principal photography. Often, actor representatives will request that the actor's trailer be *favored nations* with (i.e., no less favorable than) the trailers of other cast members of a similar stature in terms of size and amenities. Commonly requested amenities include the following: private bathroom, stereo, television, Internet access, fax machine, VCR, refrigerator, stove, bed or couch, heat, and air conditioning. Some stars request that certain food and beverages be stocked in the refrigerator, as well as other special requests. Within the confines of the studio, the star actor will usually request a first-class star dressing room with customary first-class amenities (as set out above).

Approval and Consultation Rights

Typically, the producer or studio will only grant approval and consultation rights to A-level actors or to rising stars who have attained some level of public recognition. Of course, studios and producers are generally more reluctant to grant approval rights (as opposed to consultation rights), as the studio or producer will want to protect its ability to make unencumbered business and creative decisions. More commonly, the actor will receive "meaningful consultation rights," with the understanding that the studio/producer's decision is final. The following are sometimes requested by actors:

Still Photos/Likeness and Biography Approval Rights

Actors at a certain level will be granted approval over still photos and drawn likenesses in which their image appears. The standard "give" in this regard is 50 percent approval over still photos in which the actor appears alone and 75 percent approval over still photos in which the actor appears with other cast members. This means that the actor must approve 50 percent (or 75 percent, as applicable) of the photographs submitted by the producer to the actor for use in promotional or publicity materials. In some cases (where there is a large ensemble cast, for example), the actor may only receive approval rights over photos in which he appears alone. With respect to drawn likeness approval rights, a producer may either grant one, two, or three "passes" on the likeness. In other words, depending on the actor's negotiating power, the actor will have up to three chances (if any) to submit changes with respect to such rendering.

Script Consultation/Approval

The actor might insist on approval, or at least consultation, over material changes to his role. If the studio or producer agrees, the actor will likely be required to contractually acknowledge his approval of the existing script in his employment agreement.

Co-Stars and Director Approval/Consultation

These rights are usually reserved for the very top players. The studio/producer may grant such an actor the right to effectively dictate which talent he will work with, such as his co-star(s) or director. If the actor receives approval rights, the actor's rejection of other talent cannot be overruled by the studio or producer. If the actor merely receives consultation rights, due consideration will be given to the actor's opinion, but the producer or studio's decision will be final.

Hair/Makeup and Wardrobe Approval/Consultation

Approval or consultation over hair, makeup, and wardrobe is especially important to female actors, though higher-level male actors may also request these approval rights. A-level stars will usually request that the studio hire their personal hair and makeup personnel.

Stand-In and Stunt Personnel

Some actors insist on the right to approve their stand-in or stunt person(s). In fact, some actors regularly work with a particular stand-in or stunt person and will often request that the studio hire such person or persons.

Approval Over Publicity Services, Behind-the-Scenes Footage, and EPK

Another right the actor may request is "advance notice of press on the set," as certain actors do not like to be surprised by reporters or photographers. The actor representative may further request language restricting the producer's use of outtakes or blooper footage and ask for approval over the Electronic Press Kit (EPK) and behind-the-scenes footage often included as bonus materials on the DVD.

Merchandising and Soundtracks

Talent representatives will often negotiate for payment of a royalty in the event that their client's likeness or name is used in items of merchandise relating to the film or if the actor's voice is used on the soundtrack. The standard merchandising royalty is 5 percent of 100 percent (reducible to 2.5 percent if other actors' names or likenesses appear on the merchandise) of the merchandising revenues received by the studio/producer less a 40 to 50 percent distribution fee to cover the studio's overhead and other costs associated with such merchandising activities.

Perks

An A-list actor's perks can add as much as $1 million (or more) to the actor's already enormous salary. Some of these hot actors require the studio to employ entourages of up to ten people, including hairstylists, nannies, personal trainers, assistants, chefs, and makeup stylists. Of course, even lesser-known actors will receive certain perks, particularly if the production is governed by SAG. The following are some of the perks that agents and other talent representatives might request along with those that the SAG agreement requires:

Travel

If the film is shooting in a city outside the actor's principal residence, travel issues need to be addressed. The SAG Agreement requires that actors travel first class and by air, if appropriate. Typically, producers will provide air transportation to locations in excess of seventy-five miles from the actor's residence.

Some actors are able to negotiate such distance requirement to fifty miles. As one would expect, the bigger the star, the greater the number of first-class round-trip tickets the producer will agree to supply. As mentioned above, star actors typically receive first-class tickets not only for themselves, but for their families, assistants, nannies, hairstylists, and others. Leonardo DiCaprio allegedly required MGM to fly his friends to Paris (first class) to visit him on the set of *The Man in the Iron Mask.* The average actor, however, will typically receive one first-class round-trip ticket only. However, if he is married or has a significant other, the studio or producer may agree to provide an extra ticket for that person (first class or coach, depending on the actor's leverage), provided that the actor is "required to remain on location for at least fourteen consecutive days." Per SAG, actors must also be driven to and from all airports, hotels, and the set. Actor representatives will usually request that such ground transportation be "exclusive" (i.e., that the actor will be driven alone), although the studio may only commit to nonexclusive transportation. In some cases, the actor will accept nonexclusive transportation if it is to be shared "with ***above-the-line*** talent only." This means that although the actor may not be driven privately, he will only be required to share rides with other cast members or with the producers, the writer, and/or the director, rather than with grips or other below-the-line crew. Of course, a star actor is likely to receive a private chauffeur-driven limo. The middle-tier actor will frequently be driven by a production assistant along with other cast members of similar stature. Depending on the location, actors may request use of a rental car (ranging from full-size luxury to economy, depending on the actor's stature). Assistants and other members of an entourage will often be provided with rental cars as well.

First-Class Hotel Accommodations

The SAG agreement does not require that actors be housed in first-class hotels. Thus, the degree of luxury of such accommodations must be negotiated. Most studios will, nevertheless, agree to house the actors in first-class hotels. Again, depending on the actor's stature, he may negotiate accommodations ranging from a standard hotel room to a three-bedroom suite or even an extravagant home rented for his use. Many contracts now specify that the hotel room must include WiFi/Internet access. The celebrity's entourage will usually be housed in first-class accommodations as well.

Assistant

Actors of a certain stature frequently employ personal assistants to help manage their schedules and, in some cases, their production companies. These actors typically insist that the producer pay their assistant's salary (usually about $1,000 per week) during the course of production, as well as provide the assistant with accommodations, travel, and per diem. Often, the producer/studio will house the assistant in a lower class of hotel than that provided to the actor and will furnish the assistant with crew-level per diem (as opposed to the higher per diem granted to above-the-line talent). Some actors even request on-screen credit for their assistant. Producers are reluctant to acquiesce, but sometimes agree to accord such credit (usually in the end titles). In certain locations, local union requirements might restrict a producer's ability to hire nonlocal workers. In such cases, the producer may refuse to allow the actor to bring his personal assistant and instead might require him to employ a local hire.

Premieres/Film Festivals

An actor will generally request invitations for himself plus at least one guest to all celebrity screenings and premieres of the film. The actor may also request that first-class expenses be paid by the producer or studio in connection with the actor's attendance. Major studios have recently scaled back on both premiere invitations and expenses. At many studios, only the principal cast members will be reimbursed for expenses incurred in connection with attending such premieres, while supporting cast members may not even be contractually guaranteed an invitation. Of course, star actors will not need to concern themselves with this provision in most instances, as such actors' attendance is generally desired by the studio. Typically, the expenses, accommodations, and travel for those receiving such perks will be equivalent to that provided during shooting of the picture. Where appropriate, an actor may also ask that expenses be paid in connection with his attendance at all major film festivals. In most cases, if the actor is playing a lead role in the film, the producer will want the actor to attend these festivals in order to promote the film and, therefore, will agree to furnish travel and expenses. Often, independent producers will insert language in the contract stating that such expenses are subject to the distributor's approval (since the distributor is likely to be the entity paying such costs).

DVD/Blu-Ray

Most producers will indulge the actor's request for a copy of the completed film on DVD and/or Blu-Ray format when (and if) it becomes commercially available. Movie stars sometimes also request a 35mm print of the film for their personal use.

Right to Keep Wardrobe

Actors often request the right to retain their wardrobe at the end of the shoot. Studios do not typically like to grant this, as they may need these items in the future in connection with a sequel or remake. In some cases, rather than giving the actor the wardrobe gratis, the studio or producer will allow the actor to purchase specific non-rented items at 50 percent of the studio's cost, though only after all shooting and post-production has taken place.

Other Perks

Other perks typically reserved for stars include lavish per diems, and full reimbursement for personal trainers, masseuses, makeup artists, hairdressers, and/or physical therapists for the duration of film production. If applicable, these service providers may receive travel and expenses as well. In addition, actors with children will, in most cases, require that the producer pay for the accommodations and travel of their family members, as well as the children's nanny, and sometimes even a salary for their nanny. In some cases, actors will request that a security person or team be hired to protect them. In addition, if justified by the role, an actor may ask that a dialogue and/or acting coach be furnished, at the expense of the producer or studio. The list of perks is endless, and many celebrity actors actually have "perk lists" specifying each item the actor typically receives when rendering services.

Deal Point Summary:
FEATURE ACTOR AGREEMENTS

1. Compensation
- Guaranteed Fee
  - Escrow
  - Payment Schedule
- Contingent Compensation/Bonuses
- Loan-Out Corporations

2. Services
- Start Date
- Employment Period
- "Pay-or-Play" Language
- Work Conditions and Guild Applicability
- Pension, Health, and Welfare

3. Credit
- Placement
- Position
- Size
- Paid Ads

4. Approval and Consultation Rights
- Still/Likeness/Bio
- Script Changes
- Director and Cast
- Hair/Makeup/Wardrobe
- Stunt and Stand-in
- Publicity Services and Behind-the-Scenes Shooting

5. Trailer/Dressing Room

6. Perks
- Travel, Accommodations, and Expenses
- Assistants
- Premiere Invitations/Expenses
- Right to Keep Wardrobe
- VHS/DVD/Laser Disc/Soundtrack Copies
- Other Perks

TELEVISION
ACTOR DEALS

*N*egotiating an actor's television series deal is similar to negotiating a writer's television series deal in that even before the parties are certain that a television pilot will be produced (not to mention proceed to series), or that the actor will be cast in such television pilot, the actor's services and fees for the pilot, as well as up to six-and-a-half years of series services, are negotiated. Traditionally, most ***test option deals,*** as these series performer deals are commonly referred to, were made during ***pilot season,*** which usually took place between January and May and was the period of time during which network pilots were cast.

These days, with the increase of original programming for cable networks (both basic cable and premium pay cable), casting can (and does) take place throughout the calendar year. In many cases, the terms of the test option deal are negotiated under serious time constraints, since before an actor is permitted to ***test*** for a role (i.e., audition or read for a role before the network), she must first sign the test option contract.

Many actors' representatives believe that the test option process heavily favors the studio, since the eager actor (in many cases an unknown) must sign the test option contract before she knows whether she will be awarded the part. The actor, therefore, has limited bargaining power and knows that if she does not agree to the studio's final offer, another actor will likely get the job. In most cases, the actor will have already signed a six-and-a-half-year deal by the time she learns that the studio wants to hire her. Sometimes, the test option deal is not closed until hours or even minutes before a test, and both parties, therefore, have little time to negotiate the finer points of the deal (often everything other than the compensation) or review the paperwork, though much of the contract is standard *boilerplate.* The counterargument on behalf of the studio and network is that, if they waited until after the creative executives selected the actor they "must have" in a given role to complete the deal, the studio and network would have a significant bargaining disadvantage.

It is important to note that most established actors are not required to test (or, depending on their ego, may refuse to test!) for a pilot or series role. Such actors will frequently be given an outright offer to play a role, which is often the lead or colead. It should be noted, however, that with fewer original series being produced (due to the explosion of reality television as well as the economic downturn), a greater number of film actors (such as Glenn Close and Holly Hunter) have taken roles in television series. While the marquis or A-list actors still expect to receive outright offers, some film actors have been asked to informally audition or "read" for the role.

For those actors who are testing, the process generally works as follows: The studio's casting director will meet with dozens of actors auditioning for various roles. The network, studio, and executive producer will decide which of those actors they are most interested in for the show. At this point, the field is often narrowed down to three to five actors per role. The studio, which produces the program, will ask these actors to read (i.e., audition) for a certain role in the series; this audition is generally referred to as a "studio test." If the studio likes the actor's performance, the actor will proceed to the network that will air the program to formally test for the role (at or before which time such actor must sign the test option deal negotiated by her representative). If the studio is unhappy with the actor's performance, she will not proceed to the network test, unless the network expresses serious interest in meeting with the actor in question. In most cases, the network will have final approval over the selection of the cast. Once the actor is selected to render services in the pilot, the studio and network will have the further option to employ the actor in the series if the show is picked up by the network or, alternatively, to replace her at that time.

NEGOTIATING THE DEAL

In most cases, the test option deal is negotiated between the actor's representatives and the studio's (as opposed to the network's) *business affairs department.* Of course, in some instances, the deal is negotiated directly between the actor and the casting director. This does not mean that the network does not play a role in the process. The network generally maintains final approval over all deals relating to the pilot and potential series, including such issues as position of credit, fees, and number of episodes guaranteed to the actor (all discussed in greater detail below).

In some cases, a studio will produce a *presentation,* essentially, a shorter version of a pilot, as it usually is cheaper and takes less time to produce. This allows the studio to reduce its risk to some degree, since most pilots do not receive a series order from the network. If the presentation generates a series order, the studio will often complete the presentation to the length of a pilot and air it as such.

Pilot Option Period

After the actor tests for the role, the studio is usually given a certain period of time, referred to as the *test option period* or *pilot option period,* to determine whether or not it will employ the actor in question to render acting services on the pilot. The studio will usually want as much time as possible to make a decision, while the actor, who may have the opportunity to test for another television project, will want an answer as soon as possible. Customarily, the studio will have five to ten days to make its decision. Keep in mind that the actor is not paid for this option or "hold" on her services; rather, the actor is granting an exclusive option (i.e., right) to the studio in return for the *possibility* of being cast in the series. Given the fact that the actor is not yet guaranteed any compensation, she will, in most cases, refuse to grant an option period exceeding ten days. In some instances, the network will agree to give the actor an answer within as few as twenty-four hours if the actor is in great demand or has an offer to test for another project. If the studio will not agree to a short enough option period, the actor's representative may ask for *preemption language,* which allows the actor to take other offers, subject to the producer's right to preclude the actor from taking such job by guaranteeing the actor employment. Such preemption language might read as follows:

> During the Test Option Period, Actor may accept a third party offer of pilot or series employment if, prior to accepting such engagement, Actor notifies Producer of the third party offer of employment. Producer will then have the opportunity to preempt such other employment by making actor "pay-or-play" for Producer's pilot within 48 hours of receipt of actor's notice.

In some circumstances, a studio will permit an actor to test in "second position" (i.e., such studio will have the option to employ the actor in a pilot only if the first studio with the "first position" pilot option does not elect to hire her). However, many studios do not want to waste time auditioning and negotiating with an actor who may ultimately be unavailable, and thus will only agree to test the most sought-after actors in second position.

Travel and Expenses for the Pilot Test

The SAG Agreement does not govern travel for a test, or an audition, as tests are not deemed to be employment services. Thus, while everything is negotiable, in most cases, the studio will only grant coach travel for the test, rather than first-class, and agree to pay the actor SAG minimum per diem (i.e., a daily expense allowance) currently in the range of $60. Accommodations will often be "of studio's choice." Ground transportation to and from airports, hotels, and the test, as well as the use of rental cars, must also be negotiated.

Pilot Acting Fee

The pilot acting fee is one of the most important points of negotiation for the actor. Assuming that she is selected as a performer in the pilot (i.e., the test option is exercised), the pilot fee may be the only compensation she will receive in connection with the project, as the pilot may not proceed to series. Unlike film deals, even neophytes regularly receive more than SAG minimum (which currently is in the range of $2,700 per week) for pilot acting services on a network show. Child actors traditionally receive lower pilot fees than adults. On a network show, for example, a relatively unknown child actor might receive $15,000 and up for a half-hour pilot or $20,000 and up for a one-hour pilot, while novice adult actors might earn $30,000 for a half-hour show and $35,000 for a one-hour show. Star talent will receive significantly higher pilot fees.

The actor's pilot fee is usually higher than, and may be as much as double, the actor's series episodic fee. The rationale is that, not only is the production schedule usually longer on the pilot episode, but more importantly, the studio gets an extra benefit—it gets a hold or option on the actor's services (generally lasting three to six months), during which the actor cannot commit to any long-term project that might cause her to be unavailable in the event she is picked up for the series. Industry practice dictates that the actor should receive some compensation in exchange for granting this hold.

Of course, pilot fees will vary from actor to actor and pilot to pilot, based largely on the following factors:

The Actor's Quote

As with most entertainment deals, the quote plays a key role in determining an actor's pilot fee. In some cases, the actor will have rendered services in another pilot and/or series or may have tested for other shows in which she ultimately did not get the role. The studio will usually consider both of those numbers. The actor will want her quote to be the starting point for negotiations. In many cases, an actor may have limited or no television acting experience, and thus, will not have any relevant quotes. In some cases, other quotes may be considered, such as salaries for stage roles.

The Length of the Pilot

Typically, the actor will receive greater compensation for services on a sixty-minute program than on a half-hour show, given that the work schedule for a half-hour show is generally shorter. Half-hour sitcoms typically require up to fifteen days of services, while one-hour dramas require up to twenty work days for the pilot episode. Similarly, if the studio produces a "presentation" (i.e., an abbreviated, lower-cost version of the pilot) rather than a pilot, the actor's fee will generally be lower, as the number of work days are fewer. However, the actor will usually receive additional compensation (that was prenegotiated as part of the test option deal) if further services are required to complete the presentation to the length of a pilot and/or it is ultimately aired as a pilot.

Heat

Another factor to be considered is the heat surrounding the actor in question. For example, has she just starred in a hit film or just completed a successful run on another series? As is the case with writers and directors, if the actor is in demand or of name stature, then she will likely be able to secure a larger fee or even an up-front episodic guarantee in order to agree to do the role. Alternatively, if the actor is relatively unknown, she will not have much bargaining power.

The Nature of the Project/Who Is Producing?

Two other considerations are the nature of the project and the entity that is producing. For example, an actor will usually receive a higher fee for a network pilot than for a cable pilot. Typically, cable networks pay lower fees, arguing that their audience base is more limited or that the economics of cable television do not support such "exorbitant" fees. Similarly, daytime soaps, children's programming, and "strip" shows (such as *People's Court*) usually pay significantly less than network shows. Reality series and/or hosting roles on such shows typically offer lower compensation (other than out-of-the-ballpark hits such as *American Idol*, for which a judge can earn upwards of $1,000,000 per season).

In addition, even on a network series, if an actor is anxious to work with a particular producer/creator, she might agree to accept a lower fee. For example, it is rumored that many actors working on *The Big Apple,* which aired on CBS, accepted salaries below their quotes in order to work with David Milch, who created and produced the series. Unfortunately, the show was not as successful as CBS had hoped and was cancelled during its first season.

Contingencies

Once the test option is exercised, the actor might still not be guaranteed her pilot fee unless and until certain conditions are met. For example, in many cases, the agreement will state that the producer's obligations are "subject to closing of the license fee/broadcast agreement." What this generally means is that before the actor's compensation is guaranteed, the studio producing the show and the network airing the show must agree on the amount that the network will pay for the right to broadcast the series. Actors' representatives will want to remove this language from the contract and make the actor pay-or-play (for the negotiated pilot fee) upon exercise of the pilot option, so that even if the contingency is not met, the actor will need to be paid. In many cases, the studio will only remove this contingency for A-level actors or in instances where the studio is practically certain that no problems will be encountered when finalizing the license agreement. This has become less of an issue now that many studios produce shows for networks under common ownership.

Another frequent condition is a casting contingency. A cast-contingent offer to an actor requires that all outstanding pilot roles be cast before the producer's obligations to pay such actor becomes binding. In other words, if, at the time the test deal is made, other roles remain to be cast and the studio is concerned that it may not find the "right" actor for one such role, or that it will not be able to close its deal with the actor of choice for that role, the actor's deal (at the studio's insistence) might be subject to the successful casting of those other roles. Some savvy representatives ask for preemption language, which would provide that until the condition is lifted, the actor can accept third-party offers of firm employment unless the studio waives the contingency and makes the actor pay-or-play within a certain time period (usually between forty-eight and seventy-two hours). If the studio concedes this point, then when faced with a legitimate third-party offer competing for the actor's services, it will either be required to pay the actor's pilot fee or release the actor from her contract, so that she can render services for the other party.

Pilot Services

A pilot episode generally takes longer to produce than a single series episode. This is because more rehearsal is usually required for a pilot, as the actors have not yet grown accustomed to their characters. In addition, sets often need to be created when a pilot is first produced, while such sites will already exist when the series commences production. Also, there is a greater likelihood that scenes will be rewritten or reshot, since both the studio and the network are prone to submit copious notes to the producers in an effort to get the pilot as close to "perfect" as possible, so as to warrant the production of additional episodes. As mentioned previously, most one-hour pilots are scheduled for production periods of fifteen to twenty days, while half-hour pilots are normally completed within fourteen or fifteen days. Presentations, as mentioned above, are usually shot over seven to ten days.

Pilot Expenses

In the event that an actor is required to travel to a distant location to render services on the pilot, SAG mandates that the actor will receive first-class travel, accommodations, and expenses. Of course, the nature of such expenses and transportation, such as the number of additional plane tickets or the amount of the actor's per diem, is negotiable, depending on the actor's leverage and the budget of the production. It should be noted that pilot budgets have shrunk in recent years due to the changing economics of the television business.

Series Services Option

Subject to the pilot being produced and the applicable actor rendering services thereon, the studio will secure an exclusive option, often referred to as the "series services option" or "series option," to elect to engage the actor on the series or, alternatively, to terminate the contract without further obligation. During the option period, the actor's series services for the studio will usually be in "first position," and such actor will not be permitted to render conflicting television services for any third party. Many studio test option deals provide that the series option must be exercised by June 15th or June 30th of that year. These dates generally track (or coincide with) the network "up-fronts," (i.e., the networks' announcements of their fall schedule to advertisers in May) and afford the studios a limited period of time to recast roles if necessary, rather than exercising the prenegotiated options of the existing cast members. In some cases, with respect to the first year only, the studio will negotiate for a "second bite" (i.e., an ability to delay its decision to exercise the first series-year option for such actor), in order to reserve the right to extend its exercise date, usually until December 30th of that year. This enables the pilot to be considered for pickup as a mid-season replacement for one of the network's failed series. Some actors' representatives will request that, if the date is extended until December, the studio pay an additional fee to continue to hold the actor beyond June 15th. Many studios get "two bites" to pick up the actor (i.e., until December of that year) without additional compensation.

In some cases, the contract language will provide that the studio's option exercise date for the actor will be the *earlier* of June 15th or "ten days after pickup" (i.e., ten days after the network formally picks up the show). Although the "ten days after pickup" language was once standard fare, most studios no longer agree to include such language. Their rationale is that in the event that the network grants an early pickup, the studio can take advantage of the additional lead time in order to decide cast changes, if any.

Series Fees and Annual Guarantees

The next deal points to be negotiated are the series episodic fees and the number of episodes that will be guaranteed per season (i.e., the minimum number of episodic payments that must be made regardless of the number of episodes in which the actor appears or the number of episodes actually produced). As with pilot fees, the actor will rarely receive SAG or AFTRA minimum (which is the same for both a pilot and a series episode) other than with respect to non-scripted reality programs. For example, an unknown child actor typically earns at least $15,000 per episode for a one-hour network series and $10,000 and up for episodes of a half-hour network series, while adult actors rarely receive less than $15,000 per episode as series regulars in half-hour shows or $17,500 per episode in one-hour series. Of course, the same factors as those considered in determining pilot fees will play a role in determining episodic fees.

First-Year Fees and Guarantees

Ideally, an actor's representative would like the actor to be guaranteed all episodes *ordered,* as opposed to all produced, since, in many cases, a show is cancelled before the full order is produced. However, in most cases, unless a major star is involved, the studio will only agree to guarantee (at best) all episodes *produced,* with a minimum guarantee of between six and twelve episodes in the first year and between thirteen and twenty-two episodes thereafter, depending on the actor's stature and bargaining power. A-list stars, such as Bette Midler, might be guaranteed twenty-two episodes even in the first season. Alternatively, some lesser-known actors or those with smaller "sidekick" roles (often referred to as "recurring characters") may only be guaranteed a percentage of all episodes produced, usually with a minimum of seven (for example, 7/13 of all episodes produced or 10/13 of all episodes produced, with a minimum of seven episodes). These actors' guarantees may be increased to all episodes produced in second or subsequent years if the actor's continued participation is desired by the studio. Some actors' representatives will argue that the pilot episode should be excluded from the episodic guarantee, unless the first episode of the series is produced within sixty days of completion of the pilot. In addition, actors' representatives will often try to ensure that a presentation will not be applied against the actor's guarantee unless it is aired. The actor's representative is likely to also try to ensure that the minimum guarantee cannot be reduced in the event that the series is cancelled.

Annual Increases

Customarily, the actor will receive 5 percent annual bumps in salary (or, at some studios, 3 to 5 percent, depending on the license fee) in each subsequent series year. In some cases, the actor's representative will request a larger than 5 percent increase in salary in the second season or even for the *back nine* episodes (i.e., additional episodes that may be ordered by the network in the first season beyond the initial order). If such larger increase in the second year is granted, in most cases, the deal will specify 5 percent annual increases thereafter. For example, a contract may read as follows:

Contract Year	Compensation	Minimum Guarantee
First Year	$12,500	7/13 All produced, minimum 7
Second Year	$15,000	7/13 All produced, minimum 7
Third Year	$15,750	10/13 All produced, minimum 10
Fourth Year	$16,538	All produced, minimum 13
Fifth Year	$17,365	All produced, minimum 13
Sixth Year	$18,233	All produced, minimum 13
Seventh Year*	$19,145	All produced, minimum 13

*only applies if the show is a mid-season pickup

Mid-Season Pickup

Most network television series premiere in the fall. However, networks are all too aware that some new programs fail miserably after debuting on their airwaves. Consequently, a network may pick up several additional series as "backups" to their fall schedule, i.e., series that will premiere sometime after September, to replace one or more cancelled series. Accordingly, some pilots receive orders for a mid-season debut on the network. Other times, pilots are produced outside of pilot season (typically in the summer, rather than late winter/early spring), specifically for consideration as a mid-season show. The studio will often include language in the contract stating that if the show is a mid-season pickup, the actor's fee for the second year will be the same as in the first year (until a total of twenty-two episodes have been produced in years one and two). Clearly, the actor's representative will resist this provision and argue resolutely to have this language removed.

Back-End Participation

It is not very common for actors (other than A-level stars responsible for getting a show made) to receive contingent compensation for series acting deals. Those that do typically receive an adjusted gross receipts participation in the neighborhood of 2.5 percent, vesting over a number of years. Chapter 10 further discusses negotiations relating to profit participations.

Relocation Fees

In some cases, an actor will be required to relocate in order to render services on a pilot or series. For example, if a Los Angeles–based actor is employed by HBO's *Sex and the City*, which shoots in New York, the actor will be required to move to New York to work on the series. With increasing frequency, productions are being relocated to Canada, so that a studio can take advantage of the weak Canadian dollar and possible tax advantages or benefits offered by the Canadian government. The amount of the relocation fee is subject to negotiation, but is typically a flat one-time sum ranging from $5,000 to $25,000, depending on the studio, the stature of actor, and the location in question. In some cases, an actor will receive a monthly living allowance instead of a flat fee. Child actors often receive slightly higher relocation fees, as the child's parent or guardian must also relocate.

Some actors' representatives will try to secure an additional relocation sum in the first season in the event that there is a *hiatus* between completion of the initial order and production of the back nine (such that production is shut down and the actor is later recalled). In addition to the relocation fee, some studios will provide the actor with one or more first-class round-trip air tickets, either per season or on a one-time-only basis (i.e., for the first season only). Of course, the number of tickets an actor will receive is subject to negotiation and can range from one to twenty, depending on the actor's bargaining power (and size of her entourage!).

Credit

In most cases, a *series regular* performer will receive on-screen credit on a separate card in the main or opening titles for both the pilot and the series. Though many people regularly interchange the terms "main titles" and "opening titles," there is a subtle difference. Many television programs display a limited number of credits (usually little more than the title of the series, the lead cast credits, and the "Created by" credit) prior to the actual episode commencing, usually while the musical main-title theme is played. These credits are correctly referred to as "main title credits." Subsequently (typically after a commercial break), additional credits are displayed "over picture," while the episode is playing. These generally include credits for all the producers, guest stars, the writer, and the director. These credits are referred to as "opening titles," as they appear during the opening sequence of the actual episode.

Producers and actors need to be aware of these terms when negotiating credit provisions. An actor's representative will usually request that the actor's credit also appear in paid advertisements relating to the series. Studios try to resist any contractual commitment to credit the actor in paid advertising, since the studios will want the flexibility to focus certain ad campaigns on just one or two cast members. Sometimes, it is hard for the studio to determine who will become a breakout star. An actor originally envisioned as a minor character might become the primary focus of the initial advertising campaign. Similarly, a more established actor might be relegated to a supporting role as the series evolves. Moreover, a long-running show may hire new cast members over time, some of whom might be major stars. Studios are, therefore, reluctant to assume an obligation to accord credit to a particular cast member throughout the life of a series.

An actor's representative will also likely request that the studio tie the size and type of the actor's credit to other cast members, in an attempt to ensure that no other actors receive larger or more prominent credit. Studios will sometimes agree to this request for "credit protection," but might exclude actors of a star stature. In terms of position, the most desirable is usually first, second, or third, respectively (i.e., first, second, or third among cast credits). Often, if an actor cannot secure first- or second-position credit, she will request the last credit, preceded by "and [actor's name] as [character name]" or "with [actor's name]." The conventional wisdom is that it is desirable to differentiate the actor's credit from the "pack" in some manner, in that it will draw attention. Sometimes, billing will be alphabetical. Like most other issues, credit is negotiable and will depend largely on the actor's stature and the size of the role.

Publicity Services/Promotion

As part of the actor's services, the studio usually requires that the actor render a reasonable amount of free publicity services, including personal appearance tours, in order to promote the series. Often actors' representatives will attempt to limit appearances to three per season. The actor will also want to ensure that her obligation to render promotional services will be subject to her professional availability and reasonable approval (i.e., the actor will not have to render services that she is not comfortable with). In most cases, the producer will agree to this request, provided that the services occur outside the normal production period. In addition, the actor's representative will usually insist that the actor receive first-class travel and expenses in connection with such publicity services.

Exclusivity

The issue of exclusivity (i.e., whether the actor can render acting services for a third party during the term of her contract with the studio) is often an important point for both the actor and the studio. Among the restrictions that the studio imposes are that it will not permit the actor to accept engagement as a series regular or recurring character on another series during the term of her contract (though studios sometimes make exceptions to this rule), and any permissible services rendered for third parties will be in second position to the actor's series services for the studio. This exclusivity applies even during the hold period under the series contract (i.e., during the period when the studio has the right to engage the actor for further seasons). Often, test-option deals grant the producer "the maximum exclusivity rights permitted under the SAG Television Agreement." The SAG Television Agreement sets forth exclusivity restrictions with respect to other television roles and commercials. For example, under the SAG agreement, studios have the right to prevent most series regulars from appearing in commercials advertising products or services that are competitive to a major sponsor of the network. In addition, most performers are barred from portraying or parodying the pilot/series character in another program. In addition, the SAG Agreement grants the producer the right to restrict the actor from performing in continuing or regular roles on other television series. SAG bestows upon all series performers the right to make up to three television guest appearances every thirteen weeks and the right to make unlimited radio guest appearances. The number of permissible guest appearances on talk shows, game shows, news, panel, and award shows is also unlimited, although the studio can require that such shows will not air during the regularly scheduled initial broadcast of the series.

Actor representatives will often request that the actor be permitted to render services in connection with an unlimited number of unidentifiable voice-over ads and foreign commercials. The studio will usually agree to such requests, since these services are less likely to compete with the show (or overexpose the actor). Actor representatives may also ask to exclude preexisting recurring roles if the actor has already appeared repeatedly on another series. Some cable networks do not permit their series actors to appear in MOWs (movies-of-the-week) produced for competing cable networks. Most broadcast networks do not impose an MOW restriction.

In addition, with respect to roles (such as hosting or judging) in reality television, many actors will insist on remaining exclusive only within the context of reality television, thereby retaining the ability to render services on scripted series as well as motion pictures, stage plays, and other types of media. Whether the actor has sufficient leverage to win this point will be determined on a case-by-case basis.

Program Commercials

In many cases, the producer will have the right to require the actor to perform free services in *lead-ins* and *lead-outs* (i.e., fifteen- to thirty-second "stay tuned" spots) to the program. In addition, actors are usually required to perform in commercials advertising the series. Most producers agree to pay double the applicable SAG minimum fee for such commercial services.

Approval and Consultation Rights

As in film deals, television actors frequently request certain approval rights, which may or may not be granted, depending on the artist's stature. The following are commonly requested by actors:

Photo, Likeness, and Bio Approval

An actor's representatives often request that the actor receive still photo, likeness (i.e., artistic rendering), and bio approval rights (approval over the text of the actor's biography, which may be disseminated by the studio in connection with its promotion of the series). A typical photo approval provision, or "still" approval provision (as it is often called), may read as follows:

> Producer shall submit to Actor a reasonable number of still photographs which Producer intends to use for advertising, publicity, and promotional purposes, and Actor shall approve not less than 50 percent of such photographs in which Actor appears alone and not less than 75 percent in which Actor appears with others, within 72 hours of submission.

In some cases, the actor may only be granted approval over stills in which she appears alone, particularly if there is a large ensemble cast involved. Also negotiable is the length of time in which the actor must approve the pictures, usually ranging from twenty-four hours to ten days. As for likeness approval, the actor may receive one, two, or even three "passes" on the drawn likeness, depending on the actor's negotiating power. What this means is that the actor will have the opportunity to request changes to the drawn likeness, which the studio will be required to incorporate, up to three times. Bio approval is generally granted by the studio, even for novices, since the "official" bio distributed by the studio is usually supplied by the actor (or her representative).

Hair/Makeup/Wardrobe

Another common request is for hair, makeup, and wardrobe consultation or approval. In most cases, the actor will receive "meaningful consultation" (rather than approval rights) over hair, makeup, and wardrobe, if at all. In some cases, depending on the actor's stature, she may be able to require the studio to hire her personal hairstylist and/or makeup person and require that such person service her only.

Creative Controls

In rare instances, such as when a show is developed specifically for a certain star, the actor in question may receive consultation or even approval rights over such creative elements as the director, other principal cast members, and even script approval. Such rights are rarely granted, as the studio and network typically insist on retaining control over material creative elements.

Dressing Room

The size and quality of the actor's dressing room will depend upon the usual factors (such as the size of the role, stature of the actor, and availability of trailers). In many cases, the actor's representative will ask that the actor's dressing room be favored nations with (i.e., no less favorable than) other cast members' facilities. The studio may agree to this if it is certain that the dressing facilities will be uniform for the entire cast. Otherwise, it will exclude certain performers from the favored nations clause. For example, the studio may agree that the actor's dressing room will be no less favorable than that provided to any other cast member, *excluding* that of the lead star. If the show has not been fully cast, the exclusion might be phrased broadly, so as to except "actors of star stature." Some studios are hesitant to include favored nations language, because of past experiences in which an actor claimed a breach for minor differences in style, size, or even color of the dressing facility. In some cases, the actor will insist that the dressing room be equipped with a laundry list of amenities, such as a private bathroom, bed or couch, heat, air conditioning, stove, fridge, telephone, television, VCR, stereo, CD player, and even particular food and beverages.

Nudity

While nudity is rarely an issue for the broadcast networks (although it can be—recall the bum-baring in *NYPD Blue*'s first season), it sometimes comes into play at the pay cable networks, such as Showtime and HBO. The SAG

Agreement comprehensively regulates performer services, both in connection with nudity and simulated sex, and SAG's restrictions apply in television as well as film. One form of protection afforded by the SAG Agreement provides that an actor cannot be required to appear nude unless she has executed a document that clearly references any script pages containing nudity. In other words, an actor cannot simply agree to appear nude in the abstract; rather, she must execute a document, referred to as a "nudity rider," acknowledging her consent to such appearance in each instance.

This SAG provision (which cannot be waived by the actor) poses a problem unique to series producers, in that only the pilot script exists at the time that the actor's agreement is negotiated. Thus, while specific script pages can be referenced and signed off on by the actor in connection with the pilot, the studio cannot ensure that the actor will continue to agree to render such services in subsequent episodes. While there is no foolproof way around this problem, it is important for studio business affairs executives to discuss the potential for nudity at the time that the actor's agreement is negotiated (particularly if nudity is *not* required in the pilot, but is envisioned for the series). At a minimum, the studio can avoid a situation in which an actress is cast in the pilot, renders services, and then (at the time a series is ordered) informs the producers that she doesn't "do" nudity (and never has) and was never alerted to the possibility that nudity might be requested. Accordingly, when negotiating agreements for these types of series, the business affairs executives should mention the possibility of nudity, so that, in the event that an actor objects on absolute terms, the studio will discover this at the earliest stage possible.

Once this "threshold" matter is resolved, and the actor is willing to sign off on the requisite nudity, several issues typically arise when negotiating the terms of the nudity rider (which, per SAG, must be signed). These include:

★ A request by the actor (usually agreed to by the studios) that the set be "closed" to all nonessential personnel during the filming or taping of nude scenes

★ An agreement by the studio that no still photographs will be taken during the filming or taping of such scenes

★ Actor approval over "body doubles"

Studios usually insist that they be permitted to use body doubles in the event that the performer is uncomfortable with a particular angle or scene, or even unavailable to shoot footage. Actors will often seek approval (or consultation) over the selection of the body double, since the viewing audience is likely to believe that they are watching the performer. Accordingly, the performer has an interest in how she is portrayed (even though it is not actually her on screen). Some actors request specific language prohibiting the producer from exceeding the confines of the nudity rider when shooting the double. In other words, if the nudity rider permits only above-the-waist nudity, the actor may insist that no below-the-waist nudity appear in the episode, even if the waist in question belongs to the double, since the actor may not want the viewing public to believe that the actor consented to that degree of nudity.

A sample nudity rider is included in appendix A.

Miscellaneous

High-level television actors may secure significant perks, such as voice coaches, personal trainers, masseuses, etc., during production periods. Actors with children may require the studio to pay for travel and related expenses for their children as well as their nannies. Actor representatives will commonly negotiate for the following additional items:

Merchandising/Soundtrack Royalty

A studio will want the right to use the actor's name and likeness not only in the show, but also for merchandising and advertising. In addition to the approval rights discussed above, actor representatives will often request that a merchandising and/or soundtrack royalty be paid in the event that the actor's likeness or voice is used in merchandising or on the soundtrack. In most cases, the studio will agree to a customary royalty of 5 percent of 100 percent of net receipts. When dealing with items of merchandise in which more than one actor's likeness appears, studios initially take the position that the 5 percent royalty will be reduced (pro rata, based on the number of actors whose likenesses appear on such items). Savvy negotiators will insist that the royalty be reduced only when their client's likeness appears alongside other *royalty-bearing* participants, so that, if the studio is not obligated to pay a royalty for the other images, the actor in question would be entitled to the full 5 percent. In addition, many actors are able to negotiate a floor, in the event that the royalty is reduced. The typical floor is 2.5 percent. In other words, the royalty for any item of merchandise cannot be lower than this amount, regardless of the number of likenesses appearing on such merchandise.

DVD/Blu-Ray Copies

The actor will often request a copy of the pilot and all episodes in which she appears on Blu-Ray or DVD, if and when available. In some cases, the studio will not contractually agree to this request, although in practice, the actor will seldom encounter any difficulty in obtaining such copies.

Right to Convert to Loan-Out

The savvy agent will always request that the television actor (who has not yet established a loan-out corporation) be granted the right to assign her agreement to a loan-out company (as discussed in chapter 7) at a later date. This is important, because the benefits of incorporation generally do not exceed the costs until an individual earns a minimum of approximately $250,000 per year. Accordingly, many actors do not form such corporations until a pilot in which they appeared is ordered to series, as the pilot fee alone is not sufficient to warrant incorporation by the actor.

Guild Applicability

As mentioned in chapter 7, SAG generally governs filmed programs, while AFTRA governs taped programs. Certain shows, such as most soap operas, will be governed by AFTRA (not SAG), which has somewhat different requirements. In addition, studios are producing an increased number of programs in Canada under the ACTRA agreement, which also imposes requirements that vary from the SAG agreement. Among other differences from the SAG Agreement, the ACTRA agreement permits the studio to buy out residuals in advance by making a lump sum payment to the actor.

RENEGOTIATION

Notwithstanding the fact that most television actors testing for pilots are required to sign a comprehensive agreement covering at least six years of series services, if a series becomes a hit, the actor's representative is likely to try to renegotiate the actor's salary and perks. As mentioned previously, at the time that the initial deal was negotiated and signed, neither party could have anticipated the great success of (and concomitant profits generated by) a hit series. In many cases, the actors (who might now be household names) were unknowns at the time the pilot was cast. Once the success of the series becomes a certainty, resulting in enormous profits for both the studio and network, the actor (and her agent) often demands her fair share. Even though the studio has entered into a binding agreement with the actor specifying prenegotiated episodic salaries, the studio, nevertheless, is likely to agree to renegotiate with the actor if the show is a hit, because it does not want an unhappy actor on the set. This renegotiation can take place at any time during the life of the series, but often occurs prior to the second or third season and may occur more than once during the life of a successful show. This is the time when an actor's representative will likely ask not only for an increase in salary, but also for a profit participation. In some cases, the actor will request the right to direct episodes or to enter into some sort of producing arrangement. In return, the studio will often require the actor to extend the length of the term of the agreement (i.e., the studio demands options for additional years). Sometimes, the actor will commit to perform in one or more television movies for the studio at a set fee as part of the renegotiation.

One of the more highly publicized examples of such renegotiations was the *Friends* renegotiation that took place in 2000. Each of the ensemble cast members reportedly asked for $1 million per episode. Following heated negotiations, it was reported that the studio agreed to pay each of the actors $750,000 per episode, plus a share of the lucrative syndication sales of the show. Each cast member was purportedly earning $125,000 per episode the previous season. Of course, when the show first aired, these actors were essentially unknowns (Courtney Cox was probably the most recognizable actor). Previously, in 1996 (after one or two seasons), the cast renegotiated as a team to raise their then $40,000 salaries to $125,000. It has been reported that Jerry Seinfeld, Helen Hunt, Paul Reiser (*Mad About You*), and Tim Allen (*Home Improvement*) each received $1 million per episode during the final season of their series. Reportedly, Kelsey Grammer recently negotiated a rate of $1.6 million per episode for the tenth and eleventh seasons of *Frasier.* Of course, all these shows are rare breakout hits, which attract millions of viewers each week. In some cases, the studio will not agree to the actor's demands. Litigation may result, or the parties might agree to part ways, with the studio agreeing to recast the role or to write out the character. This was purportedly the situation with David Caruso of *NYPD Blue*.

Clearly, the nature and degree of the renegotiation will depend on various factors, including the degree of success achieved by the series, how integral the actor's character is to the show, and the ways in which the series was exploited to date. In addition, the issue of whether the network will contribute to the increase, either directly or indirectly (e.g., by increasing the license fee), will play a role in the outcome.

HOLDING DEALS

When holding deals (a.k.a. "hold deals") are made, it is often the network, rather than the studio, that enters into such an arrangement with the actor. The purpose of the commitment is to (1) hold the actor off the market for a limited period of time in an attempt to cast the actor in one of the many pilots being developed for the network, or (2) in the case of higher-level performers, to keep them off the market in order to develop a project specifically for them. In addition to pilot/series hold deals, networks sometimes make MOW (also known as "MFTs," or "movies-for-television") commitments. For higher-level performers, the networks may commit to develop a pilot/series or MOW specifically for the actor, with the option to cast the actor in other projects if the developed project does not pan out. For others, the commitment is more likely to be strictly a casting option, without a development component.

Sometimes, holding deals are made with actors already working on a series, in order to hold them beyond the run of the series, not only with the intention of finding a new project to subsequently place the actor in, but also to prevent such talent from defecting to a competing network. Other times, such hold deals (for actors already engaged on a series) are entered into merely to sweeten the actor's series deal. Sometimes, MOW commitments are made for similar reasons. Most pilot/series hold deals expire after one season. Movie commitments tend to have longer terms. Hold deals are made with all levels of talent, and the fees can range from $25,000 to $1 million (although deals at this higher range are very rare). Issues that arise in holding deal negotiations include the length of the hold deal, whether or not the actor is currently on a series, the applicability of the hold fees to series acting services (i.e, whether and how much of any advance or initial guarantee paid to the actor can be recouped by the studio against subsequent fees paid to the actor for actual services), exclusivity under the hold deal, and the extent of the actor's approval rights. Holding deals have become less common in recent years.

MOVIES FOR TELEVISION/MOVIES OF THE WEEK

Negotiating an actor agreement for services in an MFT or MOW is similar to negotiating a feature film deal for an actor. The principal differences are that the salaries are, in most cases, lower (as is the budget), the work periods are shorter, and the perks are less extravagant. Often, an actor's representative will request a *theatrical release bonus* be paid to the actor in the event that the movie is released theatrically, either before or after it airs on television. The rationale is that the actor has been paid a television movie fee, as opposed to a customarily higher feature movie fee, and the studio/producer should not be able to release the movie theatrically without compensating the actor accordingly. While it is rare that television movies are released theatrically in the United States, it is more common in the overseas market. Customarily, the theatrical release bonus will be paid in accordance with a *100/50/50* formula. What this means is that the actor will receive a bonus equal to 100 percent of her compensation (fixed and contingent) under the MOW deal if the movie is released theatrically in North America *prior* to being shown on television. If, however, the movie is released theatrically in North America *after* being shown on television, the bonus would equal only 50 percent of the actor's compensation under the television movie deal. In accordance with this provision, if the film is released theatrically outside North America, the actor would be entitled to a bonus in the amount equal to 50 percent of her initial acting fee. In most cases, the producer/studio will include language providing that "in no event will the actor's bonus(es) total more than 100 percent of her compensation under the original agreement." In other words, if the movie was released theatrically in North America prior to airing on television and also was released theatrically in the foreign market, the actor's total bonus would be 100 percent (rather than 150 percent) of her compensation under the original contract.

Deal Point Summary:
TELEVISION ACTOR AGREEMENTS

1. Pilot versus Presentation

2. Length of Test Option Period

3. Pilot/Presentation Fee

4. Contingencies (License Fee/Casting)

5. Pilot Travel and Expenses

6. Pilot Start Date/Work Period

7. Series Option Date

8. Series Episodic Compensation and Annual Increases/ Annual Episodic Guarantee

9. Annual Option Date

10. Billing (Pilot/Series)

11. Program Commercials

12. Exclusivity

13. Publicity and Promotional Services

14. Relocation Fee/Plane Tickets

15. Dressing Room

16. Nudity

17. Guild Applicability

18. Miscellaneous

  • Approval Rights (Hair/Makeup, Stills, Likeness, Bio, etc.)
  • DVD/Blu-Ray Copies
  • Merchandising/Soundtrack Royalties
  • Right to Convert to a Loan-Out
  • Other Perks (Trainer, Voice Coach, etc.)

CREW
(Below-the-Line)
AGREEMENTS

$\mathscr{T}$elevision and film project budgets are typically broken down into two sections: above-the-line costs (which include underlying rights payments, as well as fees payable to writers, actors, directors, and producers) and below-the-line costs (which include all other costs associated with producing a film or television program, such as salaries of crew members, lease payments, equipment rentals, the cost of film, cameras, etc.). Production budgets actually separate these two sections on their cover page, with the "above-the-line" costs appearing at the top of the page and "below-the-line" at the bottom.

The employment of individuals hired to serve on a film or television crew, such as grips, art directors, costume designers, makeup artists, lighting technicians, drivers, caterers, etc. (essentially, everyone other than the cast, director, writers, and producers), are referred to as "below-the-line" hires. In some cases, the line producer will negotiate employment terms directly with the individual being hired. Many crew personnel do not retain agents to secure and negotiate terms of employment. Among the exceptions are typically the so-called department heads, DPs (directors of photography, also called cinematographers), music supervisors, composers, the editor, and costume designers, who typically garner high salaries and, in some cases, perquisites. There are some agencies that exclusively represent below-the-line talent (though such agencies generally focus on the higher-level hires).

Many below-the-line hires are subject to strict budgetary parameters that are not as fluid as those set for above-the-line talent. Whether justified or not, producers and studios typically believe that many of the lower- to mid-level crew members (i.e., grips, drivers, lighting technicians, assistant camera personnel, etc.) are more easily replaceable than above-the-line talent. Consequently, producers are frequently less willing to stretch the budget in order to secure the employment of a particular crew member. As a result, negotiations are often less contentious and progress relatively quickly. Of course, in some cases the director may insist on having his favorite DP, his editor, or his costume designer, and the studio may or may not cater to his demand.

Notwithstanding the foregoing, there are a number of highly sought-after department heads that command extremely high salaries. Often, these are individuals that are specifically requested by the director (e.g., Steven Spielberg may only be willing to work with a particular casting director or costume designer). Other times, a studio may be worried about an escalating budget and therefore choose to impose its own line producer (someone who, while expensive, has a proven track record in cost cutting). In recent years, the negotiations over deal points related to the engagement of such high-level department heads has approached the complexity and detail of many above-the-line negotiations.

Many crew members belong to a union (most commonly, IATSE—the International Alliance of Theatrical and Stage Employees, now known as the International Alliance of Theatrical and Stage Employees, Moving Picture Technicians, Artists and Allied Crafts) and some workers engaged on a production (for example, drivers) will simply be hired at the union-prescribed minimum rates, based on their seniority. In such cases, formal negotiations will not take place.

Studios have adopted varied practices relating to the engagement of the higher-profile below-the-line personnel, such as costume designers, casting directors, cinematographers, and music supervisors. At some studios, business affairs executives will handle such negotiations. At others, studio production executives will oversee such agreements. In some instances, the on-set line producer will negotiate all below-the-line deals (subject, of course, to studio approval).

As stated above, most below-the-line deals are typically simpler to negotiate than talent deals. As there is generally a customary range of salary and perks associated with each crew function, most deals involve little more than negotiating (1) length of service, (2) exclusivity, (3) guaranteed compensation, and (4) credit.

In many cases, particularly with respect to negotiations over credit, the parties will settle on some form of favored nations provision. For example, the producer may promise the costume designer prominent credit in form and placement no less favorable than that accorded to the director of photography, or to the production designer. These provisions serve as shorthand that prevents the need for lengthy contractual credit provisions.

As any moviegoer knows, most credits appear in the end titles of a film or television program. Precious few crew members will be able to negotiate for a main-title credit. Crew members that are generally credited in the main titles of feature films include: Costume Designer, Production Designer, Cinematographer (also known as Director of Photography), Casting Director, Editor, Composer, and (though not in all cases) Music Supervisor. These crew members are also often able to negotiate for credit in the billing block of certain paid advertisements. Of course, there are exceptions to every rule. A studio releasing a motion picture containing an abundance of special effects, for instance, might accord a main-title credit to the visual effects supervisor. Nonetheless, location managers, assistant hairstylists, sound mixers, transportation coordinators, and security personnel (among many other crew members) will rarely be credited in the main titles of a film.

At times, a formal contract will not be created to memorialize the terms of these agreements. Instead, a letter setting forth the key terms will be exchanged between the parties. Other times, a brief deal memo (similar to those set forth below) will be drafted by the producer or studio executive, with a copy sent to the crew member for her files.

It is not uncommon for deal letters/memos to contain "services" provisions that are fairly vague. In other words, the services description may be quite broad, stating only that the crew member be required to render "customary first-class services" or "services commensurate with those rendered in connection to prior seasons" or "services of a level consistent with industry standards." While such provisions may be effective in minimizing the time required to draft deal memos, the danger is that, in the event of a dispute, the parties might find that their expectations differed dramatically.

When hiring crew members on television pilots, producers/studios will occasionally request options for such person's services in the event that the pilot proceeds to series. The studio's purpose in negotiating for this option is twofold: (1) to lock in the price at an early stage (rather than at a point in time where pilot services are complete, in which case the executive producer may feel that such crew member is "indispensable" and the negotiating leverage will shift to such crew member), and (2) equally important, to ensure that such individual will be available to render any necessary series services. Producers often favor continuity on their sets and may be willing to forego hiring a talented crew member on a pilot if such person will be unavailable to render additional episodic services due to prior commitments.

Studios frequently arrange screenings of completed films or television programs for the cast and crew. One reason for holding such screenings is that many of the crew members (and even a fair number of the supporting cast) may not be invited to the film's premiere. These screenings are designed to acknowledge the contributions of such crew members. Some crew members will specifically request language in their agreement guaranteeing them an invitation to a cast-and-crew screening. Of course, some of the higher-profile crew hires (such as the composer) will often secure an invitation to the actual premiere.

Following are examples of deal memos outlining the employment terms of certain of the higher-profile crew hires.

Sample Deal Memo: Feature Film Composer

SERVICES: Artist shall compose, arrange, orchestrate, and record original music on a "package basis" for the above-referenced Picture. Artist shall utilize a minimum of 15 musicians when recording the score. Artist's services shall also include discussing music needs with the Producer and the Director, assisting in the production of music cue sheets, participating in the final mix, and providing all other customary music composer services for an assignment of this nature. Artist shall be solely responsible for contracting in Artist's name and at Artist's expense for all equipment, facilities, instruments, and services by any third party in connection with all music, excluding only third-party music licensing, the music editor, and vocalists, if any. Artist warrants and represents that all music shall be an original creation of Artist's. Artist agrees that the music created under this agreement will not contain any musical elements from Artist's engagement on any other project. Artist agrees that Producer shall be deemed the owner of all music herein and that all music shall be deemed a work-for-hire.

Artist agrees to deliver all music to Producer on a timely basis in accordance with Producer's schedule and delivery requirements.

COMPENSATION: As full compensation for the above-described services, and all rights therein, Artist shall receive the aggregate sum of $750,000. Such fee will be payable ⅓ upon signature of certificate of authorship and commencement of services, ⅓ on commencement of recording, and ⅓ upon completion of services.

SCREEN CREDIT: Subject to full performance, and provided that no less than 75 percent of the final score contained in the Picture has been created and recorded by Artist, Artist shall receive a credit in the main titles of the Picture, on a separate card, substantially in the form: "Music by _____," and in the billing block portion of paid ads issued by or under Producer's direct control, subject to customary exclusions and practices, whenever a full credit block is used.

MISCELLANEOUS: All music is provided on a music package basis. Artist's services shall include composing music to accompany the Picture's credits. Artist must attend all scheduled *spotting* sessions. Artist is affiliated with BMI.

A-level film composers (such as Elmer Bernstein and James Horner) can earn upwards of $1 million when engaged to score a big-budget motion picture. In addition to the above provisions, composers are sometimes able to negotiate to retain a portion of the publishing royalties collected by the studio in connection with its exploitation of the musical score. Such income includes license fees (if the studio licenses such music to third parties), as well as performance royalties (paid by television stations, radio stations, and others who publicly perform copyrighted music). Under federal copyright law, the publishing income derived from exploitation of a musical composition, even if commissioned as a work-for-hire, must be divided equally among the writers of the music and the employer/owner (sometimes referred to as the publisher). However, high-level composers will sometimes be granted a portion of the publisher's (i.e., studio's) share of such income (in addition to the "writer's share," which they are automatically entitled to). Studios sometimes grant such publishing income in an effort to attract top composers at a bargain rate (i.e., when they cannot or will not match the composer's current quote).

It should be noted that in the sample composer deal outlined above, the studio paid an "all-in" sum to the composer. The composer was, therefore, responsible for the salaries of any musicians hired to record the music, as well as for the cost of engineers and the rental of a studio where the score would be recorded and produced. Many times, composers and film studios structure the deal in a different manner, pursuant to which the composer is paid a "creative fee," which she retains for herself. The studio, in turn, would be responsible for all other costs relating to the creation and delivery of the score. Some composers prefer the creative fee structure, as they like to know the precise amount of money that they will end up with in connection with the project. Others are more comfortable making third-party deals and working within a budget, knowing that they will retain underages (although they will also be responsible for overages, as the studio will have paid a lump sum to the composer as an all-in package fee).

> **Sample Deal Memo: Television Pilot/Series Casting Director**
> CONTRACTING PARTY: Star Finder, C.S.A. [i.e., "Casting Society of America"]
> PILOT SERVICES/COMPENSATION: Casting services on the above-referenced sixty (60) minute pilot ("Pilot"), in consideration of $35,000, payable ⅓ upon commencement of services (and signature of certificate of engagement), ⅓ on or before the fourth week of Artist's services, and ⅓ upon completion of Pilot services. Artist's services shall be in-person and first priority, excluding only 5 days in March in which Artist is on vacation, at which time she will continue to be available by telephone.
>
> ASSISTANT: Studio shall pay directly to Artist's casting assistant the sum of $500 per week.
>
> SERIES SERVICES: In the event Studio elects to proceed to production on a series and provided that Artist casts at least ⅔ of the Pilot lead roles, Artist shall be hired as casting director for the first series year at the rate of $3,600 per episode. Studio shall continue to pay Artist's casting assistant at the rate of $500 per week.
>
> SCREEN CREDIT: Subject to Artist casting ⅔ of the Pilot lead roles, Artist shall be accorded screen credit in the main titles of the Pilot (if aired) as follows: "Casting by Star Finder, C.S.A." If Artist renders casting services on the series, Artist will receive screen credit in substantially the form accorded on the Pilot for each episode with respect to which Artist renders services. If Artist does not provide

episodic services but casts ⅗ of the Pilot lead roles, Artist shall be accorded credit substantially in the form "Original Casting by Star Finder" in the end titles. Credit in end titles for Artist's casting assistant.

OFFICE: During work periods, Studio agrees to reimburse Artist's reasonable business expenses, such as long-distance phone calls, messengers, and copying expenses, and any preapproved travel.

MISCELLANEOUS: Other terms shall be consistent with Studio's standard agreements.

Sample Deal Memo: Music Editor, TV Series
PROJECT: "Like Sardines in a Can" (one-hour television series).
HIRE: Steven Lawrence ("Editor").

SERVICES: Editor shall render customary first-class music editor services on a first priority, nonexclusive basis from the first spotting date of episode 1 through completion of final mix of episode 22.

COMPENSATION: $3,000 per episode, payable $1,500 on commencement of spotting each episode and $1,500 upon completion of services on each episode.

CREDIT: end-title crawl [i.e., as the credits scroll at the end of picture], placement subject to network approval.

Sample Deal Memo: Postproduction Supervisor, Feature Film
FEE: $75,000 fee.

CREDIT: Associate Producer, end titles, *clear field* [i.e., credit is in the end title "crawl," but with sufficient "empty" space both preceding and following such credit so that at the moment it reaches the center of the screen, it is the only visible credit].

EXPENSES: $300 per week toward actual, verifiable cost of assistant.

Sample Editor Agreement

As of April 23, 2010

Eddie Editor
c/o BTL Agency, Inc.
Beverly Hills, California

Ladies and Gentlemen:

This will confirm the material terms and conditions of the agreement ("Agreement") between Century Studios ("Century") and Jake Adams ("Editor") as an editor of the film that is currently entitled "My Dog Is Haunted" ("Film").

1.   Century's obligations under this Agreement are conditioned upon (i) Century's receipt of fully-executed copies of this Agreement; and (ii) Century having received confirmation that Editor has qualified for any insurance deemed necessary by Century.

2.   Provided that Editor is not in material breach of this Agreement, and subject to Century's rights of suspension and/or termination in the event of force majeure, Editor's death or disability, or Editor's Default, Editor shall render all services as editor as may be required by Century hereunder. Editor shall perform such services at the times and places directed by Century, in a competent, diligent and professional manner having due regard for the production of the Film within the budget.

3.   Editor's services shall commence on or about (i.e., seven [7] days before or after) May 19, 2011 ("Commencement Date").

4.   The term ("Term") of Editor's services hereunder shall commence on the Commencement Date and shall continue until such time when Century has determined that Editor has completed rendering services hereunder. Any services rendered by Editor in excess of the Term are subject to Century's prior written approval. Unless otherwise specified herein, Editor shall provide services hereunder on a consecutive or non-consecutive basis, as requested by Century, and Editor's services shall be rendered on an exclusive basis.

5.   Subject to the terms and conditions of this Agreement, and provided that Editor is not in material breach of any provision hereunder, Editor shall

receive the weekly sum of $10,000 for each week that Editor is required to render services hereunder, pro-rated for partial weeks at ⅕ thereof. Notwithstanding anything to the contrary contained herein, Editor shall be entitled to receive compensation at the pro-rated daily rate for each day that Editor is required by Century and Editor actually does travel in connection with his services hereunder; provided, however, that if Editor travels and works on the same day, Editor shall not be entitled to receive more than the applicable daily rate.

6.   If Century requires Editor to render services hereunder at a distant location, Editor shall receive first-class air transportation, first-class hotel accommodations, and a per diem to be negotiated in good faith.

7.   Upon the condition that Editor performs all of Editor's obligations under this Agreement and that Century's agreements with all guilds or unions so permit, Century shall accord Editor credit on screen in the main titles of the Film in the form "Editor: Jake Adams," and in the billing block portion of paid advertising issued by Century relating to the Film, provided a full billing block appears in such paid ad.

8.   To the extent that any provision of this Agreement conflicts with the mandatory provisions of any collective bargaining agreement applicable to and binding upon Century in connection with the rendition of Editor's services hereunder (collectively, the "Union Agreement"), the Union Agreement shall prevail; provided, however, that in such event the provision(s) of this Agreement so affected shall be curtailed and limited only to the extent necessary to permit compliance with the minimum mandatory terms and conditions of the Union Agreement. Century shall have the full benefit of all rights accorded employers under the Union Agreement. To the extent and during such period as it may be lawful for Century to require Editor to do so, Editor shall become and remain a member in good standing of any appropriate union(s). Editor agrees to the content of any and all waivers that Century may obtain from any relevant union.

9.   Century agrees to consult with Editor, subject to Editor's availability at no additional cost to Century, with respect to the selection of the subordinate editorial crew members engaged in connection with the Film.

10. Century shall have the right to suspend and/or terminate this Agreement when Editor is unable to perform his or her duties to mental or physical disability, or if Editor fails to comply with Editor's obligations hereunder or as a result of any "force majeure" event (as such term is commonly understood in the motion picture business).

11. Century shall be the exclusive owner of the results and proceeds of Editor's services hereunder, all of which shall be deemed a "work-for-hire" for Century. All right, title and interest in and to the Film and the material upon which it is based, shall be the sole property of Century.

12. Editor hereby represents and warrants that Editor is free to enter into this Agreement; Editor has the right to render services in accordance with the terms and conditions hereof; and Editor has not made, nor will Editor make, any grant or assignment, which will or might interfere with the complete enjoyment of the rights and privileges herein granted to Century.

13. Editor hereby agrees to defend and indemnify and otherwise hold Century free and harmless from and against any and all liabilities, claims, demands, damages or costs (including attorneys' fees) arising out of or resulting from any breach of this Agreement by Editor, or from any breach of Editor's representations and warranties under this Agreement.

14. The parties agree that any and all disputes or controversies of any nature between them arising at any time (whether or not relating to the Film), shall be decided by a reference to a private judge (a so-called rent-a-judge), mutually selected by the parties (or, if they cannot agree, by the Presiding Judge of the Los Angeles Superior Court), or pursuant to comparable provisions of federal law if the dispute falls within the exclusive jurisdiction of the federal courts), sitting without a jury, in Los Angeles County, California; and the parties hereby submit to the jurisdiction of such court. The private judge shall have the power to enter temporary restraining orders, preliminary and permanent injunctions. All such proceedings shall be closed to the public and confidential and all records relating thereto shall be permanently sealed.

15. Century shall, at any time, have the right to assign, license or otherwise transfer this Agreement, in whole or in part, and any or all of its rights hereunder, to any person or entity.

16. Editor agrees that, in the event of any breach of this Agreement by Century, including without limitation any failure to comply with the credit provisions set forth above, Editor's only remedy shall be an action at law for money damages, if any, actually suffered by Editor and in no event shall Editor be entitled to rescind or terminate this Agreement or to receive injunctive or other equitable relief, including without limitation enjoining or restraining the distribution or exhibition of the Film or any advertising, publicity or promotion issued in connection therewith or to recover consequential, incidental, special and/or punitive damages.

17. Century shall not knowingly require Editor to travel on any unscheduled aircraft unless (i) such aircraft is regularly used as a corporate jet, (ii) the aircraft Century is a licensed, chartered Century, or (iii) the pilot is in the business of providing chartered flights.

18. This Agreement represents the entire understanding of the parties hereto and replaces any and all former agreements, whether in writing or not in writing, and such Agreement may only be modified or altered via a written instrument signed by the parties hereto.

19. In the event of a breach or alleged breach of this Agreement by Century or any third party, the sole remedy of Editor shall be an action at law for damages, if any, and in no event shall Editor be entitled (a) to terminate or rescind this Agreement or any of the rights granted hereunder or (b) to enjoin, restrain or otherwise impair the development, production, advertising, publicizing or other exploitation of the Film or any rights therein or thereto.

CENTURY STUDIOS

_____

_____

JAKE ADAMS

DATE: _____

Deal Point Summary:
BELOW-THE-LINE AGREEMENTS

1. Union Applicability (if any)

2. Fixed Compensation

3. Payment Schedule

4. Overage Rate of Compensation

5. Deferred Compensation (if any)

6. Contingent Compensation (if any)

7. Start Date (should be specified)

8. Credit
- On Screen
- Paid Ads (if any)

9. Expenses, Transportation, Per Diem

NET PROFITS

$\mathcal{T}$here has always been a great deal of confusion surrounding the concept of studio "net profits." Most accountants define net profits as revenue minus expenses. Studio net profits, however, are not actual profits as such term is commonly understood among accountants and most business professionals. Rather, net profits in Hollywood refers to a contractually defined formula, which can vary from agreement to agreement, but which is not based on generally accepted accounting principles, or *GAAP.*

Moreover, the calculation of net profits is not static, but is continually subject to recalculation in each accounting period—i.e., the film may generate income years after the film is released, and costs will continue to accrue.

FEATURE FILM NET PROFITS

The fact that a motion picture can be profitable, even highly profitable, yet fail to generate net profits in accordance with the terms of a particular contract, has perplexed many outside the industry and some within the industry. Studios maintain that the mechanics of their net profit definitions are set forth in great detail in any given contract (sometimes taking up forty single-spaced pages). Nonetheless, after being faced with an increasing number of lawsuits (with many juries sympathetic to the "profit participant's" claim that he or she truly expected to receive a meaningful percentage of revenues), many of the major studios no longer refer to this type of contingent compensation as "net profits." Instead, the studios employ the phrase "net proceeds," "project proceeds," or some other variant of the above.

Profit participants have, in fact, challenged the studios' accounting practices in various lawsuits over the decades, most notably *Art Buchwald* v. *Paramount Pictures Corp.* in 1988. The Buchwald case involved the film *Coming to America,* which starred Eddie Murphy. Art Buchwald sued Paramount in that case over its alleged use of a treatment he wrote as the basis for the Eddie Murphy film. Paramount's contract granted Buchwald a portion of net profits using Paramount's standard definition.

The Buchwald case achieved notoriety because the presiding judge ruled that portions of Paramount's standard net profits definition were "unconscionable" (i.e., oppressive) under California law and, therefore, invalid. The court ultimately awarded Buchwald and his co-plaintiff just under $1 million based on its reformulation of Paramount's profits definition (after striking down the "unconscionable" portions).

Paramount appealed the trial court's decision, but the case settled before an appellate body rendered a binding decision. A Los Angeles superior court judge, in a later case (*Batfilm* v. *Warner Bros.*) involving similar claims concerning the film *Batman,* held in favor of the studio, rejecting the plaintiff's contention that the provisions of the net profits definition were unconscionable.

Although there have been several additional high-profile lawsuits challenging the method in which studios define and account for net profits in their talent agreements, there is still no court decision at the appellate level ruling on the intricacies of studio accounting practices. Nevertheless, profit participants continue to challenge the validity of studio profit definitions, and negotiations surrounding such definitions can be quite complex.

A sample net profit statement that talent might receive is set forth below to illustrate the method in which most studios account to such motion picture profit participants.

NET PROFIT

FILM: Timebomb

DISTRIBUTOR: Century Studios

Inception through June 30, 20XX

Participant: Roger Writer (5 percent Net)

GROSS RECEIPTS [i.e., REVENUES]

DOMESTIC THEATRICAL	$40,000,000
FOREIGN THEATRICAL	$31,000,000
NONTHEATRICAL	$8,000,000
DOMESTIC HOME VIDEO	$9,000,000
FOREIGN HOME VIDEO	$3,000,000
DOMESTIC PAY TELEVISION	$7,000,000
U.S. NETWORK TELEVISION	$3,500,000
U.S. SYNDICATION TELEVISION	$1,750,000
FOREIGN TELEVISION	$3,000,000
MERCHANDISING AND MUSIC	$1,500,000
TOTAL GROSS RECEIPTS:	$107,750,000

LESS: DISTRIBUTION FEES AND EXPENSES

DISTRIBUTION FEES:	$33,350,000 (See Table 2)

Distribution Expenses:

RESIDUALS:	$4,000,000
PRINTS AND DUBBING:	$6,000,000
ADVERTISING:	$20,000,000
FREIGHT AND INSURANCE:	$500,000
TAXES:	$600,000
TRADE DUES:	$1,000,000
CHECKING COSTS:	$300,000
OTHER:	$500,000
TOTAL DISTRIBUTION FEES AND EXPENSES:	$66,250,000

LESS: PRODUCTION COST AND INTEREST

NEGATIVE COST:	$50,469,125 (See Table 3)
INTEREST:	$8,000,000
TOTAL PRODUCTION COST AND INTEREST:	$58,469,000

NET PROFIT (LOSS):	–($16,969,000)
5 percent of net is:	0.00

Table 2:
DISTRIBUTION FEES

	GROSS INCOME	GROSS FEE	AMOUNT
DOMESTIC THEATRICAL	$40,000,000	30 percent	12,000,000
FOREIGN THEATRICAL	$31,000,000	40 percent	12,400,000
DOMESTIC HOME VIDEO	$9,000,000	30 percent	2,700,000
FOREIGN HOME VIDEO	$3,000,000	40 percent	1,200,000
DOMESTIC PAY TV	$7,000,000	30 percent	2,100,000
U.S. NETWORK TV	$3,500,000	25 percent	875,000
FOREIGN TV	$3,000,000	40 percent	1,200,000
MERCHANDISING/MUSIC	$1,750,000	50 percent	875,000
TOTAL DISTRIBUTION FEES:			$33,350,000

★ ★ ★

Table 3:
NEGATIVE COST

DIRECT COSTS OF PRODUCTION:

ACTUAL BUDGET:	$35,000,000
+ 15 percent OVERHEAD:	$5,250,000

GROSS PARTICIPATION: $6,277,500 (See Table 4)
(TO "A" LEVEL ACTOR BUCK THOMSON)

PLUS 15 percent OVERHEAD:	$ 941,625
OVERBUDGET PENALTY:	$3,000,000

TOTAL NEGATIVE COST: $50,469,125

GROSS PARTICIPATION STATEMENT
Inception through June 30, 20XX
Participant: Buck Thomson

Buck Thomson, star of *Timebomb*
Salary—$9 million against 15 percent of Gross

1. REVENUES: $107,750,000 *(as reported in Table 1)*

DISTRIBUTION FEES: N/A *(i.e., no distribution fees charged against Thomson's participation)*

Less *(only the following limited deductions)*:
Checking costs:	$300,000
Residuals:	$4,000,0000
Taxes:	$600,000
Trade Dues:	$1,000,000

2. ADJUSTED GROSS RECEIPTS: $101,850,000
   LESS EXCLUSION: $60,000,000

[Thomson's $9 million salary is an advance against his back-end participation. Accordingly Thomson begins to collect additional sums only after the studio has recouped at least $60 million, since Century has already advanced to Thomson his 15 percent gross participation on the first $60 million (which totaled $9 million). In preparing Thomson's participation statement, the studio must subtract $60 million from revenues in order to determine whether additional sums are payable.]

3. $101,850,000 − $60,000,000 = $41,850,000

4. Participant's Share (15 percent): $41,850,000 × .15

AMOUNT OF GROSS PARTICIPATION: **$6,277,500**

KEY TERMS

There are many sources of revenue that can contribute to a motion picture's income stream. The most obvious are theatrical receipts (i.e., box office revenue) and home video sales, but many films also commonly generate revenues from television sales (network, pay-per-view, cable), sales to airlines/cruise ships, merchandising, music (i.e., soundtrack album sales), Internet exploitation (including DTO [download-to-own] and streaming video), and even from the licensing of rights to theme park operators.

Each of the sources of revenue listed in table 1 above is described in more detail below.

Theatrical Receipts

Theatrical receipts are the dollars earned from the sale of theater admission tickets. Industry neophytes are sometimes confused by the distinction between box office receipts (i.e., the total dollars spent by consumers on admission tickets to theaters) and studio theatrical receipts (sometimes referred to as "film rental receipts"). In most cases, a substantial portion of box office receipts are retained by *exhibitors* (theater owners), with the balance remitted to the distributing studio. Accordingly, studios will report as revenue only the percentage of total box office receipts that they actually receive from the exhibitors.

There are various types of financial arrangements between distributors and exhibitors. A typical agreement might provide that the exhibitor retains less than 50 percent of the box office sales during the first two weeks of the film's release, escalating each week thereafter to as much as 90 percent of sales during the final weeks of release. Without delving into the complexities of the financial relationships between studios and theater owners, studios typically receive roughly half of the domestic box office receipts generated by a film and roughly 40 percent of the overseas box office take. Thus, when reading that a film "earned" $100 million in box office receipts, it is important to understand that the studio releasing the film likely earned approximately 50 percent of such amount. Exhibitors, of course, retain all of the profits generated by the sale of popcorn and other refreshments in their theaters in addition to their share of ticket sales.

In the example outlined in table 1 above, the fictitious film, *Timebomb,* generated ticket sales of $80 million domestically and $70 million overseas. The exhibitors retained their share and remitted $40 million and $31 million, respectively, to Century Studios.

Nontheatrical

Nontheatrical revenue is defined as proceeds realized by the studio through sales of its films to airlines, cruise ships, military bases, and educational institutions, such as libraries. This category of revenue generally represents a relatively small portion of the studio's potential profits.

Home Video

Many talent representatives believe that the method in which home video revenue is reported within profit statements is the most egregious example of "creative" Hollywood accounting. When Beta and VHS videos first became popular, most studios licensed video rights to their films to third parties, who in turn remitted a royalty (historically, about 20 percent) to the studio. As profits from video sales began to skyrocket, virtually every studio began self-distributing its videos (at least in the United States), yet continued to account for videos (per their net profit definitions) on a royalty basis. Accordingly, rather than including 100 percent of income in the definition of gross receipts and then deducting certain fees and expenses, studios instead typically allocate only 20 percent of the video income as revenues to be reported to profit participants. By excluding 80 percent of all income actually generated by the studios' video sales, studios retain a huge portion of the still-growing video/DVD market, without sharing such proceeds with profit participants. In fact, video exploitation represents the number one source of profits (to the studio/distributor) on many of today's films, exceeding even the studio's share of worldwide box office revenue. Studios argue that the 20 percent allocation of video revenue is appropriate, as the balance compensates them for manufacturing and related costs, as well as the financial risk associated with a video release.

In the example set forth above for *Timebomb,* the studio would have actually realized $60 million in revenues through worldwide sales of videos, DVD, and (if applicable) laser discs. However, since the studio's contract provides that the talent's participation is based on only 20 percent of the total, the studio has reported only one-fifth of actual sales in each of the domestic and foreign home video categories, for a total of $12 million.

As a result of technological advances, consumers can now enjoy films at home on their television screens by purchasing a film (either temporarily or permanently) directly from the Internet or from their satellite or cable television provider. At this point in time, the most common method for consumers to avail themselves of this technology is via "Video On Demand" or "VOD." With VOD, a menu is provided to the consumer with dozens, hundreds, or even thousands of movie titles, and the consumer can select a movie to view by pressing a series of buttons on his or her television remote, or by clicking an icon on a Web site. Most studios currently consider VOD to fall within the definition of "home video" and therefore treat revenues derived from this media platform in the same manner that DVD and Blu-Ray receipts are currently accounted for to profit participants.

Television Sales

Most theatrical films are eventually available for viewing on pay-per-view, pay cable (such as HBO and Showtime), network television, and basic cable (usually in that order). Studios also license television exhibition rights to foreign distributors and networks in many territories. The proceeds realized by the studio from each of these types of sales are reported under the category "television sales."

In many cases, television networks negotiate to purchase a group of films from a studio (rather than individual films). This is particularly true with cable networks, which often enter into multiyear deals with studios, known as *output* deals. Showtime, for example, might enter into a single agreement with Sony whereby Showtime acquires the pay television exhibition rights to every film released by Sony over a ten-year period. Within the context of such output deals, profit participants sometimes dispute the studio's allocation of proceeds among the various films included in the package (arguing, for instance, that hits should be valued higher than flops). Despite the fact that most studios currently treat VOD and Internet streaming and download revenues as video receipts, some talent representatives believe that such revenues should actually be accounted for in the same manner as television receipts. They argue that at some point in the future, all of television may become "on-demand"— i.e., consumers will select programs from a menu, and new television programs won't actually be broadcast on the air at a particular time.

Merchandising/Music

This category includes income realized by the studio through sales of t-shirts, posters, mugs, toys, and other items of merchandise relating to the film. In addition, almost every major studio release boasts a soundtrack album. Most studios license the album rights to a record label (although some record labels are in the same corporate family as the studio, such as Universal Pictures and Universal Music). In such instances, the record label incurs the expense of manufacturing and marketing the album and typically pays a royalty to the studio based on album sales. Frequently, the record company will agree to advance a negotiated sum to the studio against future royalties.

Another source of revenue included in this category is music publishing income. Most composers engaged to score a film are hired on a work-for-hire basis, granting copyright ownership of the composition to the film studio. Consequently, subject to the precise terms of the composer's contract, the studio may realize income through the licensing of the film's score to third parties.

Distribution Fees

Per most studio contracts, a set distribution fee is charged against revenues as a means of compensating the studio for its costs for maintaining distribution offices and facilities. These are generally flat rates, ranging from 30 to 40 percent of a film's gross receipts (depending on the particular medium in which the film is distributed).

After adding up all revenue, the distribution fees are almost always the first items charged against (i.e., deducted from) such revenues, which are calculated as a percentage of gross receipts. As illustrated in table 2, most studios levy different distribution fees for different media. In the example in that table, Century Studios charged a 30 percent distribution fee for domestic theatrical distribution and 40 percent in connection with international theatrical distribution. What this means to a profit participant is that the studio is immediately reducing the line items reporting theatrical receipts by approximately a third (retaining this third for its own account). The remaining 60 to 65 percent of revenues is what the studio will deem income when reporting to the participant.

What table 2 demonstrates is that over $30 million is retained by the studio as potential profit "off-the-top"—i.e., before even reaching a tally on whether there are net profits available for distribution. In other words, because studios are contractually permitted to deduct distribution fees immediately, approximately $30 million will be automatically excluded from the pool of revenue used to calculate the profit participant's net profits. Although few would deny that the studio's distribution organization is expensive to maintain, many question whether such fees are disproportionately high relative to the actual cost of running a distribution company.

Distribution Expenses

In addition to the distribution fees charged against receipts by most studios, many of the actual "hard" costs of distribution are usually deducted as well. These include the following:

Residuals

These are payments made to talent and technical staff (per union requirements) for use of the motion picture beyond its initial theatrical release. Most unions calculate the residual as a percentage of the gross receipts derived from the alternate sources of revenue (such as video and television). The bulk of these payments are attributable to IATSE, SAG, DGA, WGA, and AF of M (American Federation of Musicians) agreements.

Prints

The cost of printing copies of the movie, which are delivered to theaters across the planet, is not cheap, generally costing $1,500 each. A "blockbuster" might require over three thousand prints in the United States alone. In recent years, a new form of "print" delivery has emerged: Digital Cinema Projection (DCP). This method involves transmitting electronic copies of the movie to exhibitors, where the picture is stored on a high-capacity hard drive. The film is then projected via technologies such as LCOS in lieu of the traditional method of projecting light through film. One major benefit of DCP is that the studios no longer need to spend hundreds of thousands of dollars on film prints. Similarly, they do not need to drive these prints across the country (not only in order to deliver the prints to the theatres, but to pick them up as well). The downside, however, is that theatre chains would need to spend significant capital to replace their current projectors with digital projectors, and in the current economic climate, studios are finding it increasingly difficult to persuade the exhibitors to convert to digital technology.

Advertising

The advertising expense of $20 million included in table 1 above includes not only actual costs, but also an overhead fee of 10 percent (in accordance with the provisions of most studios' net proceeds definition). One rule of thumb suggests that the cost of advertising most studio releases is roughly equivalent to one-half of the picture's budget—so that a $40 million film will cost an additional $20 million to advertise and promote.

Freight and Insurance

This represents the cost of shipping and insuring prints and does not represent a significant expense.

Taxes

Taxes, as used here, do not include income taxes. The term refers to remittance taxes outside the United States, as well as certain box office–related taxes charged to the distributor.

Checking Costs

Checking costs are those associated with checking, or auditing, the exhibitors. In other words, after a theater owner reports ticket sales totaling $20,000 on its opening weekend, the studio may send an employee out to such theater in order to review its ledger.

Trade Dues

These are payments made by the studio to trade organizations to which it belongs, most notably the Motion Picture Association of America (MPAA). Studios will allocate a portion of their annual dues to each picture released in such calendar year.

Production Costs

After the studio tallies its revenues and subtracts distribution fees and expenses, it then proceeds to deduct the actual costs of producing the film. At this stage in our analysis, Century Studios has reported $107,750,000 in revenues and deducted $66,250,000 in fees and expenses. What has not yet been subtracted is the actual cost of producing the movie, referred to as the *negative cost* (negative not in the sense of plus/minus, but in the film/camera sense—i.e., the amount of money spent in order to create a complete negative or film plate).

In calculating the negative cost of a film, however, the studio does not merely add up all of its out-of-pocket costs, such as cast and crew salaries, rights payments, and other hard costs. Instead, the studio (again, per its contractual definition) deems "negative cost" to include any amounts paid out to gross profit participants (as opposed to net profit participants). Since gross participations are payable before net profits are reached, the studio argues that such payments should be recouped before any net profit participant receives money. In addition, almost all studios add an overhead fee (generally 15 percent of all defined production costs) to their calculation of negative cost. A byproduct of the studio's treatment of the payment of gross participations as a production cost is that the studio will tack on the aforementioned overhead fee, as well as charge interest on these costs. Table 3 above illustrates the calculation of Century Studio's negative cost.

Gross Participation

As alluded to above, most studio profit definitions treat payments to gross profit participants (i.e., payments to high-level talent or other parties receiving a gross, rather than net, participation) as costs of production, rather than expenses. The studios defend this practice by explaining that, like other production costs, cash payments to gross profit participations are payable before "breakeven" (i.e., the point at which net profits are first available for distribution). Since the studio is obligated to make such payments regardless of whether it breaks even, it argues that such payments are appropriately treated as production costs, subject to overhead and interest charges.

In the fictitious film *Timebomb,* there is only one gross participant—the star of the picture, Buck Thompson. Buck was paid $9 million against 15 percent of the gross—in other words, an up-front salary of $9 million which is deemed an advance against 15 percent of the studio's gross receipts, less only standard off-the-tops (checking costs, residuals, taxes, and trade dues). Table 4 above demonstrates the calculation of Buck Thompson's participation, which is then reported as a line-item cost (i.e., "Gross Participation: $6,277,500") in Table 3.

In some cases, the mere existence of gross profit participants on a film will single-handedly determine whether or not the picture generates net profits. This is because each time a gross participation is paid, it increases the film's "cost of production" (per the contractual definition), making the possibility of net profits more remote. This factor alone is a major reason that expensive films with huge stars and renowned directors can generate enormous box office dollars, yet fail to generate net profits. Thus, the writer of an Arnold Schwarzenegger film is much less likely to receive a check (resulting from his 5 percent of net) than is the writer of a low-budget film with a novice director and no major stars (i.e., no gross participants) that "breaks out" and becomes an unexpected hit (such as *The Blair Witch Project*).

Interest

Interest is generally charged from the day production begins and is generally levied against all budgeted production and promotion costs. The rate is usually specified as a factor of the U.S. prime rate (i.e., 125 percent of prime).

Over-Budget Penalty

Many net proceeds definitions include a provision stating that for each dollar the film exceeds its budget, an additional dollar will be charged as a cost of the film. In other words, if a $20 million–budgeted film actually costs $21 million to produce, a total of $22 million (plus interest and overhead) will be included in the negative cost, since the film exceeds its budget by $1 million. Thus, the studio, in this instance, will impose an "over-budget penalty" of $1 million. This type of provision is intended to deter profit participants from allowing the film to go over-budget.

Advances Against Profits

Talent representatives will sometimes be successful in securing advances for their clients, payable at certain defined points in time (most often based on specified levels of box office revenues). Payments made to talent at these defined "trigger-points" would serve as advances against (and be recoupable from) any contingent compensation otherwise payable to such talent. In the feature animation arena, voice talent typically participates in the film's success only in this manner (i.e., via the payment of certain box-office bonuses) rather than receiving a percentage of net or gross proceeds. These payments may be tied to domestic box office receipts, or to worldwide box office receipts. Attention should be paid to the various formulas, as some films are expected to generate more revenue in the U.S. and Canada, while others are anticipated to perform more strongly overseas. In the past, the majority of box office advances were payable at set dollar amounts of box office revenue (for example, $50,000 payable to talent when domestic box office receipts reach $100,000,000). In recent years, studios have shied away from using such simplistic formulas primarily because, at the time of negotiation, the final cost of the Picture may not be known. Accordingly, studios could find themselves in the position of paying out bonuses to various participants prior to the point at which they have recouped the film's cost. Consequently, some studios have begun implementing formulas that are based on multiples of the film's cost rather than on predetermined amounts of box office receipts. An example would be a bonus of $50,000 that is payable to an actor at the point in time at which box office receipts of the Picture exceed three times the final costs of production of the Picture.

NEGOTIABLE ISSUES/AREAS OF COMPLAINT

Set forth below are some of the more common areas of negotiation among profit participants, studios, and independent producers.

Bundling of Films

Studios sometimes sell a package of films to distributors in foreign territories. These packages may include one or two hit films and several grade-B movies. Some of the foreign distributors might even elect not to exhibit some or all of the grade-B films. In any event, when the studio accounts to the profit participants on these films, it might allocate revenue equally among the films comprising the package. Profit participants of the hit films might argue that this practice artificially decreases the revenue attributable to the hits and that the less successful films in the package should be assigned a lower value. Studios maintain that they are entitled to make any "reasonable" allocation. Disputes over such allocations of revenue are generally addressed during audits of the studio's books (conducted by talent) long after the film is released, rather than during the negotiation stage.

Over-Budget Penalty

Many studio profit definitions contain an over-budget penalty provision (defined above), regardless of whether the talent receiving such participation has any direct control over the film's budget. Depending on the leverage of the profit participant and the negotiating skill of her representative, a profit participant who does not exercise control over the budget (such as a writer or rights holder) may be successful in removing this penalty.

Interest

As mentioned above, studios generally charge interest on production costs when accounting to net profit participants. Profit participants often contend that the rate of interest charged in the contract (usually a variable of prime) exceeds the studio's actual cost of borrowing. In addition, in many cases, the studio does not actually borrow money when producing a film, or if it does, it does not borrow the full amount. In fact, some of the items on which interest is charged are costs for which the studio is not actually out-of-pocket. For example, the studio might attribute a price to the use of its vans or soundstages during filming of a movie and proceed to charge interest on such amounts.

In addition, through historical anomalies, most profit definitions calculate interest on the basis of a 360-day year (12 months × 30 days), rather than a 365-day year. While possibly making the studio's calculations simpler, such fact also results in higher interest charges to the participant.

At the request of the talent representative, most studios will agree to modify the net profits definition to provide that interest will not be charged on overhead, and that an overhead fee (see below) will not be charged on interest expenses.

Distribution Fees

Studios rarely agree to reduce or remove their distribution fees when negotiating with net participants. Some independent producers may agree to cap distribution fees or expenses at a negotiated dollar amount. Talent representatives allege that distribution fees bear no relationship to actual costs. One example sometimes cited by talent is the studio/pay cable output agreement. In the case of *Timebomb*, Century Studios has levied a 30-percent fee on its pay cable sales (to networks such as HBO). The cynical talent representative would argue that this "sale" involved, at most, a couple of phone calls, so that deducting a 30 percent fee from the proceeds of such sale seems extreme. Studios, of course, justify these fees by arguing that only they bear the financial risk of a flop. In other words, if the movie never earns a dollar, the director, writer, and actor still get paid. Consequently, if the movie is a hit, the studio argues it should receive the lion's share of the proceeds.

The distribution fees on home video revenue vary from studio to studio, with some studios declining to take any fee (since revenue is already diluted by the studio's method of accounting for video revenue on a 20-percent-royalty basis). Obviously, talent representatives vehemently object to distribution fees that further reduce the already trimmed-down share of video receipts.

Twenty Percent Home Video Royalty

Spielberg and Hanks, along with other members of Hollywood's elite, have been successful in making a significant dent in the studios' practice of including only 20 percent of video revenue within gross receipts. Most net participants will be unable to improve the definition in this regard, although, as stated above, many studios will agree not to levy a distribution fee on video receipts.

Overhead Fees

As with distribution fees, most profit participants would argue that the studio's actual overhead cost (to be properly allocated to a single film) is significantly less than 15 percent of the film's cost. Studios defend their overhead fees as reasonable. Depending on the leverage of the talent, studios might agree to reduce their overhead fee to as little as 7.5 percent.

Advertising Costs

Many studios tack on an overhead fee (usually in the range of 10 to 12 percent) to the actual, "hard" advertising costs associated with marketing a film. Talent representatives frequently argue that this overhead fee is excessive. Only the highest level of talent is generally able to negotiate a reduction in this overhead fee.

Facilities Charges

When studios assign costs to the use of their wholly owned facilities (i.e., stages, cameras, vehicles, etc.), talent agents argue that these are the very costs that the overhead charge is designed to cover. Since the studio is not actually "out-of-pocket" in connection with these expenses, profit participants often argue that they should not be reported as costs. Studios respond by contending that at any time its facilities are in use in connection with the picture, the studio is losing income, because it could be renting out such facilities to other entities. Therefore, the studio should be permitted to charge these costs to the film. Many studios maintain rate cards for each item of inventory. The studio contends that it should not be penalized for owning soundstages and catering trucks, since an independent production company without its own lot would need to spend actual dollars in order to secure such materials. The major studios do not typically agree to waive their facilities charges.

Cash versus Accrual Method of Accounting

Most businesses employ the accrual method of accounting (i.e., revenue is recognized when earned, expenses are recognized when incurred), which is favored by GAAP. In any event, businesses typically select one method (cash or accrual) in order to maintain consistency. Most studio profit definitions, however, provide that revenue will be recognized only when the cash is received, while expenses will be recognized the moment they are incurred. This has the dual effect of delaying the reporting of profits and maximizing interest charges. Studios are generally unwilling even to entertain the idea of deviating from this practice.

Foreign/Other Advances

Although studios generally credit revenue when cash is received, they sometimes argue that advances received by the studio (such as those paid by foreign distributors) should not be reported until the studio has "earned" such advance. For example, if a Spanish distributor pays $10 million to Century Studios for the rights to exhibit its film in Spain and Portugal, as an advance against box office revenue, Century might argue that it should not include such $10 million on its accounting statement until box office receipts in those territories reach the requisite level. Talent with sufficient clout should be able to persuade the studio to recognize advances when paid, rather than when earned. Persistent talent representatives possessing less leverage should at least extract a commitment from the studio to report nonrefundable advances when paid (since even if such advance is not ultimately earned by the studio through sufficient sales, the studio will still retain the funds).

Cross-Collateralization

Cross-collateralization involves offsetting profits from one project with losses from another. Studio profit definitions technically permit this practice when one writer, director, actor, or other participant is involved in separate projects at the studio. Woody Allen's legal battle with his longtime producer, Jean Doumanian, involves allegations that net losses from some of Woody's films were allowed to reduce net gains from others. In the TV arena, studios might like to cross-collateralize several series created by a writer, so that the studio's huge losses on a failed series can be applied against the enormous profits of a successful series. Studios will normally acquiesce to talent's request for a provision barring cross-collateralizing separate projects when calculating net profits.

Double Deductions

Talent representatives frequently request that the studio's profit definition be modified to reflect the disallowance of double deductions. In other words, the talent wants the studio to acknowledge that a single item of cost or expense will not be deducted multiple times (in varied sections) within the profit definition. Most studios readily agree to this request and will provide the talent with a brief addendum to the studio profit definition that specifically disallows double deductions.

Audit Rights

Studios and profit participants commonly negotiate issues relating to the participant's right to audit the studio's books, the frequency with which the studio will prepare and deliver accounting statements, and dates (i.e., time limitations) for objecting to items on such statements. Talent representatives will sometimes request that the studio agree to pay for audit costs, which can be quite expensive, in the event that the audit demonstrates a discrepancy of 5 percent or higher in the studio's calculation. The rationale is that talent should not be discouraged from pursuing their audit rights by the costs involved. While the studio might refuse to pay for all audits conducted by talent (so as not to encourage frivolous claims), many studios will agree to reimburse the talent's audit costs if a discrepancy of sufficient magnitude (5 percent or more) can be shown. Typically, the right to audit is limited to once per twelve-month period during regular office hours and upon reasonable advance notice.

Third-Party Reductions

In instances where profit participants must "bear third parties" (i.e., the number of "points" assigned to such talent is reduced by the points given to others), talent representatives will request that such reduction be "dollar for dollar" rather than "point for point." For example: Paulie Producer is granted 50 percent of the net proceeds, reducible by third-party participants to a floor of 25 percent. Paulie will request that at such time as the value of his net proceeds are calculated, the value of third-party "points" will be calculated as well (in the event that Paulie's definition varies slightly from others—typically as a result of negotiations surrounding such definition), and that Paulie's proceeds will be reduced by actual dollars owed to third parties. This is preferable (to Paulie) to the alternative, in which Danny Director's fifteen points would automatically reduce Paulie's fifty points to thirty-five, prior to being calculated. If Danny's points are less valuable than Paulie's (again, due to negotiation of the respective profit definitions), Paulie will prefer that the actual dollars owed to Danny reduce Paulie's total payments, rather than Danny's (less valuable) points reducing the number of Paulie's (more valuable) points.

Merchandising

Sometimes, studios will agree to separate or "break out" merchandising, calculating such revenues as a "separate pot" from other sources of revenue derived from exploitation of the project. This can be particularly lucrative in connection with animated projects (such as *The Simpsons* or *South Park*), which can generate hundreds of millions of dollars in merchandise. If merchandising is accounted for on a "separate pot" basis, the studio will only be able to deduct merchandising expenses and distribution fees from proceeds, rather than its entire deficit in the project. If, for example, a picture performed dismally at the box office, but generated healthy t-shirt sales, the probability that the participant will receive proceeds based on merchandising sales will significantly increase if such participant was able to negotiate for a separate accounting of merchandising.

Soundtrack Royalties

Similarly, studios will sometimes grant talent a royalty based on soundtrack album sales and account to such talent on a "separate pot" basis. With the sea change brought about by mp3 players such as the iPod, the negotiation and calculation of such "separate-pot" soundtrack royalties has become increasingly complex. Music CDs are no longer the prevailing delivery system for soundtrack albums, as digital music files have become the dominant vehicle for sales of all music.

Hybrid Costs

Profit participants may be successful in characterizing certain "hybrid" costs (such as music clearance costs) as distribution expenses, rather than production costs, particularly when negotiating with independent production companies. This will benefit the profit participant in that distribution expenses do not carry interest or overhead charges. Hybrid costs are those that can reasonably be described as both distribution and production costs.

Foreign Tax Credits

Talent representatives often request specific language providing that foreign tax credits received by the studio or distributor will be reflected in the participant's accounting statement. Since studios deduct the payment of foreign taxes from their receipts, talent representatives generally insist that the benefit of foreign tax credits be reflected as well. The relative clout of the profit participant will generally determine whether the studio will agree to reflect such credits.

Favored Nations

If a talent representative believes that there will be profit participants of higher stature than her client on a particular project, such talent representative may attempt to shortcut the negotiation process by tying her client's definition to other talent (i.e., "my client's definition shall be no less favorable than that accorded to any other individual profit participant on this picture"). Studios are generally reluctant to agree to such a broad favored-nations provision, particularly in instances where talent remains to be hired (so that if the studio subsequently grants a generous participation in order to attract a major star, the studio will not be forced to extend such benefit to the original participant). However, studios may agree to tie a particular individual's profit definition to that of one or more, specifically identified participants.

There are additional provisions in any particular distributor's net proceeds definition that can be modified through negotiation—some quite complex—and a skilled entertainment lawyer is probably best suited to spearhead such negotiations.

GROSS AND ADJUSTED GROSS RECEIPTS (AGR)

Numerous definitions of contingent compensation fall between "net profits" and "first-dollar gross" by altering, in one way or another, the items deductible from gross receipts. As previously discussed, first-dollar gross, or "pure gross," is a bit of a misnomer, as the back-end deals of even the uppermost echelon of Hollywood players generally permit the deduction of certain distribution costs classified as off-the-top, such as taxes, customs duties, and guild-mandated reuse payments.

A pure gross deal would provide for the payment of a percentage of the studio's gross receipts, beginning with the first dollar earned by such studio, prior to the studio recouping any costs whatsoever.

An "adjusted gross receipts" (AGR) definition is one in which the studio will deduct its customary off-the-top deductions as well certain other contractually stipulated distribution costs (for instance, advertising costs). The allowable distribution expenses in an AGR definition are generally more limited than those deducted in a net deal. In addition, overhead and interest provisions are generally more favorable to the participant. The principal way in which AGR differs from net is that distribution fees are generally not charged against receipts.

In many cases, what industry insiders refer to as "AGR" is actually a "modified adjusted gross" (MAG) participation (sometimes called "MAG" or "Modified Adjusted Gross"). An MAG participation is essentially a net participation with negotiated distribution fees (that will be lower than those set forth in net deals). Sometimes, talent will receive MAG as an advance against net profits, rather than in lieu of net profits. For example: "Director shall receive 10 percent of 100 percent of the Adjusted Gross Receipts attributable to exploitation of the Picture, against 25 percent of 100 percent of the Net Proceeds." Since the point at which AGR is payable is earlier than the point at which net proceeds are available, the AGR payable to the director in the foregoing example will be deemed an advance against, and be recouped from, any net proceeds ultimately owed.

TELEVISION NET PROFITS

The calculation of profit participations in the television arena is quite similar to that of feature films. The primary difference is that box-office receipts do not generally appear as a source of revenue, as few television productions are released theatrically.

Accordingly, a studio's revenue in connection with a television project will be derived principally through license fees (paid by networks for the right to exhibit the program), foreign television sales, and syndication sales. Other sources of revenue may include merchandising, music, and home video. While it is less common for television programs to generate soundtrack albums than it is for feature films, many of today's popular series (such as *Ally McBeal* and *The Sopranos*) have launched successful albums. Similarly, not all television movies or series are sold via Internet, VOD, iTunes, and DVD, although this practice is becoming increasingly common as shows are being sold as "boxed sets" (e.g., season 1, season 2, etc.). Boxed sets of TV series such as *24* and *Sex and the City* have sold very successfully. Like film studios, television distributors generally report one-fifth (i.e., 20 percent) of total home video revenue to profit participants, justifying the exclusion of the remaining 80 percent as an appropriate return on its significant investment.

Studios will levy distribution fees against revenues in much the same way as shown in table 2 above. For example, when studios sell their television programming overseas, they will deduct the contractually specified distribution fee.

Finally, the studio's method of calculating its cost of programming is essentially identical to that with respect to films. In addition to the program's budget, the studio will include any over-budget penalties (if applicable), gross participation payments, overhead, and interest.

Television is sometimes regarded as an all-or-nothing business. While approximately only 15 percent of feature film net profit participants will actually receive payments thereon, almost all successful television series (i.e., those that are ultimately syndicated) will reach the point where net profits are payable. In the case of enormously successful television series, the largest contributor to gross receipts will be U.S. syndication sales. As referenced in chapter 3, previously aired episodes of *Seinfeld* have generated over $2 billion in syndication sales to date.

Imputed License Fees

As discussed in chapter 4 (in reference to television writer/producers), studios and networks have historically been distinct entities, with studios retaining ownership of their programs. Accordingly, a studio was able to report as revenue the dollar amount of any license fee paid by a network for the right to broadcast the program. In recent years, the line between network and studio has blurred, either because such entities are co-owned by a single conglomerate or because networks have begun to produce their own programming.

Leaving aside the issues raised by *vertical integration* (in other words, when profit participants challenge the financial terms of agreements entered into between a studio and its sister company, claiming that such studio did not, in fact, bargain at arms length or secure the highest price for the rights it granted), networks that produce programming for their own airwaves typically need to impute, or artificially assign, a value to the exhibition rights exploited by such network.

Since most networks pay significant license fees for the right to broadcast programming, it would be hard to defend a position where the studio must recoup all of its costs from ancillary sources (such as video and merchandising) before recognizing net profits. Thus, even if the network is not actually receiving cash (from itself or from a wholly owned subsidiary) in exchange for broadcast rights, it will typically be willing to assign some value to those rights.

Contractual provisions reflecting this concept might resemble the following:

> In lieu of actual revenues derived at any time from any distribution or exhibition of the Program by means of Broadcast Television (as defined herein) in the Territory (as defined herein) over any programming services owned or controlled by Producer, Producer shall be deemed to have received, upon the date nine (9) months following completion of principal photography of the Program, Gross Receipts in an amount (the "Imputed Amount") equal to Seven Hundred Thousand Dollars ($700,000) for each one-hour Episode of the Program.

Some studios will impute a percentage of the approved budget, rather than a fixed dollar amount (i.e., "Producer shall be deemed to have received 55 percent of the final approved budget of each applicable episode upon the date nine (9) months following completion of principal photography of such episode.").

Issues that are negotiated in connection with the imputation of a license fee include: (1) the amount that will be imputed; (2) whether the imputed episodic license fee increases in subsequent seasons, and by how much (studios will usually agree to a 4- to 5-percent annual increase); (3) how many exhibition days such imputed license fee buys (i.e., can the network continue to air such episodes forever without attributing more revenue?); and (4) whether the network must undertake any efforts to syndicate the programs, or whether it can simply continue to air prior episodes on its own service. Networks will usually reserve the right to make such business decisions, but may agree to impute additional amounts in the event that they continue to exhibit episodes in lieu of syndication.

Agency Commissions/Package Fees

Another cost sometimes associated with television programming that does not generally apply to feature films is the talent agency "package fee." This fee, which is typically calculated as a percentage of the license fee paid by the network to the studio producing the television program, is sometimes paid by the studio to a talent agency that represented one or more of the key players involved in the project.

For example: Studio A wants to develop a program to be written by Steven Bochco that will star David Schwimmer. Agency X represents both Bochco and Schwimmer. Agency X negotiates to receive a package fee equal to between 3 and 6 percent of the network license fee for each episode ultimately produced. It should be noted that if the agency secures such a fee, it will serve in lieu of the agency's customary 10 percent commission on the salaries of its clients serving on the project.

In addition to a set percentage of the license fee, agencies often negotiate to receive additional, deferred compensation, payable out of profits (if any) generated by the program, as well as a share of revenue from the off-network exploitation of the series. Sometimes an agency may negotiate a package fee in connection with a feature film, though such fees are much rarer. While studios resist the payment of package fees to agencies, such fees are common in the marketplace. The payment of any such fees, like other costs, will be reflected in the profit participation statements generated by the applicable studio.

Advances Against Profits

Some television studios will agree to advance the payment of negotiated sums upon reaching certain episodic milestones. For instance, a studio might agree to advance $3 million to a series creator at such time, if ever, as the sixty-seventh episode is completed. This payment will be subsequently recouped from profits otherwise payable to such creator. The rationale for such a provision is that if a sufficient number of episodes are produced, the studio will almost certainly realize enormous syndication revenue and, therefore, should agree to advance a portion of the participant's share of expected profits.

CONCLUSION

A well-known anecdote is often told in Hollywood circles:

In the 1950s, as the motion picture industry was developing on the west coast, AT&T sent three of its engineers to Los Angeles to meet with certain technicians at the burgeoning studios. As AT&T was rumored to closely watch its costs, its travel guidelines required the three travelers to share a room.

Upon checking in to the local hotel, the desk clerk informed the engineers that the cost was $30 per night, with payment of the first night's fee due upon check-in. Dutifully, the three employees each contributed a $10 bill.

Hours later, the desk clerk realized that AT&T had negotiated a corporate rate with the parent company of the hotel chain and that, consequently, the travelers were overcharged by $5. The desk clerk instructed the bell captain to inform the engineers that the actual cost of the room was $25, and to return the $5.

The bell captain was not the most scrupulous fellow and decided to keep some of the money. Accordingly, he knocked on the guests' door, informed the engineers that a mistake had been made, and that the correct rate for the room was $27. He therefore returned $1 to each of the men and pocketed the remaining $2.

The AT&T employees ultimately spent $27 on the room ($9 each), and the bell captain kept $2, bringing the total to $29. The puzzle is as follows: What happened to the thirtieth dollar that the engineers initially parted with? The answer, apparently, is, "That's Hollywood accounting!"

What one should glean from this story, and from this chapter as a whole, is that when negotiating back-end deals, it is essential to remember that, unlike the generic definition of profits (i.e., profits equal income minus expenses), the entertainment industry definition is contractual and a function of negotiation.

Deal Point Summary:
NET PROCEEDS NEGOTIATIONS

1. FEATURE FILMS
- Gross Receipts
  - Theatrical
  - Nontheatrical
  - Home Video
  - Television
  - DVD, VOD, NVOD, Internet Download to Own
  - Merchandising and Music
- Distribution Fees
- Distribution Expenses
  - Residuals
  - Prints and Dubbing
  - Advertising
  - Freight and Insurance
  - Taxes
  - Trade Dues
  - Checking Costs
- Production Costs
  - Interest
  - Gross Participations
  - Over-Budget Penalty

2. TELEVISION PROGRAMS
- Imputed License Fees
- Agency Package Fees
- Advances Against Profits

THE BASICS

of

COPYRIGHT LAW

*I*t is useful for anyone involved in entertainment dealmaking to have a general understanding of the basic tenets of copyright law. A motion picture is a form of intellectual property that is subject to the laws of copyright, not only in the United States, but abroad. Successful motion pictures and television programs are frequent targets of litigation emanating from claims of copyright infringement. As most motion pictures originate in written form (i.e., in the form of a screenplay, which may be based on a book or play), it is crucial for any writer, producer, studio, or distributor to understand the rights that they acquire when they purchase a screenplay or register copyright in a motion picture or script.

QUESTIONS ABOUT COPYRIGHT

The following discussion addresses the most common issues regarding copyright protection.

What Is Covered Under Copyright Law?

Many people mistakenly believe that copyright law can protect an idea. In fact, copyright law only covers the unique *expression* of an idea, not the idea itself. Moreover, even when an expression is copyrightable, the underlying idea is not protected (i.e., someone else may create their own unique expression of such idea). Consider the following example: Joe tells his friend Jill that he'd like to write a film about a love triangle that ends in murder. Jill goes home and writes a screenplay about a love triangle that ends in murder and sells it for $1 million. While Joe may be angry, there is no legal principle preventing Jill from writing or selling her script.

Of course, not every expression is copyrightable. In order to qualify for copyright protection, the work must meet each of the following criteria:

★ It must be an original work
★ It must be in a fixed, tangible medium of expression, such as paper, video, film, or sheet music, from which the work can be perceived, reproduced, or otherwise communicated either directly or by way of machine or device
★ Notice must be given if the work was published (i.e., first distributed to the public) before March 31, 1989, i.e., it must have "copyright " or © written on it along with the date of publication and the author's name (works created after that date do not require a copyright notice; see Who Can Claim Copyright Ownership? below)
★ It cannot be a utilitarian or purely functional work, such as a table of weights or a calendar

What Types of Work Are Copyrightable?

The following types of works are copyrightable, provided that they meet the above-mentioned criteria:

★ Literary works, such as screenplays or books
★ Musical works (including accompanying words)
★ Dramatic works (including accompanying music), such as plays
★ Pantomimes and choreographic works
★ Pictorial, graphic, and sculptural works
★ Motion pictures and audiovisual works
★ Sound recordings
★ Architectural works

What Cannot Be Copyrighted?

Certain types of works are not copyrightable, such as the following:

★ Inventions, procedures, typeface designs, systems, or industrial-designs. Although many of these works may be protected under patent law or otherwise, they are not protected under copyright law. Similarly, works consisting exclusively of common information, such as standard calendars, height and weight charts, or tape measures, are also not copyrightable.

★ Ideas, concepts, or themes, as mentioned above, are not protected under copyright law, since such protections are regarded as contrary to public policy.

★ Titles are not copyrightable, although they may be protected in other ways discussed below.

★ Works in the *public domain* are not protected. When a copyright expires, the work falls into the public domain (i.e., it is essentially available to all), and thus, anyone may use the work without compensation or permission. For example, all of Shakespeare's works are in the public domain and, therefore, are not protected by copyright law. Thus, if a writer wants to create a modern-day *Romeo and Juliet,* for example, such writer will not need to obtain any underlying rights from Shakespeare's heirs. However, one would need to be careful not to infringe on other Shakespearean adaptations, which may be protected under copyright law, such as the *Romeo and Juliet* film starring Claire Danes.

★ Improvisational speeches or unrecorded live performances are not covered.

★ Real-life events are not copyrightable per se, although the unique expression of such events may be copyrightable.

Who Can Claim Copyright Ownership?

One of the greatest misconceptions about copyright law is that a creator must register his work with the copyright office in order for the work to be protected under copyright law. While this was true prior to passage of the Berne Copyright Convention in 1988, the Berne Convention stipulates that "everything created privately and originally is copyrighted and protected whether it has a copyright notice or not." Accordingly, copyright in a work now immediately vests with its author or authors (equally, unless agreed upon to the contrary) upon creation, whether the work is registered with the U.S. Copyright Office or not. Thus, the creator does not need to take any action in order to become a valid copyright owner, except in the following cases:

★ Works-for-Hire: If the work is created within the scope of employment, the employer (rather than the work's creator) will be deemed its "author" and own the copyright in the property. For example, if a studio hires a writer to write a screenplay, the studio will own the copyright in the screenplay. Commissioned works or works specifically ordered for use will be considered works-for-hire as well, unless the parties agree otherwise in a signed contract.

★ Transfer of Ownership: If an existing work is acquired by a person or entity by written copyright assignment, the assignee will be the copyright holder. In such cases, an assignment must be filed in the U.S. Copyright Office within one month of the assignment. Similarly, if the work is acquired by a license, which may be of a limited (i.e., temporary) or perpetual (i.e., everlasting or permanent) duration, the rights will be owned by the licensee for the duration of the license term.

What Rights Does the Copyright Owner Have?

A copyright in a property bestows certain ownership rights upon its owner, similar to those held by owners of more tangible property. Such rights include the following:

★ The exclusive right to reproduce copies of the work, including phonorecords

★ The exclusive right to distribute, sell, lease, or license the work or any derivatives thereof

★ The exclusive right to publicly perform or display the work or any derivatives of the work

★ In the case of sound recordings, the exclusive right to perform the work publicly by means of digital audio transmission

There are, however, limited instances in which the use of copyrighted work will be permitted without payment or consent, for example, if the use falls within the *fair use* doctrine. This doctrine covers use of the work for purposes of criticism (such as book reviews), comment, news, reporting, teaching (including producing multiple copies for classroom use), or research. In determining whether the use in any given case constitutes fair use, the following factors will be considered:

★ The purpose of the use (including whether it is for commercial use or a nonprofit, educational purpose)

★ The nature of the copyrighted work (e.g., Is the work informational or creative, and has it ever been published?)

★ The amount used in relation to the size of the work as a whole (e.g., in determining whether nonconsensual use of a work is reasonable, a court might investigate whether the potential infringer used more of the original work than was necessary for the purpose for which it was copied)

★ The effect of the use upon the potential market for, or the value of, the work or any derivative works thereof (e.g., Does the unauthorized use negatively impact the potential sale of the copyrighted work, interfere with the marketability of the work, or diminish the demand for the original work?)

A parody, for example, which is an imitation of a serious work for a humorous or satirical effect, may fall under the fair use exception, since it is essentially a method of criticism. The factors described in the preceding paragraph will be considered by a court in determining whether a defense of fair use is valid in each instance. Alternatively, a parodist (without the requisite authorization or license) may turn to the defense of free speech principles incorporated in the First Amendment.

Is the Copyright in a Work Divisible and Transferable?

Any or all of the specific exclusive rights that make up a copyright and any subdivision of such rights may be transferred and owned separately, even though the transfer may be for a limited duration in time or place of effect (e.g., if an owner sold the foreign distribution rights in and to his work, but retained the domestic rights).

Any transfer of rights must be in writing and signed by the owner of the rights conveyed or by the owner's authorized agent. Transfer of a right on a nonexclusive basis (i.e., others may also be authorized to exploit these same rights) does not require a written agreement (for example, if an owner authorized several different theater companies to concurrently perform a stage play based on the owner's work). It is advisable that any exclusive transfer be recorded with the copyright office. It should also be noted that copyright, like other personal property rights, is subject to the various state laws and regulations that govern the ownership, inheritance, or transfer of personal property, as well as terms of contracts.

How Long Does Copyright Protection Last?

Copyright protection does *not* last indefinitely, regardless of whether the work is registered. Once the copyright expires, the work falls into the public domain, and thus, it will have no copyright protection (i.e., anyone can use the work without permission). The duration of copyright in a given property depends upon when it was created. If the work was created (i.e., first fixed in a tangible medium of expression) on or after January 1, 1978, the copyright endures for a term of the life of the author plus seventy years after his death. If there is more than one author, the term will be the life of the last surviving author plus seventy years. If the work constitutes a work-made-for-hire or if the author is anonymous or pseudonymous, the length of the copyright will be the lesser of the date of creation plus 120 years or the date of publication plus ninety-five years.

If the work was created before January 1, 1978, but not published or registered by that date, it will have been deemed to fall within the 1976 Copyright Act (which took effect in 1978) and will be given federal copyright protection. The duration of copyright in these works will generally be computed in the same way as for works created on or after January 1, 1978 (i.e., the life of the author plus seventy years, or the lesser of the date of creation plus 120 years or the date of publication plus ninety-five years). This is because under the 1909 Copyright Act (the statute in effect immediately prior to the 1976 statute), the copyright term did not commence upon creation, but upon publication or registration. The 1976 Act further provides that in no case will the term of copyright for works in this category expire before December 31, 2002, and for works published on or after December 31, 2002, the term of copyright will not expire before December 31, 2047.

Under the laws in effect before 1978, copyright was secured either on the date a work was published with a copyright notice or on the date of registration, if the work was registered in unpublished form. In either case, the copyright endured for an initial term of twenty-eight years from the date it was secured. During the last (i.e., the twenty-eighth) year of the first term, the copyright was eligible for renewal for an additional twenty-eight years. The Copyright Act of 1976 extended the renewal term from twenty-eight to forty-seven years for copyrights that were subsisting on January 1, 1978, for a total term of protection of seventy years. A law enacted in 1998 further extended the renewal term of copyright still subsisting on that date by an additional twenty years, providing for a renewal term of sixty-seven years and a total term of protection of ninety-five years.

Is Copyright Notice Required?

Copyright notice includes the copyright symbol (©) or the word "copyright," the year of first publication, legal name of the copyright owner, and may include "all rights reserved" (which is optional). For example, "© 2001 Jane Doe. All rights reserved."

A copyright notice is no longer required under U.S. law, although affixing such notice offers certain benefits. The primary benefit of including such notice is that it serves to eliminate the "innocent infringer" defense for purposes of mitigating damages. In other words, an infringer will be hard-pressed to argue that he didn't know that the work was protected if it has a copyright notice written on it. Notice was required under the 1976 Copyright Act if the creator chose to publish the work, but was abolished when the United States adopted the Berne Convention in 1989.

Why Register an Original Work?

Why register an original work if copyright protection is automatic? While registration of original work with the U.S. Copyright Office is not required to effect copyright ownership or obtain copyright protection, except with respect to published works with notice, it is important in that it helps establish proof of creation and enables the copyright holder to defend himself in a plagiarism lawsuit. In addition:

★ Registration is required as a prerequisite to legal action for infringement, unless it is a foreign work registered under the Berne Convention

★ It allows the owner to seek statutory damages and costs if copyright registration was made before infringement or within three months of publication

★ If registration is made within five years of creation, it is *prima facie* evidence of validity of copyright

What Is the Process for Registering a Script with the U.S. Copyright Office?

To register material with the copyright office, the creator must send the following three items to the U.S. Copyright Office:

★ Two copies of the material being registered
★ A completed application
★ The nonrefundable filing fee for each application

The items should be sent to:
The Library of Congress
U.S. Copyright Office
101 Independence Avenue, S.E.
Washington, D.C. 20559-6000

Registration is effective on the date of receipt, although processing of the application can take up to eight months. The registrant will be sent a certificate of registration once processed or a letter explaining why the work was rejected.

What Is the Process for Registering a Script with the WGA?

Registration with the Writers Guild of America (WGA) does not have the same effect as registration with the U.S. Copyright Office, although it can offer additional evidence of the date of creation. The WGA will register scripts, treatments, synopses, outlines for television, radio, and theatrical motion pictures, as well as DVDs, videocassettes, computer disks, interactive media, stage plays, novels, short stories, poems, commercials, lyrics, and drawings. Script registration is handled by the WGA's Intellectual Property Registration Office. The registration fee is currently $10 for guild members and $20 for nonmembers. Along with the fee, the registrant must send one copy of all materials with the title and legal name of the writer(s). A numbered receipt will be sent by the WGA to confirm receipt of the work. WGA registration is valid for five years and may be renewed on or before the expiration date for an additional five years. Any material that is not renewed is destroyed by the WGA. The WGA's Web site, *www.wga.org*, provides additional information on this procedure.

Are There Electronic Methods of Registration?

It is now possible to register works electronically through a service called *firstuse.com*.

Firstuse offers time-stamping and authentification of digital files, including screenplays, novels, short stories, and poems. The site provides details as to the specifics of this process.

How Does One Order a Copyright/ Title Search and Report?

The records of the Copyright Office are open to the public for inspection and search. In addition, the Copyright Office will perform searches for a fee. For more details, the inquiring party should contact the U.S. Library of Congress Copyright Office at (202) 707-3000 or visit the U.S. Copyright Office's official Web site, *www.loc.gov/copyright*, where copyright information, fee information, circulars, regulations, copyright registration forms, and other related materials are available.

What Are the Remedies for Infringement of One's Copyright?

The owner of a copyright may bring suit in the case of any unauthorized use of the copyrighted material, such as unauthorized copying or adaptation of the protected work. In the event an infringement is determined, remedies may include:

- ★ Confiscation and destruction of the infringing works
- ★ Statutory damages and/or a requirement to pay the owner of the copyright actual damages equal to any profits the infringer received (or could have received)
- ★ Attorney's fees if the copyright owner registered the work within three months of its first publication
- ★ A court order requiring the infringer to stop producing or distributing the infringing item
- ★ Anyone who willfully infringes the copyright to reproduce a motion picture for commercial advantage or private financial gain may be subject to criminal penalties

How Does One Protect a Title?

As mentioned earlier, titles are not protected under copyright law in the United States, although they may be protected in other ways. The Motion Picture Association of America (MPAA), a trade group that represents the major studios, has implemented a system to prevent its members from using the same film titles. MPAA members and independent producers may register a title with the MPAA Title Registration Bureau for a fee. The first party to register the name has the right to use it. The protection lasts for a year and is renewable. However, it is important to note that the protection afforded to those who register is limited, as it applies only against other parties to the MPAA Agreement. It offers no protection against a party that is not a signatory.

A television series title may be protected under trademark law. However, trademark registration does not apply to a film title, except in connection with merchandising or a "franchise motion picture" (which is a series of related motion pictures such as the James Bond films). A title of a series of books may also be protected under trademark law. A film title (or television show title, book title, or play title) may be protected under the law of unfair competition if the title has become so closely associated with a certain film that it has acquired a "secondary meaning" under the laws of unfair competition, such as *Casablanca* (i.e., even though Casablanca is a city, a publishing company may conclude that it would be illegal to publish a book with that title). It is important to note that a title may infringe the rights of the owner of another title of a motion picture, television series, book, play, or other trademark. For example, it may not be permissible to title a film *My Crappy Mercedes*.

What Are Submission Release Forms?

In order to avert claims of copyright infringement, producers, studio executives, agents, and managers will usually require that individuals wishing to submit a script or other literary work for consideration sign a materials release form, or *submission release form,* before the work is evaluated. Such forms are standard and are used to avoid situations in which an individual submitting a script, which is rejected by the agent, producer, studio, etc., later claims that such party copied (or plagiarized) his script. There are only so many stories out there, and the odds that two or more individuals came up with a similar idea are not slim. Such releases usually include language stating that the individual submitting the work understands that the party reading the work has access to materials and ideas that may be similar or even identical to the individual's story and that there is no confidential relationship between the individual and the party reading the script or other literary work. The form also typically stipulates that the individual has retained at least one copy of the work, so that he cannot sue in the event that the submitted copy is lost.

A sample materials release form can be found in appendix A.

THE DIGITAL MILLENNIUM COPYRIGHT ACT

What is the DMCA's Purpose?

The Digital Millennium Copyright Act (DMCA) was enacted by Congress in 1998 to (i) empower copyright owners to prevent online infringement of their copyrights, and (ii) protect online service providers (such as AOL and Earthlink) from being unfairly subject to liability for copyright infringement committed by its users.

To that end, the DMCA provides a takedown notice provision whereby copyright holders can protect their copyrights, as well as a "safe harbor" provision for service providers to shield themselves from liability (each is further discussed below). The act also implements various anti-piracy measures that prevent unauthorized access to and copying of copyrighted works.

Who Does the DMCA Target?

The DMCA targets two categories of wrongdoers:

1. Circumventors of technological anti-piracy measures (e.g., so-called hackers).

2. Traffickers (such as manufacturers, sellers, or distributors) of technologies, devices, or products used to circumvent technological anti-piracy measures built into commercial software (e.g., Napster, Kazaa, DVD-Ripper, CD-Key Generator).

What Prohibitions Does the DMCA Establish?

Circumventors are prohibited from acts that circumvent anti-piracy measures designed to prevent access to copyrighted materials. However, circumventors are not prohibited from acts that circumvent anti-piracy measures designed to prevent copying of copyrighted materials. Because the copying of works may be a "fair use" under certain circumstances, this distinction is included to ensure that the public will have the continued ability to make fair use of copyrighted works without fear of liability under the DMCA.

Traffickers are prohibited from manufacturing, selling, or distributing products that are used to circumvent anti-piracy measures that prevent either *access* or *copying* (e.g., Napster, Bit Torrent).

Exceptions to the DMCA's Provisions

There are a number of exceptions to the DMCA's prohibitions, many of which apply to acts taken by libraries, educational institutions, and law enforcement.

What Type of Penalties are Imposed for Violating the DMCA?

Penalties for violating the DMCA may include (1) civil remedies (such as injunctive relief, seizing of devices, damages, costs, and attorneys' fees), and (2) criminal penalties for those who act willfully and for purposes of commercial advantage or private financial gain (up to a $500,000 fine or up to five years in prison, or both, for a first offense, and up to a $1,000,000 line or up to ten years in prison, or both, for any subsequent offense).

How Does the Safe-Harbor Provision Work?

As previously mentioned, the DMCA provides immunity for online interactive service providers in cases where content on the provider's Web site infringes another's copyright, so long as the service provider doesn't exercise direct control over the content in question that it could be said that the provider, in some sense, transmitted the content itself. In order to qualify for DMCA immunity, the provider must:

★ Not be aware, actually or constructively, of the existence of infringing content

* Receive no financial gain directly attributable to the infringing content
* Respond promptly to notices from copyright holders that infringing content appears on its Web site.

If the service provider appears to have had some involvement in the creation or transmission of the posting (e.g., by editing, but not removing, infringing content), the provider is not entitled to DMCA protection. Similarly, if the provider is aware (or reasonably ought to be aware) of the existence of infringing content and does nothing, the provider is not entitled to protection. The DMCA requires that a service provider remove any infringing content upon learning of its existence, whether through a DMCA takedown notice or of its own initiative by, for example, regular monitoring of site content, a service provider must also ban repeat infringers from its service.

In addition to removing the content and the abuse conditions, a service provider must (1) adopt a policy that provides for the termination of service access for repeat copyright infringers in appropriate circumstances; (2) implement that policy in a reasonable manner; and (3) inform its subscribers of the policy. One facet of such a policy is that the service provider must have a designated agent for service of takedown notices.

Current case law establishes that search engines such as Google, whose services may provide access to infringing content, are entitled to DMCA immunity, provided they comply with the provisions of the DMCA. Of course, Web sites that "invite" infringement, such as peer-to-peer file-sharing networks such as Napster and Bit Torrent, do not benefit from DMCA immunity.

What is the Procedure for Issuing Takedown Notices?

If aware of infringement, a copyright owner may send a takedown notice to a service provider that substantially complies with the DMCA's takedown notice requirements. A valid takedown notice must:
* Be signed under penalty of perjury
* Attest to the accuracy of the information in the notice, including that the person issuing the notice is authorized by the copyright holder
* Attest to the good faith of the claim
* Adequately identify the allegedly infringing material

Once such a notice has been sent, the service provider becomes obligated to remove the infringing content (if it is in fact infringing content). Service providers are required to take appropriate action when they obtain knowledge of infringing content, or when they reasonably should have knowledge of infringing content. One way they may obtain this knowledge is through receipt of a valid copyright takedown notice, signed under penalty of perjury by someone authorized to represent the copyright holder. Another is through the existence of "red flags," or apparent infringing activity; for example, a takedown notice failing. It is essential to substantially comply with the requirements of the DMCA in order to shift the burden to the service provider to locate and remove the infringing content.

Monitoring and Control of Content

A service provider is not required to police its users, e.g., to determine if a user is a repeat infringer, nor is it obligated to determine whether content on its Web site enables copyright infringement. It follows, therefore, that a service provider that does not regularly monitor content on its site will not be assumed to know of infringements (except where such infringement is so blatant that the provider should reasonably know about it).

There is some question, however, as to when a service provider's implementation of a monitoring policy might result in a waiver of DMCA protection. A provider who regularly monitors its Web site would certainly have greater access to "red flags" that could indicate infringement, however, there does not appear to be case law addressing the extent to which voluntary-monitoring may increase the purview of a provider's constructive knowledge of the existence of infringing content.

In any event, service providers should take care in crafting monitoring policies, and should ensure that such policies are rigorously followed.

Another act to be aware of is the Communications Decency Act (CDA) enacted by Congress in 1996. While it was intended to regulate the use of pornographic material on the internet, the CDA's section 230, which deals with *Internet service provider* (ISP) liability, has garnered much of the attention. In essence, section 230 provides ISPs with immunity from certain claims against them. The CDA directs that "[n]o provider or user of an interactive computer service shall be treated as the publisher or speaker of any information provided by another information content provider." Courts have broadly applied the CDA, granting the protection to listserv moderators (e.g., moderators of discussion forums), providers who had notice that they were hosting infringing content and even providers who had an active role in producing the content that was the basis for the lawsuit. The CDA, along with the DMCA, provides ISPs a substantial shield with which to defend themselves in court. For a copy of the CDA, check out *www.fcc.gov/Reports/tcom1996.txt*.

REALITY TELEVISION

*U*nscripted television is hardly a new concept—in fact, it's been around for a long time in some form or another, from the old *Candid Camera* series (in the late 1940s) to *The Newlywed Game* and *The Dating Game* (in the late 1970s) to MTV's *The Real World* (starting in the '90s and still going strong today). However, as discussed in chapter 1, the popularity and prevalence of reality television has really exploded since the early 2000s, and such shows as *American Idol* and *Survivor* have not only taken up primetime slots, but they've led the TV ratings in recent years, with millions of viewers each night.

Why the increasing appeal? Many reasons have been suggested as to why these shows have become such a huge part of our popular culture. Whether it is because they satisfy our innate desire to see others humiliated, that they offer hope to the millions of people looking for fame, or that they are cheaper to create and are therefore a product of the changing economics of television (or, more likely, a combination of all these reasons), reality television seems to be here to stay—at least for a while.

WHAT IS REALITY TV?

Reality television can mean different things to different people. A wide variety of programming is considered to fall under the umbrella of "reality TV" these days, including:

1. Documentary-style shows such as *Big Brother* or *The Real World,* where the viewer watches the participants going about their daily activities. In some shows, such as *The Simple Life* or *The Osbournes,* the "participant" is a celebrity rather than an unknown individual. Within this category are also the "docu-soaps," such as *The Real Housewives of Orange County* and *Jon & Kate Plus 8.*
2. Talent contests and variety shows such as *Dancing With The Stars* and *American Idol,* where celebrities (and those seeking to become celebrities) showcase their skills and compete for the top spot and prizes (e.g., a record deal or cash).
3. Modern game shows like *Deal or No Deal* and *Who Wants to Be A Millionaire.*
4. Competition or elimination shows like *The Apprentice, The Biggest Loser,* and *The Bachelor,* where contestants compete for such things as a high-level career, money, prizes, or even a marriage proposal.
5. Home renovation shows like *Extreme Makeover: Home Edition,* where the viewer watches needy families receive entire home makeovers, and *Designed To Sell,* where homeowners get help fixing up their houses before selling them.
6. Hidden-camera shows such as *Punk'd* and *The Jamie Kennedy Experiment.*
7. Entertainment news or "magazine" shows like *Entertainment Tonight* and *The Insider.*

Within these categories, of course, are numerous subcategories, and several shows could certainly fall into more than one category.

Agreements for Reality TV

The fact that reality shows are referred to as "unscripted" and professional actors are not being utilized (except as hosts in some cases, or as celebrity contestants such as on *Celebrity Apprentice*) does not mean that there will be fewer agreements to negotiate. In fact, this type of programming raises new legal concerns and often involves numerous contracts. Of course, what agreements will be needed will vary depending on what type of show is proposed.

Performer Agreements for Reality TV

Generally, on-camera performer agreements for reality shows fall under the following categories:

1. **Host Agreements** (e.g., Ty Pennington on *Extreme Makeover: Home Edition* or Howie Mandel on *Deal or No Deal*). These agreements are usually similar to an actor's television pilot or series deal, as the producer will routinely have multiple consecutive options to employ the host in subsequent seasons (as well as a special, should the show—and the actor—be a success. Fees and perquisites for these services vary widely, but they are typically much lower than for network scripted series television. The amounts paid are dependent on the usual factors such as budget, network vs. cable or other media (such as Internet productions or mobisodes), guild applicability, length of show, and who the host in question is (i.e., is he or she a celebrity, and at what level, or is he or she known) amongst other factors. One of the key issues of negotiation for these types of deals is "exclusivity" of the performer. A savvy representative will try to limit the parameters of the actor's exclusivity to reality television and maintain the right to render services in a scripted series (as well as commercials and all non-television series productions such as films and MOWs). In terms of credit, high-profile hosts or those who helped develop the concept (or for whom the show was developed) may be able to secure a producer credit of some form in addition to their customary "host" credit. Other important provisions are promotional services and the use of "behind the scenes" and "making of" footage. These host agreements are often not subject to any guild, or if they are guild, they often fall under AFTRA's jurisdiction. Of course, like all series deals, if the show proves to be a success in its first or second season, these deals will likely be renegotiated by the talent's representatives, and the studio and network will likely comply even though they aren't legally obligated because everyone wants a happy host (or judge, as the case may be).

2. **Judge Agreements** (e.g., Paula Abdul and Simon Cowell on *American Idol*). These agreements are structured in a similar manner to the host agreements discussed above.

3. **Contestant/Participant Agreements** (e.g., Jason Mesnick on *The Bachelor* or Denise Richards on *Dancing With the Stars*).

Contestants are asked to sign detailed participant agreements setting forth the rules of the show, stipulating numerous representations and warranties that the contestants must make about their physical and mental wellbeing and specifying strict confidentiality provisions. Contestants must also sign comprehensive waivers, releases of liability, and assumption of risk agreements (which are particularly important for the producers of shows like *The Amazing Race* and *Fear Factor*, where personal injury is a real possibility). These releases typically contain broad waivers of any and all potential claims, including claims for defamation, invasion of privacy and disclosure of embarrassing personal facts, and right of publicity, as well as, where appropriate, claims regarding bodily injury or emotional harm. These agreements will often grant the producer an option to engage the participant for a reunion episode or other type of special. Perquisites (dressing room, travel, and expenses) are usually nominal, although "celebrity" contestants can usually secure some added benefits. A sample participant agreement is included at the back of the book, although such forms vary based on the specific nature of the show in question. Family members and/or friends of participants who appear on the show are required to sign waivers and releases, including a depiction release (discussed further below).

4. **Other Talent Services Agreements**. These include agreements and releases, and are for those appearing on camera as "experts" or guest panelists on reality shows.

5. **Depiction Releases**. These releases are for those who appear on hidden-camera "surveillance television" shows like ABC's *What Would You Do?* These releases authorize the producer to use the footage taken of the then-unsuspecting participant on television and waive all claims against the producer for such use. In some cases the individuals are paid, in others they are not. Problems, of course, occur when the participant refuses to sign off on the producer's use of him or her in the show and is not presented with a release until after the footage is shot (since having a release signed prior to filming is usually not possible given the "surprise" element of these shows). A sample depiction release is included at the back of the book.

In some cases, non-participants such as audience members may be asked to sign releases if they appear identifiably on camera, although signs posted prominently indicating that filming is taken place are often considered sufficient notice.

Show Creator Agreements for Reality TV/Rights Deals

Show creator agreements are structured very much like scripted show creator deals and address essentially the same key deal terms: development services, development fees, pilot and series services and fees, contingent compensation, ownership, and credit. However, compensation and perks will generally be less favorable as the budgets for reality shows are typically lower than those for scripted shows. Moreover, most of these shows are not produced under the jurisdiction of the major Hollywood guilds (although some of them hire directors under the DGA Agreement). Accordingly, the types of credits accorded on such programs may differ (e.g., a "created by" credit may be replaced by a "based on the concept by" credit). Other factors relevant to the dealmaking process for reality television include the creator's precedent (most important would be precedent for reality shows, if they have any), the nature of the show (e.g., is it a game-show format, competition-type show, surveillance-type show), whether the show is intended for network or non-network exploitation, whether it is intended for primetime or non-primetime, and the length of show. In some cases, rather than a pilot episode, the network or studio will decide to produce a one- to two-hour "special" to test out the concept and determine whether it gets any traction before proceeding to a series, in which event the network and studio will retain an option (on talent, rights, and director) to proceed to series. In addition, the extent of services to be provided by the creator of the show will be an important factor (e.g., whether the creator will act as the "show runner" or merely render non-exclusive, non-material services).

Ownership of the "format" rights to the show is a key issue of negotiation as well. Several show formats, such as *Who Wants to Be a Millionaire* and *Survivor,* have been successfully sold across the world. Typically, when pitching a show to a studio or network, the studio (or network) would insist on complete ownership of the show, including the format rights. Established reality creators (such as Mark Burnett, the creator of *Survivor*) often have their own production companies and produce the shows themselves. Such creators may then license the shows or the formats to networks worldwide but could retain ownership rights. In addition to show creator deals, there may be certain rights that may need to be obtained for a show. For example, if the show is about showgirls at a certain Las Vegas casino, and the casino's name is being used, an agreement with the owner of the casino would need to be made in order to use the casino's name, logos, etc., in addition to a location agreement.

Writer Agreements for Reality TV

Although, as previously discussed, reality television is considered to be "non-scripted," writers are often engaged to create dialogue, scenarios, sketches, plot outlines, synopses, routines, and other narratives for these shows. The form of such agreements will vary depending on the type of services required, whether the contract is subject to guild jurisdiction (discussed below), and other customary factors such as the writer's quote and the budget of the program.

Guild Applicability

In the past, most reality shows were produced "non-guild." However, in recent years, the guilds have been pushing to get these shows under the jurisdiction and have been working with the studios and networks to do so (although many reality shows are still produced outside any guild's jurisdiction). For example, some shows currently or previously covered under the WGA Agreement include *Intervention, The Weakest Link, Jeopardy,* and *The Dog Whisperer.* The guild is often willing to negotiate more favorable terms for the producers of these shows if the budget or production constraints make the current WGA minimum terms unworkable. The DGA also covers reality TV and will negotiate more favorable terms for basic cable reality shows that fall under their purview. In terms of the actors unions, several reality shows are produced under AFTRA's jurisdiction.

DIGITAL CONTENT DEALS

*A*greements relating to the creation of digital content do not fit into established frameworks in the way that television and motion-picture dealmaking (which, while evolved, have been around for nearly one hundred years) fall within a consistent structure. Digital deals are still relatively new and, unlike the motion picture business (in which even today, there are fewer than a dozen major studios), there have been thousands of financiers of digital content, since the start-up costs associated with launching a Web site pale in comparison to forming a television production company or motion-picture studio. For this reason, there is a lack of uniformity in this area.

Accordingly, there are many variations of the digital deal and a plethora of ways to negotiate (and document) these types of transactions. Set forth below are some of the key issues relating to the negotiation of a deal between the owner of a Web site (hereinafter referred to as the "Web site") and a content creator, such as a writer.

RIGHTS GRANTED: COPYRIGHT IS KEY

Unlike television and motion-picture deals, in which there is a very small likelihood that a screenwriter will be able to retain copyright ownership of the program to be produced, new-media agreements vary widely on this issue. A Web site might allow content creators to retain ownership of their work in return for the Web site's right to host such content.

Alternatively, a Web site may agree to pay a license fee to a content creator in exchange for the right to broadcast a particular work (such as a short film) on said Web site for a fixed period of time. In this type of arrangement, the content creator will receive a fee and will typically retain ownership of the work.

In other contractual arrangements, a content creator will grant full ownership of her work to the Web site and will render all services as a work made for hire, in a manner not dissimilar to the traditional television and motion-picture writing agreements.

METHOD OF TRANSMISSION

An important element of the negotiation related to the grant of rights is the manner in which the final product will be delivered to consumers. For example, the agreement might specify that the work can be broadcast only on the Internet Service Provider's ("ISP's") primary Web site (e.g., *www.hulu.com*), and cannot be sold separately as a download or on any type of digital media device. In other cases, there may not be any limitation whatsoever on the method of transmission of the work, including methods "not yet known or devised."

TYPE OF SERVICE

Similarly, the type of service on which the work is exhibited may be a Web site or might be something completely different, such as VOD on a cable television or satellite service. If the product is offered via VOD, the consumer will locate the work by perusing a menu on the cable or satellite service and, after selecting the program, will be asked to press a button on the remote control confirming a decision to purchase the program for viewing. Alternatively, the work may be sold to the public via iTunes, which would be viewable on a computer monitor as well as on a traditional television screen via such products as Apple TV. Particularly with respect to Web site exhibition, the agreement must specify whether the program can be made available for permanent download ("DTO," or download to own), or only as a streaming video.

AUTHORIZED DEVICES

Another part of the analysis when structuring these types of deals is an examination of which devices other than computers accessing the Internet (e.g., cell phones and/or other handheld portable devices), if any, will be granted a license to display the program. "Mobisodes" refer to short programs that are intended for initial exhibition on a cellular telephone. "Webisodes" refer to short programs (often part of a series) that are intended to be exhibited initially on the Internet. The savvy negotiator might want to limit the devices that are authorized to exhibit the work. The program might be made exclusively available for viewing on a PSP (Play Station Portable) or on the Amazon Kindle. For example, there are certain games and applications that are available exclusively for iPhone.

FEES/ALLOCATION OF COSTS

The compensation that a content creator will secure in a new media deal varies widely. In fact, there are often no minimums and no maximums. A writer might work for free or be paid hundreds of thousands of dollars. Unlike most "Hollywood" deals, many of the guild agreements do not yet govern these transactions, in which event they cannot dictate minimum compensation levels. The WGA Agreement that was ratified in 2008 covers certain types of made-for-Internet programming, and most of the remaining major guilds are currently seeking jurisdiction over these types of deals. Irrespective of whether set minimums need to be adhered to, there is often insufficient history or tradition to rely on when negotiating such deals.

The main types of fee arrangements for new media deals with writers are (i) work-made-for-hire fee structures, (ii) license-fee payments, (iii) barter arrangements, or (iv) some combination or hybrid of the foregoing.

In the work-made-for-hire arrangement, the Web site would engage the content creator to create a particular program, which would be owned by the Web site. The writer might be paid a one-time fee at the outset, although the parties might negotiate for bonuses (based on Web site "hits," for example) or other additional payments. Moreover, a deal can be structured to resemble a first look or overall television deal, in which any work created by the writer for the designated term of the agreement would be owned by the Web site. In such cases, the writer might be given office space at the host company and/or receive monthly payments (in addition to bonuses once programs are created).

If the deal is structured as a license, the Web site will obtain a license from the creator (rather than ownership of the copyright) allowing it to broadcast or otherwise exploit the work (including the possibility of sub-licensing the work, as more fully described below) for a set period of time, all of which would be subject to negotiation. At times, the Web site will negotiate for options to extend the length of the license term (in which event the extension would typically be accompanied by a license fee). Even after negotiating a fee (whether a one-time lump sum payment or an episodic-type fee), the parties need to reach some agreement as to allocation of costs relating to the operation of the Web site or applicable service platform. In some cases, the creator of the work may participate in certain ad revenues generated on the Web site or may even be willing to allow free access to the work.

BARTER DEALS

One advantage to the "Wild West" mentality of digital dealmaking (in which policy and precedent do not impose the same obstacles to creative dealmaking that sometimes exist in the motion picture and television arena) is that content creators are sometimes able to participate in the advertising revenue generated on Internet Web sites. The opportunity for the writer to share in such revenues (and lack of reluctance by the Web site to enter into this type of arrangement) has made the barter deal one of the key revenue models for new media deals. In this type of arrangement, in lieu of or in addition to receiving an up-front cash fee as consideration for the license, the content creator will forgo the fee (or take a reduced fee) in exchange for a percentage of the advertising revenue realized on such site. The percentage granted to a Webisode creator, for example, and whether an advance payment (recoupable out of future ad revenues) will be payable is a matter of negotiation between the parties. In success, a barter deal such as the one described herein can be quite lucrative for the writer/creator.

RESERVED RIGHTS

The reservation of rights (if any) in these types of deals ties in closely to the negotiation of the bundle of rights that is granted. A Webisode creator might grant to the Web site owner all rights to produce and distribute the series on the Internet, but may retain the right to create any form of derivative production (such as a remake or sequel) based thereon. Other categories of rights that might be reserved by the content creator include print publication, motion picture rights, television rights, stage rights, theme park rights, and/or interactive game rights.

SUBLICENSING

Due to the ease of duplicating digital files, the issue of sublicensing (i.e., the right to allow third parties to broadcast and possibly to alter the program) takes on added importance. It is important for content creators to be very specific when entering into this type of agreement about what venues might be permitted to exhibit or even to provide links to the actual program. Web site operators, as well as cable and satellite providers, will usually desire maximum flexibility with respect to this issue, particularly if the ISP owns multiple Web sites. The content creator may agree that the program should be disseminated as widely as possible or, alternatively, may choose to limit the number and types of Web sites at which the program will be available to consumers.

SECURITY MEASURES

The savvy writer of content for new media should be concerned about the level of Internet security maintained by the Web site. The Web site should have sufficient piracy prevention and anti-copying software in place so that the content creator can feel reasonably assured that his work will not be copied illegally and disseminated widely (without compensation to him or to the Web site). Accordingly, the writer might insist on a provision in the agreement obligating the Web site to maintain reasonable controls in accordance with industry standards.

TERM

Another crucial element in digital deal negotiations is the term or length of the license. As discussed above, if the content creator is granting all rights to the ISP in perpetuity, as a work made for hire, the transfer of ownership is complete and there is no need to limit the term of the arrangement. However, if the deal is structured as a license in which the ISP is granted limited rights to stream the program (similar to the manner in which television networks often acquire the rights to broadcast each television episode over a limited time period), the term of the license needs to be set forth in the agreement. As digital dealmaking is still in its infancy, there is no prescribed time period that works as an across-the-board policy. Terms can vary from six months (as a form of test-run) to three or even five years.

REPORTING FREQUENCY

Because of the fast-paced nature of new media, particularly the Internet, traditional motion-picture accounting principles may not easily translate to deals of this type. Most studios account to motion-picture participants on a quarterly basis until eighteen to twenty-four months after initial release of the film, at which point accountings are rendered annually or semi-annually. A mobisode or Webisode creator might negotiate to receive accountings (particularly in instances where she is entitled to a percentage of advertising revenue) as often as monthly when entering into a negotiation with an ISP.

WARRANTIES AND INDEMNITIES

Perhaps not surprisingly, the warranties and indemnity provisions that are found in these types of agreements are similar to those discussed in connection with other rights and writing agreements. From the ISP's perspective, the creator will need to warrant that the material is original (or otherwise available for use) and does not infringe on the rights of any third parties. Conversely, the creator will look for protection from the licensor in connection with litigation or other costs that might arise from claims or lawsuits that are not related to the misconduct or breach of the content creator.

SUBSEQUENT PRODUCTIONS

Many of the issues relating to the production of subsequent programs (such as remakes and sequels) resemble those that are extant in the television/film arena, but there are some important differences as well. The differences relate to the fact that so many of these digital deals have a limited scope in terms of the rights that are granted, unlike the traditional television, motion-picture rights, or writing deal, in which the studio will acquire almost all of the "universe" or rights. Because it is not uncommon for the creator of a Web program to retain remake/sequel rights, the issues that arise when discussing these terms relate primarily to the timing of such subsequent productions. For example, if the ISP agrees to allow these rights to vest with the content creator, the ISP will usually insist on a holdback, so that production of any sequel or remake might not be permitted for a minimum of two years after expiration of the license term (so that, for example, a remake of the new media production would not be made available until after the last episode of the original program was broadcast on the Web site). In addition, the Web site operator may request a right of first negotiation or the right to cofinance any subsequent productions.

If the Web site owner acquires remake/sequel rights to the digital program at the outset, the writer/creator of such program may attempt to secure the first opportunity to be engaged as the writer of such subsequent production, or to negotiate certain passive payments or royalties in the event such programs are subsequently created. It is important to remember that the vast majority of these types of programs are not covered by the Writers Guild agreement and, consequently, if the creator of such program does not negotiate for a minimum royalty, he or she will not receive any payment by virtue of the collective bargaining agreement.

CONSULTATION AND APPROVAL RIGHTS

Content creators of new-media productions will generally insist on a high level of approval rights, primarily because it is relatively inexpensive to produce content for the Internet, and the Web site (unlike a motion picture studio) may not be adamant about retaining the "final cut" when the dollars spent on any particular Web program may not be terribly significant. In fact, some of the deals that are structured give the creator near carte blanche to deliver a program to the Web site. In such cases, the Web site may negotiate for consultation and/or approval rights with respect to particular elements. At a minimum, the Web site will seek to retain the right to alter the program to conform with running time and/or censorship requirements.

GUILD APPLICABILITY

Several years ago, ABC television issued a press release announcing that several of the writers of the hit series *Lost* would write and produce a series of two-to-three-minute shorts related to the *Lost* series, which would be titled *Lost: The Missing Pieces* and be available for viewing on ABC's Web site as well as on cellular telephones. These shorts were produced under the jurisdiction of a side-agreement with the WGA that reportedly took five months to negotiate. It should be noted that this agreement covered this particular program only and was signed by ABC rather than the entire motion picture and television alliance. The *New York Times* reported in 2007 that the writers of these shorts were paid an upfront fee (reported to be approximately $800 per episode) as well as residuals arising out of exploitation of the shorts on the Internet. In 2008, after a one-hundred-day writers' strike, the motion picture and television association concluded a three-year agreement with the WGA that covers, on a going-forward basis, certain types of new-media writing deals. While readers of this book should refer to the current WGA Agreement for further details, the parties essentially agreed that if a writer is engaged by a guild signatory company to render writing services for new media (e.g., the Internet), the writing services will be covered by the WGA if one of the following conditions is met: (a) the program is based on a preexisting program that is already covered by the WGA; (b) the writer qualifies as a "professional writer" as defined in the WGA Agreement (i.e., has been accorded some writing credit, is a published novelist, or has been engaged to write for film, television, or radio for a minimum period); or (c) the budget for such new-media program exceeds certain minimum amounts set forth in the WGA Agreement. If a program meets one of these conditions and the writer is engaged by a motion picture studio (or other entity that is a signatory to the WGA Agreement), the writer of such a program will be entitled to a minimum fee and the guild's pension health and welfare provisions will apply to such productions. In addition, the WGA will be the final arbiter of credits with respect to such programs. Finally, if a covered new-media program is reused in traditional media, certain residual obligations will be imposed on the employer.

Deal Point Summary:
DIGITAL CONTENT AGREEMENT

1. Rights to Be Granted
    - License
    - Ownership
2. Method of Transmission
3. Type of Service
    - VOD
    - Streaming
    - Other?
4. Authorized Devices
5. Fees/Allocation of Costs
6. Rights Reserved
7. Sublicensing
8. Term
9. Cash Only or Barter?
    - Minimum Guarantee?
10. Reporting Frequency
11. Warranties and Indemnities
12. Subsequent Productions
    - First Opportunity to Write
    - Passive Payments/Royalties
13. Consultation and Approval Rights
14. Guild Applicability

SAMPLE
CONTRACTS/FORMS

CERTIFICATE OF AUTHORSHIP/CERTIFICATE OF EMPLOYMENT

Reference is hereby made to that certain motion picture ("Picture") presently entitled "_____" for which _____ ("Employee") is to perform services as director and producer pursuant to an agreement ("Agreement") dated as of July 19, 2001, between [Name of Loan-Out Company] ("Lender") and Century Studios ("Company").

Lender and Employee, for good and valuable consideration (receipt of which is hereby acknowledged), hereby certify and agree that (i) all of the results and proceeds of the services of any kind heretofore rendered by and hereafter to be rendered by Employee in connection with the Picture and (ii) all ideas, suggestions, plots, themes, stories, characterizations, and other material, whether in writing or not in writing, at any time heretofore or hereafter created or contributed by Employee which in any way relate to the Picture or to the material on which the Picture will be based are and shall be deemed works "made for hire" for Company. Lender and Employee further acknowledge, certify, and agree that as between Employee and Lender, on the one hand, and Company, on the other, Company is and shall be deemed the author and exclusive owner of all of the foregoing for all purposes and the exclusive owner throughout the world of all of the rights comprised in the copyright thereof, and of any and all other rights thereto, and that Company shall have the right to exploit any or all of the foregoing in any and all media, now known or hereafter devised, throughout the universe, in perpetuity, in all languages as Company determines. Lender and Employee will, upon request, execute, acknowledge, and deliver to Company such additional documents as Company may reasonably deem necessary to evidence and effectuate Company's rights hereunder, and hereby grant to Company the right as attorney-in-fact to execute, acknowledge, deliver, and record any and all documents which Employee and/or Lender fail to execute within five (5) days after so requested by Company.

Lender and Employee warrant that except as contained in material furnished Employee and/or Lender by Company, all literary, dramatic, musical, and other material and all ideas and designs ("Material") of Employee used in connection with the Picture are wholly original with Employee or in the public domain; shall not infringe upon or violate any copyright of, or, to Employee and Lender's best knowledge (including that which Employee and Lender should have known in the exercise of reasonable prudence), infringe upon or violate the right of privacy or any other right of any person or entity, and are not the subject of any litigation or claim that might give rise to litigation; and that Lender and Employee are free to grant all rights granted and make all agreements made by Lender and Employee herein. Lender and Employee agree to hold Company and its successors, licensees, and assigns harmless from and against all damages, losses, costs, and expenses (including attorneys' fees) which Company or any of its successors, licensees, or assigns may suffer or incur by reason of any breach of any of the warranties made by Lender and/or Employee herein or in the Agreement. Company hereby agrees to hold Lender and Employee harmless from and against all damages, losses, costs, and expenses which Employee may suffer or incur by reason of any breach of any warranty made by Company in the Agreement and any other claim arising from Company's development, production, distribution, or exploitation of the Picture in respect of which Lender and Employee have no obligation to indemnify Company hereunder or under the Agreement.

In the event of any breach by Company of the Agreement, the sole remedy of Lender and Employee shall be an action for money damages, and Lender and Employee shall not have any right to enjoin, restrict, or otherwise interfere with Company's rights in the Material.

Executed as of July 19, 2001

_____   _____
By: By:

NUDITY RIDER

Reference is made to the Agreement, dated as of July 19, 2001, (the "Agreement") between Century Studios ("Company") and [Actor's Loan-Out Company] ("Lender") for the acting services of _____ ("Artist") in connection with the theatrical motion picture currently entitled _____ ("Picture").

Artist understands that the role of "_____" shall require Artist to appear wearing lacy lingerie (which may reveal portions of her breasts and buttocks) while dancing in a sexual manner as set forth in scene 18 (pages for which are attached hereto), and shall require Artist to appear topless (with her breasts revealed) in scene 51 (pages are attached hereto) of the screenplay ("Screenplay") draft dated _____. Company acknowledges that in no event shall genital nudity be required of Artist. Artist hereby agrees to perform all of such scenes as set forth in the Screenplay and acknowledges that Artist's refusal to perform said scenes as set forth in the Screenplay shall constitute a material breach of the Agreement.

In the event that the Screenplay is rewritten or otherwise altered and Company wishes to make material changes in such scenes, or Company wishes to include additional nude and/or sex scenes, Company shall consult in good faith with Artist as to such changes, and Artist shall have the right to refuse to perform such additional scenes and to deny Company the option to use a nude body double to portray Artist in such scenes. If Artist has agreed in writing to appear in any such scene and subsequently withdraws her consent, Company shall have the right to utilize a nude double for said scene, provided, however that the extent of such double's nudity shall not exceed that agreed to in writing by Artist. Provided Artist is available as reasonably requested by Company and subject to the exigencies of the production, Artist shall have the right to designate Artist's body double, provided that in the event of a disagreement, Company's decision shall be final and controlling.

All such scenes and any other nude and/or sex scenes shall be shot on a set closed to all persons not having an essential purpose in connection with the filming of such scenes.

Company shall not authorize any still photographs or likenesses of Artist in the nude to be taken or reproduced in any manner whatsoever from any frame, footage, or outtake of the Picture or otherwise used for any purpose whatsoever, including, but not limited to, in connection with advertising, publicity, trailers, or otherwise without Artist's prior written approval, provided that the foregoing shall in no way limit the Company's right to use such footage as part of the final edited version of the Picture.

Pursuant to the terms and conditions of the Agreement, Company shall own all results and proceeds of Artist's services rendered pursuant to the Agreement and shall have the exclusive right to use, license, and exploit the Picture and Artist's performance therein, throughout the world in perpetuity in any and all media, whether now known or hereafter devised.

All the terms of the Agreement shall remain in full force and effect without modification or change.

AGREED AND ACCEPTED:

PUBLISHER'S RELEASE

In exchange for good and valuable consideration, the receipt and sufficiency of which is hereby acknowledged, the undersigned hereby acknowledges and agrees, for the express benefit of Century Studios, Inc. and its representatives, successors, and assigns forever, that the undersigned has no claim to or interest in the worldwide motion picture or television rights or customary ancillary or subsidiary rights or any other rights of any kind other than print publication rights heretofore granted to the undersigned, in or to that certain literary work published by the undersigned and described as follows:

TITLE: _____

AUTHOR: _____

DATE/PLACE OF PUBLICATION: _____

COPYRIGHT REGISTRATION: #_____

The undersigned hereby consents to the publication and copyright by and/or in the name of said author, author's heirs, representatives, licensees, and assigns, in any and all languages, in any and all countries of the world, in any form or media, of synopses, excerpts, and summaries, not exceeding 7,500 words in length each, of said literary work, based principally upon said literary work, for the purpose of advertising, publicizing, and/or exploiting any such motion picture, television, or other version. There shall be no limitation in length, however, with respect to any motion picture, television, or other version not based principally upon said work, including, but not limited to, sequel motion pictures and television series.

SIGNED: [BOOK PUBLISHER]

MATERIALS RELEASE/SUBMISSION RELEASE

DATE:

Gentlemen/Ladies:

1. I am submitting to you herewith the following material (hereinafter referred to as "said material"):

TITLE:

FORM OF MATERIAL (e.g., story, screenplay, treatment, novel, play):

PRINCIPAL CHARACTERS AND BRIEF SUMMARY OF THEME/PLOT:

WGA REGISTRATION NUMBER:

NUMBER OF PAGES:

2. I request that you read and evaluate said material, and you hereby agree to do so, and if I subsequently make a written request, you agree to advise me of your decision with respect to the material.

3. I warrant that I am the sole owner and author of said material, that I have the exclusive right and authority to submit the same to you upon the terms and conditions stated herein, and that all of the important features of said material are summarized herein. I will indemnify you of and from any and all claims, loss, or liability (including reasonable attorney's fees) that may be asserted against you or incurred by you, at any time, in connection with said material or any use thereof.

4. I recognize that you have access to literary materials and ideas which may be similar or identical to said material in theme, idea, plot, format, or other respects. I understand that no confidential relationship is established by my submitting the material to you hereunder.

5. I understand that you have adopted the policy, with respect to the unsolicited submission of material, of refusing to accept, consider, or evaluate unsolicited material unless the person submitting such

material has signed an agreement in a form substantially the same as this agreement. I specifically acknowledge that you would refuse to accept, consider, or otherwise evaluate my material in the absence of my acceptance of each and all of the provisions herein. I shall retain all rights to submit this or similar material to persons other than you.

6. I have retained at least one copy of said material, and I hereby release you of and from any and all liability for loss of, or damage to, the copies of said material submitted to you hereunder.

7. I enter into this agreement with the express understanding that you agree to read and evaluate said material in express reliance upon this agreement and my covenants, representations, and warranties contained herein, and that in the absence of such an agreement, you would not read or evaluate said material.

8. I hereby state that I have read and understand this agreement and that no oral representations of any kind have been made to me, and that this agreement states our entire understanding with reference to the subject matter hereof. Any modifications or waivers of any of the provisions of this agreement must be in writing and signed by both of us.

9. If more than one party signs this agreement as submitter, the reference to "I" or "me" throughout this agreement shall apply to each such party jointly and severally.

10. Should any provision or part of any provision be void or unenforceable, such provision or part hereof shall be deemed omitted, and this agreement with such provision or part hereof omitted, shall remain in full force and effect. This agreement shall at all times be construed so as to carry out the purposes hereof.

Very truly yours,

_____   _____
Signature   Street Address, City and Zip Code

_____   _____
Print Name   Phone Number

ANNOTATION GUIDE

For each element in the written material (whether such element is a character, an event, a setting, or section of dialogue), furnish the following information by written notation in the margin:

1. Whether the element presents or portrays:
   - An actual person or fact, in which case, the note should indicate whether the person's name is real, whether (s)he is alive, and whether (s)he has signed a release
   - Fiction, but a product of inference from fact
   - Wholly fiction, not based on fact

2. Source material for the element:
   - Book
   - Newspaper or magazine article
   - Recorded interview
   - Trial or deposition transcript
   - Any other source

NOTE: Source material identification should give the name of the source (e.g., the *Los Angeles Times*), page reference (if any), and date. To the extent possible, identify multiple sources for each element. Retain copies of all materials, preferably cross-indexed by reference to page numbers. Coding may be useful to avoid lengthy, repeated references.

PERSONAL DEPICTION RELEASE

Dated as of: _____

(NAME)
(ADDRESS)

Re: Personal Depiction Release

Dear Sirs:

I, _____, understand that _____ ("you") is developing a television project (the "Program") to be based upon my life (the "Property"). As the Program may include a portrayal and/or depiction of me, I hereby grant to you the following rights:

1. For good and valuable consideration, receipt of which is hereby acknowledged, I hereby grant to "you," which term shall include not only yourself, but your employees, agents, affiliates, parent, directors, officers, successors, licensees, and assigns, the irrevocable right and license to depict, use, and simulate in any and all media worldwide and in perpetuity my name, likeness, and life story, including, but not limited to, my interviews, actions, activities, career experiences, and personal biography, both actually and fictionally, in connection with the Program, and any remakes or sequels based thereon. I further grant to you all right, title, and interest in and to any ideas that I may have conveyed to you during any interviews with you for use in or in connection with the production, distribution, exhibition, advertising, and other exploitation of the Program. The rights herein granted to you shall include the right to depict and/or portray me, my personal history, and biographical facts, and to fictionalize my name, face, likeness, personal history, and biographical facts to such extent and in such manner as you in your sole discretion may determine in connection with the Program.

2. Further, you shall have the right to distribute, exhibit, or otherwise exploit the Program, and any and all remakes or sequels based thereon,

in whole or in part, worldwide and in perpetuity, by any method and in any media whether now known or hereafter devised, including, but not limited to, theatrical, nontheatrical, and all forms of television, cable, DVD, and videocassette, and to grant and/or assign such rights to third parties without limitation.

3. In making this grant, I understand that you will rely thereon in proceeding with the development and production of the Program, and the other exploitation thereof, and that you will incur substantial expense and contractual obligations based upon such reliance.

4. I warrant that I have not been induced to execute this document by any means or statements made by you or your representatives as to the nature or extent of your proposed exercise of any of the rights herein granted, or otherwise, and I understand that you are under no obligation to exercise any of the rights, licenses, and privileges herein granted to you. I further warrant and represent that I have not entered into any agreement inconsistent with the terms of this agreement, and that I have not conveyed or granted to any third party any of the rights granted to you hereunder.

5. I hereby release and discharge you forever from any and all liability arising out of any injury of any kind, including but not limited to any and all claims of defamation, libel, slander, invasion of privacy, copyright infringement, or any other infringement of any personal or proprietary right, which may be sustained by me from participation in or in connection with the making or utilization of the Program (or any remakes or sequels based thereon), or from the exploitation of the Program (or any remakes or sequels based thereon), in any media throughout the world, by reason of the exercise by you of any of the rights granted to you hereunder.

6. All rights granted and agreed to be granted by me to you under this Agreement shall be irrevocably vested in you and shall not be subject to rescission by me or any other party for any cause. I acknowledge that in the event of a breach of any of your obligations under this Agreement, the damage (if any) caused to me thereby is not irreparable or otherwise sufficient to give rise to a right of injunctive or other equitable relief; and my rights and remedies in the event of such a breach shall be limited to

the right, if any, to recover damages in an action at law. Anywhere herein the term "you" or "your" is used, such term shall include you, your successors, and assigns, and you shall have the right to assign this Agreement to third parties without limitation. This Agreement shall be subject to the laws of the State of California applicable to agreements entered into and to be wholly performed therein, can only be amended in writing, and supersedes all prior agreements, whether written or oral, with respect to the subject matter hereof.

7. I understand that if I grant an interview to any other person respecting the Property, I am obliged to, and will so advise, such third party that I have exclusively granted to you the exclusive right to create and exploit a television program or theatrical motion picture based on my life story and that no such rights are conveyed to such third party by reason of my granting an interview. I agree to consult in advance with you respecting any requests for interviews or personal appearances on television or otherwise. I agree not to issue or authorize any publicity, advertising, or promotion respecting the Option Agreement, the Property, and/or the Program and acknowledge that the right to do so is exclusively yours.

Please confirm your agreement with the aforesaid by signing and returning to me the enclosed copy of this letter.

Very truly yours,

_____

_____

(Print Name)

AGREED TO AND ACCEPTED:

(Company Name)

By: _____
Its: _____

LIFE STORY OPTION/PURCHASE AGREEMENT

The following sets forth the agreement as of _____ ("Agreement") between _____ ("Purchaser") and _____ ("Owner") with respect to the life story of Owner (the "Property").

1. OPTION: For the sum of $_____, payable upon exercise hereof, Owner hereby grants Purchaser an exclusive and irrevocable ____-year option ("Option"), commencing as of the date hereof, to purchase all motion picture and allied rights (as specified in paragraph 5 below) in and to the Property (the "Rights").

2. EXTENSIONS: Purchaser shall have the right to extend the initial option period for an additional one-year period by notice and payment to Owner of an additional sum of $_____ at any time prior to the expiration of the initial option. The initial option period and extended option period shall be automatically extended during one or more events of force majeure, as such term is commonly understood in the entertainment industry, for the duration of such event or during the pendency of any claim involving the Owner's representations and warranties hereunder that might interfere in the timely development, production, delivery, or exploitation of the initial motion picture produced hereunder ("Picture").

3. PURCHASE PRICE: Upon exercise of the Option, if ever, Purchaser shall pay Owner the sum of $_____, less the sum paid to Owner pursuant to Paragraph 1 above, as a purchase price for the Rights. If the Picture is produced hereunder, Owner shall also be entitled to a sum equal to 5 percent of 100 percent of the Purchaser's net proceeds, if any, derived from the Picture, in accordance with Purchaser's standard definition of net proceeds, the language of which shall be subject to good faith negotiations between the parties within customary parameters.

4. SUBSEQUENT PRODUCTIONS:

   a. Sequels: If a Sequel is produced hereunder, a one-time payment of a sum equal to fifty percent (50 percent) of the Purchase Price is payable to Owner pursuant to Paragraph 3 above, payable upon commencement of principal photography of the Sequel, and a percentage participation equal to fifty percent (50 percent) of the contingent compensation is payable to Owner pursuant to Paragraph 3 above.

b. Remakes: If a Remake is produced hereunder, a one-time payment of a sum equal to thirty-three and one-third percent (33 1/3 percent) of the Purchase Price is payable to Owner pursuant to Paragraph 3 above, payable upon commencement of principal photography of the Sequel, and a percentage participation equal to thirty-three and one-third percent (33 1/3 percent) of the contingent compensation is payable to Owner pursuant to Paragraph 3 above.

c. Television Series: If Purchaser produces a Television Series based upon the Picture and Owner is not in default hereunder, Purchaser shall pay Owner a royalty for each new episode produced of such Television Series in an amount to be determined after good faith negotiations between the Purchaser and Owner.

5. OWNERSHIP: Upon exercise of the Option, Producer shall own, exclusively and forever, throughout the universe, all motion picture and allied rights in all languages in and to the Property (excluding print publication rights). Owner reserves all Print Publication Rights in and to the Property. Purchaser will have the right to publish excerpts of the work not in excess of 7,500 words with respect to the advertising and promotion of any productions produced hereunder. Purchaser may, in its discretion, make any changes in, additions to, and deletions from the Work. Purchaser may use Owner's name, likeness, and biographical material in and in connection with the exploitation of the Rights granted hereunder.

6. CONSULTATION/MATERIALS: Owner shall have a right of good-faith, meaningful consultation with Purchaser, subject to Owner's reasonable availability, to consult with Purchaser, as and when reasonably requested by Purchaser during the development, pre-production, and/or production of the Picture. All consultation rights shall be exercised in accordance with the Purchaser's budgetary parameters and scheduling requirements relating thereto, and provided Purchaser's decisions with respect to such matters will be final and controlling. Owner further agrees to furnish Purchaser, for use in the Picture, all information, data, documents, clippings, photographs, records, and other material in Owner's possession and under Owner's control relating to the Property or to any matter depicted or referred to in the Picture. Owner agrees to cooperate with Purchaser, and with such persons as Purchaser may designate, to the fullest extent possible; provided,

however, that Owner shall not be obligated to provide producer with highly-confidential, private matters.

7. TRAVEL: In the event that Purchaser requires Owner to travel to a distant location in connection herewith, Purchaser shall provide Owner and Owner's spouse with business-class round-trip transportation, hotel accommodations, and a reasonable per diem.

8. REPRESENTATIONS AND WARRANTIES: Owner hereby represents and warrants that: (i) Owner has not and will not authorize any motion picture or other production, version, adaptation of the Property during the option period (as it may be extended) or thereafter if the option is exercised; (ii) the Property and/or the information provided by Owner pursuant to Paragraph 5 above, or any part thereof, as herein granted will not, to the best of Owner's knowledge, constitute libel or defamation of, or an invasion of rights of privacy or otherwise violate or infringe upon any other right or rights of, any third party; and (iii) to the best of Owner's knowledge, there is no outstanding claim or litigation pending against the title or ownership of the Property or any part thereof or in the rights therein.

9. CHARACTERS, FICTIONALIZATION: Owner hereby grants Purchaser the full right and authority to use Owner's names, voices, likenesses, and characteristics in and in connection with the Picture. Owner agrees that Purchaser is and shall be free to fictionalize, in whole or in part, adapt, dramatize, rearrange, add to, and/or subtract from the Property and any information provided by Owner pursuant to Paragraph 5 above, in the Picture and any productions produced hereunder; provided, however, that Purchaser hereby agrees that Purchaser will not portray Owner in a defamatory manner and also that Purchaser shall use good faith efforts to portray Owner in a manner that is consistent with the spirit of Owner's story.

Owner represents and agrees that Owner will not bring, institute, or assert, or consent that others bring, institute, or assert, any claim or action against Purchaser on the grounds that anything contained in any production based upon the Property, or the advertising and publicity issued in connection therewith, is defamatory, reflects adversely on Owner, or violates any other rights whatsoever, including, without limitation, rights of privacy and publicity, and Owner hereby releases Purchaser from and against any and all claims, demands, actions, causes of action, suits, costs, expenses, liabilities, and damages whatsoever that Owner may now or hereafter have against Purchaser (except only Purchaser's failure to pay any compensation set forth hereunder), in connection with any productions based on the Property and the preparation, production, performance, broadcast, exhibition, distribution, and/or exploitation thereof, or any other use or exploitation of the rights granted to the Purchaser hereunder.

10. RELEASES: Owner agrees to sign Purchaser's standard depiction release in the form and substance reasonably satisfactory to Purchaser's counsel, and Purchaser shall be responsible for obtaining all third-party releases.

11. RESULTS AND PROCEEDS: It is agreed that all rights of any kind and nature in and to all productions produced hereunder shall be vested solely in Purchaser. Such rights shall include, without limitation, all rights of copyright. Owner agrees that any ideas, suggestions, plots, incidents, situations, and other literary or dramatic materials suggested or created by Owner, as well as the results and proceeds of any services furnished by Owner to Purchaser, shall be and become the sole, complete, and exclusive property of Purchaser, and accordingly, Purchaser shall have the exclusive and perpetual right to use the foregoing in, and in connection with, the Picture and any other productions produced hereunder, including, without limitation, any trailers therefore and the publicity, advertising, exploitation, distribution, and exhibition thereof.

12. ASSIGNMENT: Purchaser shall have the right to assign any or all of its rights under this Agreement to any third party, provided, however, Purchaser shall remain secondarily liable.

13. FORMAL AGREEMENT: The parties hereto intend to execute a more formal agreement(s) incorporating the terms and conditions hereof, together with those of Purchaser's standard contracts for agreements of this nature, and agree that until such execution, this Agreement shall constitute a binding agreement between the parties and supersede any prior understanding between the parties, whether verbal or written, with respect to the subject matter hereof.

AGREED AND ACCEPTED:

_____   _____

"Purchaser"   "Owner"

SCREENPLAY PURCHASE AGREEMENT

This memorandum of agreement ("Agreement"), dated as of November 1, 2001, sets forth the terms and conditions of the agreement between _____ ("Studio") and _____ ("Artist") with respect to Studio's acquisition of that certain original screenplay written by Artist, presently entitled _____ (the "Screenplay") in connection with the proposed feature-length theatrical motion picture based in whole or in part on the Screenplay, also tentatively entitled _____ (the "Picture").

1. PURCHASE OF RIGHTS, COMPENSATION

    1.1 RIGHTS. Artist hereby sells, assigns, transfers, and grants to Studio all rights, title, and interest, including, without limitation, all of the exclusive motion picture, television, DVD, videocassette, videodisc, computer-assisted media (including, but not limited to, CD-ROM, CD-I, and similar disc systems, interactive cable, and any other devices or methods now existing or hereafter devised), character, remake, sequel, sound record, theme park, stage play, merchandising, and allied, ancillary, and subsidiary rights, of every kind and nature, now known or hereafter devised, throughout the universe and in perpetuity in and to the Screenplay (collectively, the "Rights").

    1.2 COMPENSATION. Subject to Artist's full performance of all material obligations herein and as payment in full for Artist's grant of the Rights to Studio, Artist shall be entitled to receive the sum of $200,000 payable as follows:

        1.2.1 CASH COMPENSATION. $200,000 on Artist's signature and delivery to Studio of this Agreement and the Short Form Assignment in the form attached hereto as Exhibit "A."

        1.2.2 BONUS. If the Picture is produced as a feature-length theatrical motion picture and Artist receives sole screenplay credit therefore upon final credit determination under the Writers Guild of America Theatrical and Television Minimum Basic Agreement (the "MBA"), but not Article 7 of Theatrical Schedule A thereto ("Final Credit Determination"), then Artist shall be entitled to receive a bonus in an amount equal to $400,000 less all sums previously paid to Artist under Paragraph 1.2.1 above, which sum shall accrue and become payable to Artist upon Final Credit Determination.

If upon Final Credit Determination Artist receives shared screenplay credit, then in lieu of the foregoing, Artist shall be entitled to receive a bonus in the sum of $300,000 less all sums previously paid to Artist under Paragraph 1.2.1 above, which sum shall accrue and become payable to Artist upon Final Credit Determination. If upon Final Credit Determination Artist does not receive either sole or shared screenplay credit, but Artist receives sole "Story by" credit, then in lieu of the foregoing, Artist shall be entitled to receive a bonus in the amount of $250,000 less all sums previously paid to Artist under Paragraph 1.2.1 above, which sum shall accrue and become payable to Artist upon Final Credit Determination.

Notwithstanding the foregoing, if upon commencement of principal photography, no other screenwriter has been engaged to render services in connection with the Picture, Artist shall be paid, at such time, the sum of $250,000 less all sums previously paid to Artist under Paragraph 1.2.1 above, which sum shall be an advance against any bonus payable to Artist under this Paragraph 1.2.2, provided, however, that said advance shall be immediately repayable to Studio in the event that following such Final Credit Determination, Artist is not entitled to sole or shared screenplay credit or sole "Story by" credit. Artist shall not be entitled to receive any bonus under this Paragraph 1.2.2 if Artist does not receive either sole or shared screenplay credit or "Story by" credit as set forth herein. To the extent permitted under the MBA, any bonus payable hereunder shall be inclusive of and fully applicable against any minimum payments to which Artist may be or become entitled to under the MBA.

1.2.3 CONTINGENT COMPENSATION. If the Picture is produced and released as a feature-length theatrical motion picture and Artist receives sole screenplay credit therefore upon Final Credit Determination, then Artist shall be entitled to receive contingent compensation in an amount equal to 5 percent of 100 percent of the Net Profits, if any, of the Picture. If Artist receives shared screenplay credit upon Final Credit Determination, then in lieu of the foregoing, Artist shall be entitled to receive contingent compensation in an amount equal to 2.5 percent of 100 percent of the Net Profits, if any, of the Picture. If Artist does not receive either sole or shared screenplay credit, but Artist receives "Story by" credit upon Final Credit Determination, then in lieu of the foregoing, Artist shall be entitled to receive contingent compensation in an amount equal to 1.25 percent of 100 percent of the Net Profits, if any, of the Picture. Artist shall not be entitled to any such contingent compensation under this Paragraph 1.2.3 if Artist does not receive sole or shared screenplay credit or "Story by" credit for the Picture as set forth herein. For purposes of this Agreement, Net Profits shall be defined, computed, accounted for, and paid in accordance with Studio's standard Net Profits definition (including a 15 percent overhead charge plus charges for any Studio facilities used in accordance with the then current Studio rate card), attached hereto and incorporated herein by this reference.

1.3 ADDITIONAL DOCUMENTATION. Concurrently herewith, Artist will execute a Short Form Assignment in the form of Exhibit "A" attached hereto and, at Studio's request, Artist will execute or cause the execution of any and all additional documents and instruments reasonably deemed by Studio to be necessary or desirable to effectuate the purposes of this Agreement.

2. REPRESENTATIONS, WARRANTIES, AND INDEMNITY
Artist hereby represents and warrants and agrees to indemnify Studio as follows:

a. Artist is the sole owner of all rights, title, and interest in and to the Screenplay;

b. Artist has not previously granted, assigned, mortgaged, or hypothecated, nor will Artist grant, assign, mortgage, or hypothecate (other than to Studio as provided herein), any right, title, or interest in and to the Screenplay or any part thereof to any person, firm or other entity;

c. No rights of any third party are or will be violated by Artist's entering into or performing this Agreement. Artist has not made and shall not hereafter make any agreement with any third party which could interfere with the rights granted to Studio hereunder or the full performance of Artist's obligations hereunder;

d. The Screenplay is original with Artist, and neither the Screenplay nor any part thereof is taken from or based upon any other material except material wholly owned by Artist or material which is incidentally in the public domain (and Artist shall inform Studio as to which portions of the Screenplay are incidentally in the public domain);

e. The exploitation or any other use of the rights herein granted shall not violate any copyright and shall not, to the best of Artist's knowledge, including that which Artist should have known in the exercise of reasonable prudence, defame any person or entity nor violate any right of privacy or publicity, or any other right of any person or entity;

f. There are no adverse claims to or against the Screenplay by any person, firm, or corporation, nor is there pending any litigation or, to the best of Artist's knowledge, including that which Artist should have known in the exercise of reasonable prudence, threat of litigation concerning the Screenplay;

g. There are no other contracts, agreements, or assignments affecting Artist's right in and to the Screenplay;

h. Artist hereby indemnifies and holds harmless Studio (and its parent, subsidiaries, subsidiaries of its parent, affiliates, associates, successors, assigns, and the directors, officers, employees, agents, and representatives of the foregoing) from and against any and all damage, loss, liability, cost, penalty, guild fee, or award or expense of any kind, including reasonable outside attorneys' fees, arising (i) out of any breach of Artist's representations, warranties and agreements hereunder or (ii) out of any claim alleging facts which, if true, would constitute such a breach, if and to the extent that such claim is of a type not ordinarily covered by a so-called errors and omissions or producer's liability insurance policy. Studio shall not be entitled to indemnification under (ii) above with respect to a claim which Studio determines in its sole good faith business judgment to be a so-called "frivolous and/or nuisance" type claim. Studio shall indemnify and hold Artist harmless from any charge, loss, liability, cost, penalty, guild fee, or award or expense of any kind (including reasonable attorney's fees) in connection with the production, distribution, or exploitation of the Picture, except to the extent that Artist is in breach of Artist's representations and warranties hereunder and excepting Artist's tortuous conduct if of a nature not covered by Studio's existing errors and omissions policy; and

i. Artist acknowledges that the rights granted to Studio hereunder are of a unique, extraordinary, and intellectual character, the loss of which cannot be adequately compensated in damages in an action at law, and therefore, Artist acknowledges that Studio shall be entitled to injunctive and other equitable relief to prevent or curtail any breach of this Agreement by Artist.

3. FIRST OPPORTUNITY: THEATRICAL SEQUEL, THEATRICAL REMAKE, TELEVISION PRODUCTION

3.1 For a period of (a) ten (10) years after the initial general theatrical release (if any) of the Picture if Artist was the only writer engaged to render writing services on the Picture, or (b) seven (7) years after the initial general theatrical release (if any) of the Picture if there were other writers in addition to Artist engaged to render writing services on the Picture, if Studio elects, in its sole discretion, to have a screenplay written for the initial theatrical sequel to or initial theatrical remake of the Picture, and provided Artist receives sole screenplay credit upon Final Credit Determination for the Picture and is then active as a writer in the theatrical motion picture industry, and is available when and where required by Studio, then Studio shall first negotiate in good faith with Artist, within Studio's standard parameters, to engage Artist to write the screenplay for such initial theatrical sequel and/or initial theatrical remake (and each succeeding theatrical sequel and/or theatrical remake of the Picture, as applicable, provided that Artist received sole screenplay credit on the immediately preceding theatrical sequel to and/or succeeding theatrical remake of the Picture, as applicable) on financial terms no less favorable to Artist than the financial terms set forth herein with respect to the Picture. If Studio and Artist fail to agree on terms for Artist's services in connection with such initial theatrical sequel and/or initial theatrical remake within thirty (30) days following Studio's service of notice on Artist of the commencement of negotiations therefore, or if Artist elects not to write or is unavailable, Studio shall have the right to engage another writer(s) and shall have no further obligation to Artist with respect to such theatrical writing services hereunder except for payments of royalties (if any) to which Artist may be entitled pursuant to Paragraph 3.3 below.

3.2 TELEVISION PRODUCTION. If within seven (7) years after the initial general release (if any) of the Picture, Studio elects (in its sole discretion) to have a teleplay written for the initial television motion picture based on the Picture (i.e., a pilot, initial episode of a series, a movie-of-the-week, or miniseries, collectively, a "Television Production"), and provided Artist received sole screenplay credit for the Picture upon Final Credit Determination and is then active as a writer in the television motion picture industry and is available when and where required by Studio, then Studio shall first negotiate in good faith, within Studio's standard parameters, with Artist for Artist's writing services for such Television Production, provided, however, that Artist's engagement in connection with any Television Production shall be subject to network or licensee approval. If Studio and Artist fail to agree on terms for Artist's services on such Television Production within thirty (30) days following Studio's serving of notice on Artist (or Artist's agent) of the commencement of negotiations therefore, if Artist is unavailable, if Artist is not approved by the network or licensee, or if Artist elects not to write, then Studio shall have no further obligation to Artist hereunder, except as otherwise provided in Paragraph 3.3 below.

3.3 ROYALTIES. If Studio produces a theatrical sequel to or theatrical remake of the Picture, or a television motion picture (or television series) based thereon, and provided Artist received sole separation of rights under the MBA for the Picture and is not engaged to write for the applicable production described below, then Artist shall be entitled to receive the applicable royalty specified below; provided, however, that if Artist received shared separation of rights under the MBA for the Picture and is not engaged to write for the applicable production described below, then Artist shall be entitled to receive fifty percent (50%) of the applicable royalty specified below.

a. THEATRICAL SEQUEL. One-half (½) of the cash compensation actually paid to Artist pursuant to Paragraph 1.2.1 and 1.2.2 above, for Artist's grant of rights in and to the Screenplay for the Picture, plus, as contingent compensation, a percentage of Net Profits (if any) of such sequel, which percentage shall be equal to one-half (½) of the percentage of Net Profits to which Artist was entitled on the Picture.

b. THEATRICAL REMAKE. One-third (⅓) of the cash compensation actually paid to Artist pursuant to Paragraphs 1.2.1 and 1.2.2 above, for Artist's grant of rights in and to the Screenplay for the Picture, plus, as contingent compensation, a percentage of Net Profits (if any) of such sequel, which percentage shall be equal to one-third (⅓) of the percentage of Net Profits to which Artist was entitled on the Picture.

c. TELEVISION SERIES. The following royalties are payable for each episode of a television series based upon the Picture, as produced for a particular broadcast season:

(i) Primetime Network (i.e., ABC, CBS, NBC, FOX, or WB)

RUNNING TIME	PAYMENT
30 minutes	$1,500
60 minutes	$2,200
90 minutes (or more)	$2,800

(ii) Non-Prime-Time, Non-Network

RUNNING TIME	PAYMENT
30 minutes	$ 700
60 minutes	$1,100
90 minutes (or more)	$1,400

d. MOVIE(S)-OF-THE-WEEK AND MINISERIES. $15,000 for the first two (2) hours, and $7,500 for each additional hour of running time thereafter (prorated for portions thereof), not to exceed a maximum of $50,000, regardless of running time.

e. RERUNS AND ROYALTIES. Twenty percent (20%) of the applicable royalty set forth in subparagraphs 3.3.c and 3.3.d above shall be payable for each of the first five (5) network reruns, in the combined territory of the United States and Canada. No further rerun payments shall be made thereafter.

f. SPIN-OFFS. If Studio, in its sole election, produces a so-called "generic" spin-off series based upon a television series which is based upon the Picture, and if such spin-off series is based upon character(s) created by Artist and contained in the Picture, then Studio agrees to pay to Artist a sum equal to fifty percent (50%) of the sum contained in Paragraph 3.3.c above for each "generic" spin-off series. A "generic" spin-off series is a spin-off series in which a central character in a continuing role was created by Artist and appeared in the Picture and the original television series. No royalties will be payable to Artist for any "planted" spin-off series.

g. TIME AND FREQUENCY OF PAYMENT. Unless specified otherwise, theatrical payments due under this Paragraph 3.3 shall be payable on commencement or principal photography. Television payments shall be payable upon initial United States network broadcast, but if the television production is not broadcast in the season for which it was ordered and Studio has irrevocably received its license fee, then the applicable royalty shall be paid to Artist within thirty (30) days after the end of said broadcast season.

h. INCLUSIVE OF MBA MINIMUMS. The royalty and rerun payments set forth in this Paragraph 3.3 are inclusive of the minimum royalties and rerun fees payable under the MBA. Any additional payment required by the MBA under this or any other paragraph of this Agreement shall be payable at the minimum rate required under the MBA.

3.4 CREDIT. Credit shall be accorded as provided under the MBA.

3.5 NOVELIZATION. Novelization rights shall be in accordance with the MBA provisions applicable thereto.

3.6 OWNERSHIP AND DISTRIBUTION. Studio shall exclusively own all now known or hereafter existing rights of every kind throughout the universe, in perpetuity and in all languages, pertaining to the Screenplay, the Picture, and all elements therein, for all now known or hereafter existing uses, media, and forms, including, without limitation, all copyrights (and renewals and extensions thereof), motion picture, television, DVD, videocassette, videodisc, computer-assisted media, sound record, character, sequel, remake, theme park, stage play, merchandising, and allied, ancillary, and subsidiary rights therein, and the foregoing is inclusive of a full irrevocable assignment to Studio thereof.

3.7 NO OBLIGATION TO USE. Studio is not obligated to use the services of Artist or to produce, distribute, or exploit the Picture or, if commenced, to continue the production, distribution, or exploitation of the Picture in any territory. Regardless of whether or not Studio elects to produce, distribute, and/or to exploit the Picture (or to commence same), Studio is not obligated to use the services in whole or in part of Artist.

3.8 ASSIGNMENT. Studio may assign, transfer, license, delegate, and/or grant all or any part of its rights, privileges, and properties hereunder to any person or entity. This Agreement shall be binding upon and shall inure to the benefit of the parties hereto and to their respective heirs, executors, administrators, successors, and assigns. In the event of assignment, and provided the assignee assumes in writing all of Studio's obligations as of the date of such assignment, and further provided such assignee is a major or so-called "mini-major" motion picture studio, television network, or equally financially responsible third party, Studio shall be relieved from all further obligations to Artist hereunder accruing from and after the date of such transfer.

3.9 INSURANCE. Artist shall be covered as an additional insured on Studio's Errors and Omissions insurance policy in connection with the Picture during customary periods of production and distribution of the Picture, subject to the limitations, restrictions, and terms of said policy. The provisions of this Paragraph shall not be construed so as to limit or otherwise affect any obligation, representation, warranty, or agreement of Artist's hereunder.

3.10 WGA BASIC AGREEMENT. If there is any conflict between any provision of this Agreement and the WGA Basic Agreement, then the latter shall prevail, but the conflicting provisions of this Agreement shall be limited only to the WGA Basic Agreement, and as so modified, this Agreement shall continue in full force and effect. All payments herein include the payments required under the WGA Basic Agreement, and any additional payment required under the WGA Basic Agreement shall be payable at the minimum rates provided therein.

4. IRCA COMPLIANCE

Artist acknowledges that any offer of employment hereunder (if applicable) is subject to and contingent upon Artist's ability to prove his identity and employment eligibility as required by the Immigration Reform and Control Act of 1986, as amended. Accordingly, Artist hereby agrees (a) to complete and execute Section 1 ("Employee Information and Verification") of an Employment Eligibility Verification ("Form I-9") at the time of his or her execution of this Agreement or commencement of services, whichever is earlier, and (b) to deliver, in person, to Studio said Form I-9, together with documentation of his or her employment eligibility, within three (3) business days of his or her execution of this Agreement. If Artist fails to complete and deliver the Form I-9 as provided above, Studio shall have the right, by notice to such effect given to Artist, to terminate the Agreement, and thereupon, Artist's employment hereunder shall cease and terminate, and neither party shall have any right, duty, or obligation to the other under the Agreement, except as shall have accrued prior to the effective date of termination.

5. NOTICES

Any notice pertaining hereto shall be in writing. Any such notice and any payment due hereunder shall be served by delivering said notice or payment personally or by sending it by mail, cable, or telex (postage or applicable fee prepaid) addressed as follows (or as subsequently designated in writing):

To Artist:

With a Courtesy Copy to:

To Studio:

The date of personal delivery, mailing, or delivery to the cable or telex office of such notice of payment shall be deemed the date of service of such notice or payment, unless otherwise specified herein; provided, however, that any notice which commences the running of any period of time for Studio's exercise of any option or Studio's performance of any other act shall be deemed to be served only when actually received by Studio.

6. GENERAL

This Agreement (together with Exhibit "A" and Studio's standard Net Profits definition) constitutes the entire agreement between the parties and supersedes all prior and contemporaneous written or oral agreements pertaining thereto and can only be modified by a writing signed on behalf of both parties hereto. Artist's sole and exclusive remedy for Studio's breach, termination, or cancellation of this Agreement or any term hereof (including any term pertaining to credit) shall be an action for damages, and Artist irrevocably waives any right to seek and/or obtain rescission and/or equitable and/or injunctive relief.

IN WITNESS WHEREOF, the parties hereto have executed and delivered this Memorandum of Agreement as of the date and year first written above.

AGREED AND ACCEPTED:

_____   _____
"STUDIO"   "ARTIST"

EXHIBIT "A"

SHORT FORM ASSIGNMENT

KNOW ALL MEN BY THESE PRESENTS: That the undersigned, for value received, hereby sells, assigns, transfers, and grants in perpetuity unto STUDIO and its successors and assigns (herein called "Assignee") the sole and exclusive motion picture, television, DVD, videocassette, videodisc, computer-assisted media (including but not limited to CD-ROM, CD-I, and similar disc systems, interactive cable, and any other devices or methods now existing or hereinafter devised), character, sequel, remake, theme park, sound record, stage play, merchandising, and allied, ancillary, and subsidiary rights of every kind and nature, throughout the universe and in perpetuity (the "Rights"), in and to the screenplay entitled _____ (which, together with the title, themes, contents, characters, and other versions thereof, is hereinafter called the "Property") written by Artist, and such rights shall include, but not be limited to, all of the exclusive copyrights (and renewals and extensions thereof), all as more particularly set forth in and subject to the terms and conditions of that certain Memorandum of Agreement for Acquisition of Rights between the undersigned and Assignee dated as of November 1, 2001.

The undersigned hereby agrees to allow Assignee to obtain or cause to be obtained all United States copyrights in and to said Property, whether or not referred to herein, and hereby assigns said Rights under said copyrights to Assignee; and the undersigned hereby irrevocably appoints Assignee as attorney-in-fact, with full and irrevocable power and authority to do all such acts and things, and to execute, acknowledge, deliver, file, register, and record all such documents, in the name and on behalf of the undersigned, as Assignee may deem necessary or proper in the premises to accomplish the same.

Assignee is also hereby empowered to bring, prosecute, defend, and appear in suits, actions, and proceedings of any nature under or concerning all copyrights in and to said Property and all renewals thereof, or concerning any infringement thereof or interference with any of the

Rights hereby granted under said copyrights or renewals thereof, in its own name or in the name of the copyright proprietor, but at the expense of Assignee, and, at its option, Assignee may join such copyright proprietor and/or the undersigned as a party plaintiff or defendant in any such suit, action, or proceeding.

DATED: _____   _____
                                ARTIST

SHOPPING AGREEMENT/ATTACHMENT AGREEMENT

As of _____

Re: " _____ **"**

Dear All:

This letter (the "**Agreement**") sets forth the agreement between
_____ ("**Owner**") and _____ ("**Producer**") in
connection with the potential development and production of a [**movie/TV
series etc.**] currently entitled "_____" (the "**Series**" or
"**Picture**") based on [**the book/screenplay**, etc.] collectively, the "**Property**").

1. Evaluation of Interest. Commencing as of the date hereof, and continuing through _____ (the "**Term**"), subject to extension by written agreement of the parties hereto, Producer will have the right to evaluate interest from financiers, licensees, networks, distributors and any other third parties (the "**Potential Financiers**") for financing, development and/or production of the Series. In connection therewith, Producer shall not have the right to create any development or promotional materials relating to the Series. Further, Producer shall only be entitled to use the Property for the purpose of creating interest in the Series. Producer shall provide Owner detailed information respecting all pitches, contacts, offers and proposals and related inquiries from Potential Financiers in connection with Owner's activities hereunder.

2. No Authority to Bind. Notwithstanding anything herein to the contrary, Producer is not authorized to, and shall not (i) execute any agreement on behalf of Owner or in connection with the Series or (ii) otherwise bind Owner to any agreement or encumber the rights in and to the Series. No agreement is binding upon Owner unless and until the same has been executed by Owner, and the terms and conditions of any agreement, including any amendments, extensions or cancellations thereof, shall be determined by Owner in its sole and absolute discretion. Owner shall be under no duty or obligation to Producer to accept the terms or conditions of any offer for the license of rights to the Series solicited by Producer, the acceptance or rejection of all such offers being determined by Owner in the exercise of Owner's sole and absolute discretion.

3. Confidentiality. The parties hereto agree that they will not directly or indirectly disclose or permit the disclosure of any of the terms, conditions, or other aspects of this agreement without the prior written consent of the other party, except with respect to each party's respective employees (on a need-to-know basis) and financial and legal advisors, and as and to the extent required by law. Producer agrees not to issue any press releases respecting this Agreement or the Series without the prior written consent of Owner.

4. No Rights. Nothing in the Agreement shall be construed to be a license or grant of rights in and to the Property or any intellectual property or goodwill owned or controlled by Owner.

5. Formal Agreement. In the event that there is sufficient interest from Potential Financiers in the Series, Owner and Producer will have the option to commence discussions respecting the co-production of the Series in accordance with industry standards, with Producer attached as a producer of the Series). If at the expiration of the Term, the parties do not elect to commence discussions respecting a co-production, or if the parties commence discussions and fail to enter into a Co-Production Agreement within thirty (30) days of the commencement of such discussions, then Owner will have no further obligations to Producer in connection with the Series or otherwise. Unless and until such time as Owner and Producer enter into the Co-Production Agreement (if ever), this Agreement shall be a binding agreement on Owner and Producer and their successors and assigns, and any actions taken by Producer in connection with the Series will indicate assent to the terms and conditions of this Agreement.

Very truly yours,

_____

By: _____
Its: _____

ACCEPTED AND AGREED:

_____

By: _____
Its: _____

PILOT/SERIES TELEVISION WRITER/PRODUCER AGREEMENT

_____ PRODUCTIONS, INC.

Effective as of [DATE]

[Name]
[Address]

**RE: [LOANOUT] ("LENDER") f/s/o [ARTIST] ("ARTIST") /
    "[PROJECT]" ("PROJECT")**

Ladies and Gentlemen:

This letter sets forth the agreement ("Agreement") between _____ PRO-
DUCTIONS, INC. ("Producer") and [LOANOUT] (Fed. I.D.
#_____) ("Lender") f/s/o [ARTIST] (S.S. #_____)
("Artist") regarding the television series project currently entitled "[PRO-
JECT]" ("Project").

1. Pilot Executive Producing Services and Fees: If Producer produces a
pilot based on the Project ("Pilot"), Producer shall engage Lender to provide Artist's Executive Producer Services (as hereinafter defined) on the
Pilot for a fee of $_____ for a [½-hour] [1 hour] [2 hour] Pilot. In
the event a presentation ("Presentation") is produced in lieu of a pilot,
the parties will negotiate a reduction of fee in good faith based upon the
budget of such presentation.

2. Series Services:
(a) Executive Producer Services—First and Second Series Years Lock: If
Producer accepts an irrevocable network order to produce a series based
on the Pilot ("Series"), Producer shall engage Lender to furnish Artist's
non-writing Executive Producer Services for all episodes produced during the first and second Series years.

(b) [Executive Producer Services—Third Series Year Option: Lender hereby grants to Producer the exclusive, irrevocable option to engage Lender to furnish Artist's non-writing Executive Producer Services for all episodes produced during the third Series year. Producer shall exercise its option for the third Series year, if at all, by written notice (the "Option Notice") delivered to Lender within ten (10) business days following Producer's written acceptance of a written licensee order therefor. Notwithstanding the foregoing, Lender shall have the one-time right, exercisable by written notice delivered to Producer within five (5) business days following Lender's receipt of the Option Notice to elect not to render non-writing Executive Producer Services in the third Series Year.]

(c) Consultant Services: If Artist has rendered all Executive Producer Services for the first and second Series years, and Producer has exercised its option to engage Lender to furnish Artist's Executive Producer Services for the third Series year, then Producer shall engage Artist's services as a non-exclusive, non-writing consultant on the Series for the life of the Series, beginning with the fourth Series year. Notwithstanding the foregoing, if Producer exercises its option to engage Lender to furnish Artist's Executive Producer Services for the third Series year, and Lender elects not to render such services as provided in paragraph 2.b. above, then Producer shall engage Artist's services as a nonexclusive, non-writing consultant on the Series for the number of years Artist rendered Executive Producer Services on the Series. Producer shall have no obligation to engage Artist's Consultant Services if Producer exercises its pay-or-play rights pursuant to paragraph 10 of this Agreement. "Consultant Services" are those services as are customarily rendered by non-writing consultants as reasonably determined by the Series executive producer/showrunner.

3. Fees:
    (a) Executive Producer Services:
        (i)   First Series Year: $_____ per episode.
        (ii) Second Series Year: $_____ per episode.
        (iii) [Third Series Year: $_____ per episode.]
        (iv) 5% annual increases thereafter.
    (b) Consultant Services: $_____ per episode, no annual increases.

4. Executive Producer Services/Exclusivity: Artist's services as a non-writing executive producer ("Executive Producer Services") in connection with the Presentation, Pilot and/or Series shall be of an actual and substantial nature and shall be consistent with the highest standards in the United States television industry. Artist's Executive Producer Services shall be exclusive to Producer in all forms of television (including internet and broadband) and shall be rendered on a[n] [non-]exclusive [in-person] basis during periods of Pilot and Series pre-production, production and post-production, as applicable. Artist's Executive Producer Services shall include such services as are customarily rendered by executive producers of programming in the television industry. Lender and Artist warrant and represent that Artist does not have any commitments or obligations that might interfere with Artist's full compliance with the terms and conditions of this Agreement. Furthermore, Lender and Artist warrant and represent that Artist shall not accept any commitment or enter into any agreement that might interfere with Artist's full compliance with the terms and conditions hereunder.

5. Series Production Bonus: If Producer produces the Series [on which Artist receives sole or shared "created by" credit], Producer shall pay Lender a Series Production Bonus of $_____. The Series Production Bonus is based on, and payable following, the actual production and broadcast during the regular broadcast season of thirteen (13) episodes, excluding the Pilot.

6. Royalty: If Producer produces the Series [on which Artist receives sole or shared "created by" credit], Lender shall be entitled to a royalty of $_____ for each episode produced and broadcast during the regular broadcast season (excluding the Pilot), payable promptly following broadcast of each applicable episode. [The royalty shall be payable on an episode-by-episode basis following completion of principal photography of the applicable episode.]

7. Profits:
(a) MAG: For the Pilot and each episode on which Artist has rendered all material services as set forth in this Agreement, Lender shall be entitled to an amount equal to 5% of the Modified Adjusted Gross receipts ("MAG"), if any, derived from the Series, [reduced on a dollar-for-dollar

basis by contingent compensation (whether in net profits, gross receipts or otherwise, however denominated) payable to all third-party profit participants other than [ ] to 2.5% MAG] derived from the Pilot and/or Series.

(b) MAG Definition: Lender's MAG shall be computed, determined, and paid pursuant to the standard television definition of MAG of Producer's distributor, which is attached hereto as Exhibit "A" and incorporated herein by reference (the "MAG Definition"). The MAG Definition includes the following:

(i) Distribution Fees:

Initial Network:	0%
Canadian Network:	25%
U.S. Pay Television:	25%
U.S. Syndication:	25%
International Television:	25%
U.S. Home Video:	30%
International Home Video:	45%
U.S. Theatrical:	35%
International Theatrical:	40%
Worldwide Non-Theatrical:	50%
Merchandising:	40%

Notwithstanding the foregoing, in the event that Producer enters into an agreement with a network for the renewal of the Series following the expiration of the initial network license and such network renewal provides for the network to pay to Producer, prospectively, an episodic license fee in excess of the pattern budget for such series, then Producer shall charge a 25% distribution fee on the amount by which the license fee exceeds the pattern budget.

(ii) Charge: The Administrative Charge will be a 15% charge on all allocable costs of the Pilot and Series.

(iii) Financing Charge: 1.5% above prime.

(iv) Third Parties "Off the Top": All third-party profit participants (and deferments and advances against profit participations, if any) shall be taken "off the top" in determining Lender's share of MAG in accordance with paragraphs IV.C. and IV.D. of the MAG Definition.

(v) Remaining Terms: The remaining terms of Lender's profit participation shall be computed, determined, and paid pursuant to the standard television definition of MAG of Producer's distributor [, subject only to such changes as may be negotiated within Producer's customary parameters]. [, within Producer's customary parameters, subject to good faith negotiations]. [subject to good faith negotiations which shall conclude prior to commencement of production of a Pilot. If Lender does not provide comments before that time, the terms herein shall govern].

(c) Vesting: Lender's MAG will vest, if at all, ⅓ upon rendition and completion of all required Pilot Executive Producer services (or if no Pilot is required, then upon rendition and completion of all required Presentation Executive Producer services); ⅓ upon rendition and completion of all required Executive Producer Services for the first Series year; and ⅓ upon rendition and completion of all required Executive Producer Services for the second Series year.

8. Distribution Control:

(a) General: Producer shall have complete, exclusive and unqualified discretion and control as to the time, manner, and terms of its distribution, exhibition and exploitation of each Series episode (including the Pilot and Presentation), separately or in connection with other programs, in accordance with such policies, terms and conditions and through such parties as Producer in its business judgment may in good faith determine are consistent with business policy and proper or expedient and the decision of Producer in all such matters shall be binding and conclusive upon Lender and Artist. Notwithstanding the foregoing, Producer shall accord good faith (meaningful) consultation with Artist with respect to the initial domestic off-network sales plan, subject to the reasonable availability and reasonable response time of Artist. Producer makes no express or implied warranty or representation as to the manner or extent of any distribution or exploitation of each Series episode (including the Pilot and Presentation) nor the amount of money to be derived from the distribution, exhibition and exploitation of each Series episode (including the Pilot and Presentation), nor as to any maximum or minimum amount of such monies to be expended in connection therewith. Producer does not guarantee the performance by any Subdistributor, licensee or exhibitor, of any contract regarding the distribution and exploitation of each Series episode (including the Pilot and Presentation).

(b) Dealings with Affiliates: Lender and Artist acknowledge that Producer is part of a diversified, multi-faceted, international company, whose affiliates include, or may in the future include, among others, exhibitors, television "platforms", networks, stations and programming services, production and production consultation, video device distributors, record companies, internet companies, so called "e-commerce companies", publishers (literary and electronic) and wholesale and retail outlets (individually or collectively, "Affiliated Company or Companies"). Lender and Artist further acknowledge that Producer has informed Lender and Artist that Producer intends to make use of Affiliated Companies in connection with its distribution and exploitation of the Series episodes (including the Pilot and Presentation), as, when and where Producer deems it appropriate to do so. Lender and Artist expressly waive any right to object to such distribution and exploitation of any Series episode (including the Pilot and Presentation) (or aspects thereof) or assert any claim that Producer should have offered the applicable distribution/exploitation rights to unaffiliated third parties (in lieu of, or in addition to, offering the same to Affiliated Companies). In consideration thereof, Producer agrees that Producer's transactions with Affiliated Companies will be on monetary terms comparable to the terms on which the Affiliated Company enters into similar transactions with unrelated third-party distributors for comparable programs. Lender and Artist agree that Lender's and Artist's sole remedy against Producer for any alleged failure by Producer to comply with the terms of this paragraph shall be actual damages, and Lender and Artist hereby waive any right to seek or obtain preliminary or permanent equitable relief or punitive relief in connection with any such alleged failure.

(c) Arbitration: Any dispute arising under the provisions of this Paragraph 5 shall be arbitrated by, and under the rules of, J.A.M.S./

Endispute ("JAMS") in binding arbitration in Los Angeles, California and before a mutually selected arbitrator experienced in the United States television industry. Although each side shall advance one-half of the fee of the arbitrator and for JAMS' services, the prevailing party in such arbitration shall be entitled to recover all costs of arbitration, including reasonable outside attorneys' fees and costs.

9. Credit: Subject to Artist's complete performance of the terms and conditions of this Agreement, for the Pilot and each Series episode for which Artist actually completes all required services the following shall apply:

(a) Executive Producer Credit: Producer shall accord Artist credit as executive producer [on a separate card in the main/opening titles, substantially similar size, style and duration as others at the same credit level].

(b) [Production Company: For the Pilot and each Series episode for which Artist actually completes all required Executive Producer Services, Artist shall be entitled to a logo credit for Artist's production company; provided, however, that if the network restricts the number or timing of production company logo credits, Producer may use only Producer's production company credit and that of any Series financing partner, to the exclusion of Artist's production company credit and that of any creator or co-creator of the Pilot/Series, if Producer determines in good faith that due to network restrictions it requires the time and space to give meaningful airing of its own credit.]

(c) Limitations: Except as otherwise set forth in this Paragraph 7, all aspects of each credit shall be at Producer's sole discretion. In addition, all credits shall be subject to network (or other licensee) and applicable guild approval. Inadvertent or casual failure to accord credit as provided herein shall not be deemed to be a breach of this Agreement. Neither Lender nor Artist shall be entitled to seek injunctive relief for a failure to accord credit. [Producer agrees, promptly following receipt of written notice from Artist specifying any such failure, to take such steps as are reasonably practicable to cure such failure with respect to future copies of the applicable episode.]

10. Ownership: Producer shall solely and exclusively own throughout the universe in perpetuity all rights of every kind and nature, including the copyright and all rights of copyright, in and to the Project, the Presentation, Pilot and/or Series and the services furnished by Lender and/or Artist hereunder, all of the results and proceeds thereof, in whatever stage of completion as may exist from time to time, together with the rights generally known as the "moral rights of authors" and the exclusive right to distribute and otherwise market and exploit the Project, Presentation, Pilot and/or Series and all components thereof throughout the universe, in perpetuity, and in any media, whether now or hereafter known or created. Lender and Artist acknowledge that all results and proceeds of such services are being specially ordered by Producer for use as a part of an audiovisual work and shall be considered a "work made for hire" for Producer and, therefore, Producer shall be the author and copyright owner thereof.

11. [Non-Network Productions: Notwithstanding anything contained hereinabove, all payments to Lender set forth herein are only payable if the Pilot and/or Series are produced for initial exhibition in network prime-time on CBS, ABC, NBC or FBC. If the Pilot and/or Series are not produced for initial television exhibition pursuant to the parameters set forth in the previous sentence, then all of the compensation hereunder shall be reduced by an amount to be negotiated in good faith by the parties consistent with decreases in budget and revenue projections.]

12. Pay-Or-Play: All of Artist's services are to be rendered on a pay-or-play basis with respect to only the compensation specified in Paragraphs _____ above. If Producer exercises its pay-or-play rights, any compensation earned by Lender and Artist in the entertainment industry during the period Producer could have required Artist to render services hereunder shall reduce Producer's obligation to pay episodic compensation.

13. Remedies: Artist's services and the rights herein granted to Producer are of a unique character of such value that the toss of these services could not adequately be compensated in damages in an action at law, and a breach by Lender or Artist of this Agreement will cause irreparable injury. Producer, therefore, shall be entitled to seek equitable relief by way of temporary restraining order, preliminary or permanent injunction or otherwise to prevent the breach of this Agreement and to secure its enforcement. The sole right of Lender and Artist as to any alleged breach by Producer shall be the recovery of money damages and the rights granted by Lender or Artist under this Agreement shall not terminate by reason of such alleged breach. Producer may choose not to use Artist's services or the results and proceeds thereof by terminating all of Producer's obligations under this Agreement except for any applicable payment required hereunder. Each of Producer's several rights, remedies and options hereunder shall be cumulative, and no one of them is exclusive of any other. No failure or delay on the part of Producer to exercise any right, power or privilege under this Agreement shall operate to waive any right, power or privilege.

14. Warranty and Representation: Lender and Artist each represents and warrants that: (a) neither is under any obligation or disability, created by law or otherwise, which would in any manner or to any extent, prevent or restrict Lender and Artist from entering into and freely performing this Agreement; (b) Lender is a corporation duly organized and existing under the laws of the state of its incorporation; (c) Lender is a bona fide corporate business entity established for a valid business purpose within the meaning of the tax taws of the United States; (d) Artist is under contract of employment with Lender for a term extending at least until completion of all services required by Producer under this Agreement; (e) any material to be furnished by Lender and/or Artist to Producer hereunder shall be wholly original with Lender and/or Artist and Producer's use of such material will not violate or infringe upon the rights of any third party; (f) there are no encumbrances of any kind upon the material; (g) Lender and/or Artist has the sole right to grant all rights in and to such material to Producer; (h) Lender shall be solely responsible for the payment of all monies payable to Artist by reason of Artist's rendering services in connection with this Agreement; and (i) each has the full right, power and authority to enter into this Agreement, to grant the rights granted by each to Producer hereunder and to perform all of the terms hereof.

15. Indemnification: Each party will indemnify, defend and hold harmless the other, the other's parents, affiliates, divisions, subsidiaries, successors, transferees, assignees, licensees, and the agents, associates, officers, directors and employees of each, from and against any and all damages, costs, expenses, liabilities, claims and causes of action in any way arising by reason of the breach of any warranty or representation hereunder by the indemnifying party or any other provision in this Agreement, including, without limitation, reasonable outside attorneys' fees and costs in the defense and disposition of such matters. Notwithstanding the foregoing, Producer shall not indemnify, defend and hold Lender harmless to the extent such third-party claim or action arises out of a breach or alleged breach of Lender's representations, warranties or agreements hereunder or out of Lender's criminal misconduct or malicious, willful, tortuous or deceitful acts. Producer shall have the right to control any such claim or litigation with counsel of its choice. Lender shall have the right as well as the obligation to consult and cooperate with Producer in connection with any such claim and, upon Producer's request, to furnish Producer any and all evidence, materials or other information relevant thereto. Lender understands and agrees that all aspects of the defense of any such claim, whether as part of any litigation, negotiations or otherwise (including any decision regarding any settlement), shall be controlled by Producer and such control shall in no way abrogate or diminish Lender's obligations under this paragraph 15. In addition, Producer shall have the right to settle and dispose of any such claim as it so determines.

16. Default; Incapacity; Force Majeure: In the event of Lender's or Artist's default or event of force majeure (any interference with or suspension or postponement of production by reason of any cause or occurrence beyond the control of Producer, including labor disputes, strikes, any acts of God, war, riot, governmental action, regulations or decrees, casualties, accidents, illness or incapacity of the director or a principal member of the cast of the Series or similar or dissimilar causes which prevent rendition of services), Producer may, at its election, terminate this Agreement by notice to Lender without payment after termination, except for payments accrued and not yet paid, or suspend services without payment during any such suspension, in which case Producer may postpone all dates in connection with this Agreement for a period equal to all or part of the suspension period by notice to Lender and/or Artist on or before the last to occur of: (i) termination of the suspension; or (ii) five (5) business days after the end of the default, incapacity or force majeure.

17. Insurance: Lender and Artist shall be covered by Producer's errors and omissions and general liability insurance policies for the Pilot and/or Series during customary periods of production and distribution, subject to the limitations, restrictions and terms of, and endorsements to, such policies.

18. Form 1-9: As an express condition to Producer's performances under this Agreement, Artist must submit a form 1-9 (Employment Eligibility Verification Form) and original documents satisfactory to prove Artist's employment eligibility.

19. FCC Compliance: In compliance with the Federal Communications Act, Lender and Artist warrant and represent that neither Lender nor Artist will accept any consideration from anyone other than Producer for inclusion of any matter in the Pilot and/or Series.

The remaining terms of this Agreement are Producer's standard terms and conditions, subject only to such changes as may be negotiated within Producer's customary parameters. If Lender does not provide comments before that time, the standard terms and conditions shall govern.

This letter is the complete agreement between the parties unless and until a more detailed formal contract is executed.

Sincerely,

_____ PRODUCTIONS, INC.

By: _____
                 An Authorized Signatory

AGREED AND ACCEPTED:
[LOANOUT]
              ("Lender")
By: _____
Its: _____
Federal I.D. _____

I have read the terms of the foregoing Agreement and fully understand its terms and agree as an express inducement to the parties entering into the Agreement to render all services, grant all rights necessary, and observe all requirements of Lender under the Agreement. If I fail to do so, Producer shall have the same rights against us personally as if I had entered into the Agreement directly with Producer.

_____

[ARTIST]   ("Artist")
TAX ID. #_____

FORM OF REALITY SERIES PARTICIPANT AGREEMENT

I ("I", "me") and [Producer], Inc. ("Producer") entered into the (1) Program Appearance Authorization and Release; (2) Request and Authorization for Disclosure and Redisclosure of Medical Information; (3) the Psychological Evaluation Release Form; (4) the Confidentiality Agreement; (5) Videotape/Stills License; and I have completed the short form Reality Show Application and the long form Participant Questionnaire; all relating to the television series currently entitled *The Reality Show* and any version thereof (the "Series"). In consideration of and as an inducement to Producer entering into this Agreement and further considering me to become a participant, as applicable, in the Series (a "Participant"), I am making representations, warranties, disclosures, covenants and agreements described below. If any disclosure, representation or warranty is false or misleading or if I breach any covenant or agreement made in this Agreement or any other form, agreement, application, questionnaire or release in connection with the Series, Producer may remove me from the Series; and Producer may make any explanation, announcement, on-air or otherwise, Producer or the network broadcasting the Series (the "Network") may choose. I deem it to be in my best interest to enter into this Agreement and I am signing this Agreement voluntarily, knowingly and of my own free will.

I UNDERSTAND THIS IS AN IMPORTANT LEGAL DOCUMENT RELATING TO MY PARTICIPATION IN THE SERIES, AND BY SIGNING THIS DOCUMENT I AM WAIVING CERTAIN LEGAL RIGHTS.

Accordingly, Producer and I agree as follows:

I. DISCLOSURE AND ACKNOWLEDGEMENTS:
A. If I am selected by Producer to be a Participant in the Series, I agree to take part as a Participant in connection with the production of the Series as and to the extent required by the Producer on such dates and at such locations as Producer shall designate in its sole discretion. I understand that interviews, meetings, psychological and/or medical evaluations, examinations and the like are or may be scheduled to take place in Seattle and possibly other locations throughout the United States (the

"Location") for casting purposes and/or during or after the production of the Series. I agree to participate in said evaluations and/or examinations and further understand and agree that any and all medical and/or psychological examiners may share with Producer the results of said examinations. I also agree that in connection with evaluating my participation in the Series, Producer may or may not conduct a background check on me. I also agree to attend any meetings or interviews required by Producer in connection with my preparation for or participation in the Series. I further agree to be available and to participate when and where Producer may require in connection with publicity, interviews and similar matters (e.g., to appear on news shows, talk shows and other programs, and to make other appearances as required by Producer) in connection with the Series as when and where designated by Producer in its sole discretion.

B. Knowledge of Series Nature and Content and Agreement to Comply with All Rules, Directions, and Instructions: I am familiar with the nature and concept of the Series. I understand that the Series is a unscripted television show, is not a game show, and will be produced for entertainment purposes.

C. Alternate Participation: I acknowledge that I may be chosen as an alternate (as opposed to a Participant) by Producer in its sole discretion. If I am chosen as an alternate, I shall remain available to participate in the Series as a Participant if and when chosen by Producer to replace a Participant. I acknowledge and agree that Producer may, at any time and in its sole discretion, add, remove or replace Participants.

D. Knowledge of Nature of Activities and Attendant Risk of Injury: I understand that the Series may involve strenuous physical activity including, without limitation, hiking, wading, swimming, diving, parasailing, water skiing, other water sports or activities, skydiving, snow skiing, ice skating, rollerblading, and other physical activities yet to be determined. I also understand that the Series may involve me being a passenger in watercrafts, land vehicles and small planes. I represent that I am familiar with the varied risks and dangers attendant to each of the activities and means of transportation and the risks and dangers described in this Agreement. I acknowledge that my participation in the

Series carries with it the potential for death, serious physical injury, mental or physical illness, and property loss. I acknowledge that Producer has advised me to consult and that I have consulted with my own physician regarding the advisability from a physical and emotional health perspective of my potential participation in the Series and that any injuries allegedly caused thereby are hereby specifically included within the matters released under paragraph V below and indemnified against under paragraph V below. I further acknowledge Producer will not provide me with any medical or psychological treatment (unless otherwise noted herein) or pay for any medical or other treatment expenses should I become sick or injured and I must look to my own insurance to cover the cost of any medical or other treatment expenses I incur. I represent I know of no reason why I should not participate in the Series.

E. Knowledge of Potential Embarrassment and Surprises: I acknowledge that interviews on or in connection with the Series may consist of another Participant and/or my statements about other Participants, personal relationships and, perhaps, the opinions and statements of my family and/or friends and other people connected with the series, and that some of these statements and/or statements by the host of the Series, Producer or Producer's employees or agents or others may be considered surprising, humiliating, embarrassing, derogatory, defamatory, or otherwise offensive or injurious to me, the viewing audience, Producer or Producer's employees or agents and/or other third parties. I also have been informed and I fully understand that any "dating" advice from "dating experts" or advice from stylists as to make-up techniques, hairstyles, dress, or the like given to me on or in connection with the Series is for entertainment only. I am free to reject any such advice in whole, or in part, and should I follow all or any part of such advice, I shall do so entirely at my own risk. Any actual or alleged consequences of my following such advice shall be included within the matters released under paragraph V and indemnified under paragraph V below. I further understand and acknowledge that I may experience one or more surprises (e.g., a secret or other unknown fact may be revealed to me) in connection with my appearance on the Series, and such surprise shall be included within the matters released under paragraph V below.

F. Isolation of Participants from Family and Friends: I understand that if I am selected to participate in the Series I will be separated from my family, my friends, and my regular environment for several consecutive weeks. These conditions may expose me to severe mental stress. I voluntarily and fully accept and assume these risks and understand and acknowledge that the waivers, releases and indemnities in this Agreement expressly apply to these risks.

G. Supplies, Services and Travel Furnished by Producer to Participants: I acknowledge that neither Producer nor any contractor or employee providing equipment or services in connection with the Series has made any warranties whatsoever with respect to equipment or services which they furnish in connection with the Series or which the Participants may otherwise use, and that there are no warranties of any kind from anyone regarding the fitness or suitability of any equipment or services for use for any purpose in connection with the Series. I hereby waive any right I might otherwise have to warnings or instructions regarding any aspect of the Series or the equipment or services utilized in connection therewith. I further understand and agree that I am solely responsible for obtaining and paying for any life, travel, accident, property or other insurance I may desire in connection with any travel and/or any other activities I undertake on or in connection with the Program, and Producer is not responsible for providing such insurance. In the event I am not transported back to my origination point immediately after taping of the Series, I understand and agree that all activities which I undertake after such taping are at my sole discretion, expense (except to the extent Producer has arranged and paid for my return travel or extended hotel lodging), risk and responsibility.

II. Grant of Rights; Ownership of Materials and Series: All rights which I have granted hereunder are referred to hereafter collectively as the "Granted Rights". It is understood and agreed that the Granted Rights may be used in any manner and by any means, whether now known or unknown, throughout the universe and either factually or with such portrayal, impersonation, simulation, imitation or other modification, in whole or in part, as Producer, its licensees, successors, and assigns, determine in their sole unfettered discretion. Producer may freely assign any or all of the Granted Rights. Notwithstanding the foregoing, I agree and acknowledge that neither Producer nor the Network shall have the obligation to exercise any of the Granted Rights (the exercise of such rights to be in Producer's and Network's sole and absolute discretion). For good and valuable consideration, the receipt and sufficiency of which are hereby acknowledged, with full knowledge, I hereby grant to Producer the following exclusive, perpetual and irrevocable rights (i.e., "The Granted Rights"):

A. Name, Likeness, Etc., Promotional Activities: The unconditional right throughout the world in perpetuity to use, simulate or portray (and to authorize others to do so) or to refrain from using, simulating or portraying, my name, likeness (whether photographic or otherwise), voice, personality, personal identification or personal experiences (including, without limitation, whether I am clothed, partially clothed or naked, whether I am aware or unaware or such photographing, videotaping, filming or recording, and by requiring me to wear a microphone at all times), my life story, biographical data, incidents, situations and events which heretofore occurred or hereafter occur, including without limitation the right to use, or to authorize others to use any of the foregoing in or in connection with the Series (or any episode or portion thereof) and the distribution, exhibition, advertising, promoting or publicizing of the Series or any Series episode by Producer, the Network, its operations, activities or programming services and with any merchandise, tie-in, product, or service of any kind where such use is made in conjunction with a reference to the series by producer, the Network, or any of its programming services, but not so as to constitute a direct endorsement of any other product or service. I understand that, in and in connection with the Series, I may reveal and/or relate, and other parties (including, without limitation, other Participants, Producer and the host of the Series), may reveal and/or relate information about me of a personal, private, intimate, surprising, defamatory, disparaging, embarrassing or unfavorable nature, that may be factual and/or fictional. I further understand that my appearance, depiction and/or portrayal in the Series and my actions and the actions of others displayed in the Series, may be disparaging, defamatory, embarrassing or of an otherwise unfavorable nature and may expose me to public ridicule, humiliation or condemnation. I acknowledge and agree that Producer shall have the right (a) to include any such information and any such appearance, depiction, portrayal, actions, and statements in the Series as edited by Producer in its sole discretion, and (b) to broadcast and otherwise exploit the series containing any such information and any such appearance, depiction, portrayal or actions. The waivers, release and indemnities in this Agreement expressly apply to any such inclusion and exploitation. I hereby consent to Producer's filming, taping and/or recording of me for use in and in connection with the Series and agree to cooperate fully with Producer in such activities, acknowledge and agree that Producer will be the sole and exclusive owner of all rights and material filmed, taped, and/or recorded pursuant to this Agreement.

B. Participant Personal Photographs, Film and Video: I understand and agree that during Series production I shall, under no circumstances, shoot or take any photographs, film or video without obtaining Producer's prior written approval. If I have previously developed said film or video, I shall provide Producer with all of such exposed film (negatives and prints) or video for Producer's and the Network's use in the Series as a Granted Right, the advertising and promotion of the Series and any and all ancillary uses of the Series (e.g., books, calendars, videos, CD-ROM). Producer and the Network shall be entitled to retain possession of the film or video. I understand and agree that no additional compensation, payments, residuals, reuse fees or otherwise shall be made to me with respect to Producer's or the Network's use of such photographs, film or video and I shall not haven the right to exhibit, distribute or exploit such photographs, film or video.

C. Ownership of Rights: Without limiting any of the rights I have granted herein, I acknowledge and agree that all of the results and proceeds of my granting of rights hereunder (collectively, the "Materials") including, without limitation, all artistic, literary, dramatic, musical, photographic (still or moving, taken during the Series preparation, preproduction or production period) and other materials which I may create or furnish hereunder, are being specially commissioned by Producer as contribution to an audiovisual work and, accordingly, the copyright and all other proprietary rights, title and interest in such Materials shall be owned by Producer as the author of such Materials, which shall be considered "works-made-for-hire," pursuant to the United States

Copyright Act. If any of such Materials are not deemed "works-made-for-hire," I hereby assign to Producer the entire copyright and all other rights in and to such Materials (and where any such Materials are riot in existence at the date hereof, by way of present assignment of future copyright), throughout the universe for the full period of copyright and all renewals and extensions thereof, and thereafter for the maximum period permitted by law. Without limiting the foregoing, Producer shall have the exclusive right to copy, reproduce, change, add to, delete from, translate, distribute, transmit, exhibit, advertise, use and otherwise exploit the Materials or any part thereof, to make or authorize any ancillary use thereof (including, without limitation, the distribution or licensing of the materials for syndication, commercial and non-commercial publishing, print publication, home video, sound recordings, Internet/online and merchandising) and to advertise and promote the foregoing, in perpetuity throughout the universe by any and all means and in any and all media whether now known or hereafter invented or devised (including, without limitation, television, theatrical, non-theatrical, cassettes, disc, and other home-video devices, the Internet and other online or computer-assisted media and print media) and to authorize others to do any of the foregoing. Producer shall have the right to make any tee it desires of any Materials (including, without limitation, the Series and my performance in the Series or the materials), without the payment of any compensation, except as otherwise stated herein. All materials which I use in connection with the Series shall be subject to Producer's prior approval. I hereby waive unconditionally and irrevocably the benefit of any provision of law known as "Moral Rights" or similar laws now or hereafter prevailing in any part of the world which might otherwise apply to the materials and I will not assert any Moral Rights against Producer or the Network. I agree that any telecast or other exploitation of the Materials or any rights therein, whether as part of the Series or otherwise, will not entitle me to receive any compensation.

D. Public Domain Material: Nothing in this Agreement shall ever be construed to restrict, diminish or impair the rights of either Producer or the Participants to utilize freely, any work or media, any story, idea, plot, theme, sequencer scene, episode, incident, name, characterization or dialogue which may be in the public domain, from whatever source.

III. CONSIDERATION/PUBLICITY/EXCLUSIVITY:

A. Consideration: If I am selected to be a Participant on the Series and provided that I am not in breach of this Agreement and that Producer has not discontinued or suspended my participation in the Series, Producer shall, as consideration for my participation and all rights I have granted hereunder to Producer in connection herewith, furnish me throughout the series production period with joint living quarters with other Participants at a location(s) selected by Producer, meals, transportation and other good and valuable consideration, the receipt of which I hereby acknowledge. I acknowledge and agree that the applicable consideration expressly set forth in this paragraph A shall be in full consideration of my grant of rights and participation in the filming and/or videotaping of the Series. Producer shall have no obligation to utilize my participation in the Series. Further, Producer shall have no obligation to produce or exhibit the Series or to use or otherwise exploit the results and proceeds of my participation in the Series. I agree that my appearance as a Participant in the Series does not constitute a performance within the parameters of a performing arts union or guild and under no circumstances will any compensation (other than that specifically referenced above), such as payment, residual, royalty, reuse or similar payments, be payable to me or on my behalf regardless of the manner and the extent to which Producer or the Network elects to exploit the Series or the results and proceeds of my services hereunder.

B. Publicity and Promotion: From the date of this Agreement and continuing for twelve (12) months following the date of network broadcast of the final episode of the series, if and when requested by Producer, I agree to be available, subject to existing professional commitments, for publicity interviews, publicity photograph sittings, still photographs, on-the-air and other publicity activities. During this time, I agree Producer may film, tape, audio/video record my likeness and broadcast or otherwise distribute such recordings worldwide in perpetuity.

C. Special Episodes: Producer and/or the Network shall have an exclusive and irrevocable right to film and/or videotape reunion and/or special episodes (collectively the "Special Episodes") in which I hereby agree to participate for no additional compensation. Any such Special

Episodes will be produced within twelve months from the premiere of the first episode of the Series. If Producer and/or the Network elect(s) to film/tape the Special Episodes, then Producer and/or the Network shall notify me of such decision at least fifteen days prior to the commencement date of principal photography or taping of the Special Episodes. I agree to participate in the production of the Special Episodes for a period of approximately three (3) days (such time will be subject to my then existing professional commitments) (the "Special Production Period") at a location which Producer and/or the Network will designate at a later date. I hereby grant to Producer and/or the Network all rights in the Reunion Episode(s) as if the same had been included as a regular Series episode and all other applicable paragraphs of this Agreement shall apply thereto. Producer and/or the Network agree(s) that if Producer elects to require my participation in the Special Episodes (though it is not obligated to do so), it shall provide transportation for me to and from the location of any Special Episodes, as well as meals and lodging at the location.

D. Cooperation and Access: I hereby agree to grant Producer access to any place, to the extent within my control, and to cooperate fully with Producer in obtaining access to other places involved with me or my services in the Series. I further agree to refrain from seeking refuge in places where the Series cameras are not allowed access. If required, I further agree to cooperate fully with Producer in obtaining access to, and executed releases from, other persons, including my parents, siblings and friends. I shall provide such executed releases to Producer within three (3) days after Producer tapes, shoots or records any such material that may require such a release.

E. Exclusivity: I agree that for a period commencing on the data of this Agreement and six months after the date of the initial broadcast of the Series finale (hereinafter the "Initial Exclusivity Period"), I shall not appear on or authorize production of or Participate in any way with any other television programming, the development or any other television programming (including but not limited to negotiation with third parties regarding the development of any type of programming), radio programming, print media, online services, or any other media outlet now known or hereafter devised (including, but not limited to the internet [including chat rooms, message boards, etc.]), or any commercials or advertisements without Producer's and the Network's prior written consent.

IV. ACKNOWLEDGMENT AND ASSUMPTION OF RISK

A. Knowledge, Awareness, and Assumption of Risks of Personal Injury and Property Loss: I am aware that the Series, Dates and/or other activities may include, but not be limited to, hiking, camping, wading, diving, swimming, climbing, skydiving, snow skiing, ice skating, para-sailing, water skiing, rollerblading, riding in water crafts, land vehicles and small planes, all of which are hazardous activities. I am voluntarily participating in the Series, Dates and related activities with full knowledge, appreciation and understanding of the dangers and personal risks involved. I hereby agree to accept any and all risks attributable to my participation in the Series, including but not limited to, illness, serious personal injury, death and/or property loss.

B. Rights to Withdraw: I acknowledge that I always have the option to discontinue my participation in the Series and to withdraw as a participant from the Series at any time (whether because of Producer's disclosures to me or for any other reason), subject to the reasonable time and logistic restraints necessary to assist me if I withdraw while on location. I also acknowledge that Producer may provide additional disclosures to me regarding the various risks to which I might be subjected in connection with my participation in the Series and that Producer may ask me to sign additional releases and waivers relating to those risks. I understand that if I refuse to sign any such releases and waivers which Producer requires or if I elect to withdraw from the Series, then I can no longer participate in the series and I forfeit any honorarium, if any, to which I would be entitled. I understand and agree that no such discontinuation or withdrawal will affect any of the rights I have assigned to Producer or any of my covenants, agreements, waivers, releases or indemnities in this agreement. I acknowledge that I may be held fully responsible for all costs and damages incurred by producer which result from my voluntary withdrawal from the series, and/or a breach of any representation or statement made by me in this agreement, and/or in any of the applications or other agreements executed by me (as set forth above) and/or after my selection as a participant, during any series pre-interview or interview of me. Such costs may include all costs of production. I understand and agree that no such discontinuation or withdrawal will affect any of the rights I have assigned to Producer or any of my covenants, agreements, waivers, releases or Indemnities in this Agreement.

C. No Representations or Warranties from Producer: I acknowledge that Producer has made no representations or warranties of any kind whatsoever to me regarding other participants, including but not limited to the mental or physical health of such participants or their career, financial history, education, or medical/emotional or personal history. I understand and acknowledge that Producer may or may not screen or conduct background checks or investigations the other participant(s) I select to go on the Dates or any other person who appears, or may appear, on the Series (including an investigation of any person's medical, professional or criminal history) and has no duty to conduct such investigation. In the event Producer chooses, in its sole discretion, to conduct background checks on other participants, Producer has no obligation to share the results of such background checks with me. I further understand and acknowledge that Producer cannot control, and is not responsible for, the events which transpire, or allegedly transpire, on any Dates or during any other interaction between myself and other participants or any other person on the Series. I agree to maintain my behavior on the Date(s) and any other interactions with any person on the Series in accordance with all applicable laws and generally accepted social practices. I understand there are risks in any such interaction, including but not limited to, the possibility of non-consensual physical contact; AIDS, HIV and other communicable and sexually transmitted diseases; or pregnancy. I expressly agree and affirm to producer that I will conduct myself with the care, good judgment and discretion that I would ordinarily exercise in similar situations. In addition, I acknowledge that I, at my sole election, may decide to participate in an activity that involves a risk of injury, embarrassment, danger or death. I assume all risk associated with such activity and understand that Producer undertakes no responsibility or liability of any kind or nature for any adverse effects or problems of whatever kind or nature, which I may experience as a result of undergoing such activity. I agree that any injuries, damage or harm allegedly suffered by me in connection with any Date(s); any other interaction between myself and other participants or any other person on or connected with the Series; or any other activity in connection with the Series, are hereby Specifically included within the matters released under paragraph V below and indemnified against under paragraph V below. I hereby waive any right, claim or dispute I might otherwise have with respect to Producer's decision not to conduct any background investigation(s) or, in the event Producer chooses to conduct background checks, for any negligently or improperly conducted background checks, or Producer's failure to share the results of such background checks with me and I agree that any injuries, damages or harm allegedly suffered by me in connection therewith are hereby specifically included within the matters released in paragraph V below and indemnified against under paragraph V below.

D. Knowledge of and Assumption of Other Risks: I acknowledge that the foregoing is not an exhaustive list of the risks, hazards and dangers I will be exposed to as a result of the Series activities. I voluntarily and freely accept and assume these and all other risks, hazards and dangers I may encounter or be exposed to and understand and acknowledge that the waivers, releases and indemnities in this Agreement expressly apply to these risks, hazards and dangers.

V. RELEASES, WAIVERS AND INDEMNIFICATIONS

A. Definition of "Releasing Parties": As used in this Agreement, the term "releasing parties" means and refers to each of me, my heirs, next of kin, spouse, guardians, legal representatives, executors, administrators, successors and assigns.

B. Definitions of "Released Parties": As used in this Agreement, the term "released parties" means and refers to each of Producer, the Network and their respective parents, subsidiary entities, affiliates, successors, licensees and assigns, and their respective directors, officers, employees, agents, contractors, partners, shareholders, attorneys, representatives and members.

C. Waiver of All Claims and Suits; Released Claims: I and the other releasing parties hereby irrevocably agree that I and the other releasing parties will not sue or claim against any of the other participants in the series or the released parties for any injury, illness, damage, loss or harm to me or my property, or my death, howsoever caused, resulting or arising out of or in connection with any defect in and/or failure of equipment, warnings or instructions, or my preparation for, participation and appearance in or elimination from the series or activities associated with the Series. In addition, I and the other releasing parties hereby unconditionally and irrevocably release and forever discharge each of the other participants in the Series and the released parties from and against any and all claims, liens, agreements, contracts, actions, suits, coats, attorneys' fees, damages, judgments, orders and liabilities of whatever kind or nature in law, equity or otherwise, whether now known or unknown, suspected or unsuspected, and whether or not concealed or hidden arising out of or in connection with my preparation for, participation and appearance in, withdrawal from, or elimination from the Series, the Dates or other activities associated with the Series or the production and exploitation of the Series, including, without limitation, claims for any injury, illness, damage, loss or harm to me or my property, or my death (collectively, the "released claims"). The released claims shall include, but not be limited to, those based on negligence or gross negligence of any of the released parties, the Series production staff, or any of the other participants in the Series, products liability, breach of contract, breach of any statutory or other duty of care owed under applicable laws, libel, slander, defamation, invasion of privacy, publicity or personality, negligent or intentional infliction of emotional distress and infringement of copyright.

D. Indemnification: I and the other releasing parties irrevocably agree to defend, indemnify and hold Producer, the Network, their parent, subsidiary and related companies, and their officers, directors, employees, agents, attorneys, licensees, successors, and assigns (each, the "Indemnitee") from and against any claim, loss, penalty, liability, cost and expense, including without limitation reasonable legal fees, arising out of (1) any actual or threatened breach of any agreement, warranty, representation or undertaking made by me in this Agreement and (2) my preparation for, participation and appearance in or elimination from the Series or the activities associated with the Series.

E. Assumption of Risk of Unknown or Undiscovered Facts, Claims or Defects, and Release of Released Parties: I and the other Releasing Parties acknowledge that there is a possibility that after my execution of this Agreement, I or they will discover facts or incur or suffer claims which were unknown or unsuspected at the time this Agreement was executed and which, if known by me or them at that time, may have materially affected my or their decision to execute this Agreement.

I and the other Releasing Parties acknowledge and agree that by reason of this Agreement, and the release contained in the preceding paragraphs, I and the other Releasing Parties are assuming any risk of such unknown facts and such unknown and unsuspected claims. I and the other Releasing Parties have been advised of the existence of Section 1542 of the California Civil Code which provides:

A GENERAL RELEASE DOES NOT EXTEND TO CLAIMS WHICH THE CREDITOR DOES NOT KNOW OR SUSPECT TO EXIST IN HIS FAVOR AT THE TIME OF EXECUTING THE RELEASE, WHICH IF KNOWN BY HIM MUST HAVE MATERIALLY AFFECTED HIS SETTLEMENT WITH THE DEBTOR.

Notwithstanding such provisions, this release shall constitute a full release in accordance with its terms. I and the other Releasing Parties knowingly and voluntarily waive the provisions of Section 1542, as well as any other statute, law, or rule of similar effect, and acknowledge and agree that this waiver is an essential and material term of this release and this Agreement, and without such waiver Producer would not have accepted this Agreement or my participation in the Series. I and the other Releasing Parties hereby represent that I and they have been advised by our legal counsel, understand and acknowledge the significance and consequence of this release and of this specific waiver of Section 1542 and other such laws.

VI. MISCELLANEOUS

A. Producer's Right to Suspend or Terminate This Agreement: Producer shall have the unconditional right to terminate this Agreement, in Producer's sole and absolute discretion, with or without cause. Without in any way limiting the foregoing, Producer may elect to terminate my participation in or in connection with the Series if any of the following occur: (i) if the Series is canceled or the Series format is materially altered; (ii) in the event of an occurrence of an event of force majeure (as defined below) which lasts for more than fourteen (14) days; (iii) in the event of my incapacity (including physical or mental disability, default; (iv) in the event of my conviction of a misdemeanor or felony; or (v) any other conduct of mine which, in Producer's reasonable judgment, would adversely affect my ability to represent Producer and the Network properly or to participate hereunder. Producer shall have the right, in its sole discretion and for any reason, upon notice to me, immediately to suspend and/or discontinue my participation hereunder and shall, during such period of suspension or, upon termination, be released from any further obligations to me whatsoever. Producer may terminate any period of suspension at any time in Producer's sole discretion and I shall thereupon resume my participation hereunder. As used herein, an "event of force majeure" shall mean any act of God, inevitable accident, terrorism, fire, lockout, strike or other labor dispute, riot or civil commotion, act of public enemy, law, enactment, regulation, rule, order or act of government or governmental instrumentality (either Federal, state or local, foreign or other), failure of technical facilities; or other cause of similar or different nature beyond Producer's control which materially interferes with, prevents, or impedes production of the Series or Producer's or the Network's operations. Any potentially illegal behavior or activity including, but not limited to, drug use, violence, threats, harassment, intimidation or assault, during and after the period that this Agreement is in effect will result in immediate termination of my participation. I agree that I shall immediately leave the premises where the Series is being filmed after receiving said verbal notice of termination, or as otherwise instructed by Producer's personnel and Producer shall have no further obligation to me.

B. Restrictions on Use of Trademark: I shall not at any time use any of Producer's names, logo, trade names, or trademarks (including, but not limited to, the title of the Series and/or the trademarks of Warner Bros., Telepictures Productions, any broadcaster, or of any of Producer's related companies) in connection with any kind of advertising, promotion, publicity, merchandise, tie-in, product or service, other than as provided in this Agreement.

C. Representations, Warranties and Indemnities:

(1) I hereby represent and warrant as follows:

Eligibility
[a] I am over 25 years old.
[b] I am a legal resident of and am residing in the United States and have a valid passport through.
[c] I have full right, power and authority to enter into and fully perform this Agreement.
[d] I will abide by all Participant rules of conduct, all U.S. laws and all applicable local laws.
[e] I represent and warrant that I am not presently a candidate for any type of political office ("Candidate") and will not become a candidate from the time this Agreement is executed until one (1) year after the initial broadcast of the last episode of the Series in which I appear.

D. Confidentiality/Disclosure: Any and all information disclosed to or obtained by me concerning or relating to the Series, the Participants, the events contained in the Series, the outcome of the Series or any Series episode, Producer, the Network and the terms and conditions of this Agreement shall be strictly confidential. I agree that I shall NOT disclose or cause to be disclosed to any third party any information to which I have had or will have access or learn concerning the Series, the other Participants, their friends or families, Producer, the Network, or the Network's programming or other services, or the terms and conditions of this Agreement, except as required to fulfill my obligations hereunder; as expressly authorized by Producer in writing; or as required by law. I also agree that I shall not disclose or cause to be disclosed any such information to any Participant, individual or entity including, without limitation, any members of the press. I acknowledge that any direct or indirect disclosure of such information will constitute a material breach of this Agreement and will cause Producer and the Network substantial and irreparable injury and will cause substantial damages in excess of Five Million Dollars ($5,000,000), entitling Producer (and/or the Network, as a third-party beneficiary of this provision) to, among other things: (1) injunctive or other equitable relief, without posting any bond, to prevent and/or cure any breach or threatened breach of this paragraph by me;

and (2) recovery of the Producer's and/or the Network's damages and attorneys' fees and court costs incurred to enforce this paragraph. I also agree not to make any personal appearance for anyone other than Producer and/or Network or make any statement to any media person or service with respect to the Series without Producer's and Network's prior written approval as set forth in this Agreement. In addition to this paragraph D, Producer and I have agreed to enter into a separate Confidentiality Agreement. In the event the provisions of this Agreement and the confidentiality Agreement differ, the terms of the Confidentiality Agreement shall control.

E. Remedies: I acknowledge and agree that the rights I have granted hereunder and my participation related thereto are unique, unusual, special and extraordinary, the loss of which would not be adequately compensable in damages in an action at law. I further agree that, in addition to any rights or remedies which Producer may have under this Agreement or otherwise, Producer therefore would be entitled to all available equitable remedies in case of my breach or threatened breach of this Agreement. Any remedies, rights, undertakings and obligations contained in this Agreement shall be cumulative. No remedies, rights, undertakings, or obligations shall be in limitation of any other remedy, rights, undertaking, or obligation of either party. No breach of this Agreement shall entitle me to terminate or rescind the rights granted to Producer or the Network herein. I hereby waive the right, in the event of any such breach by Producer or the Network, to equitable relief or to enjoin, restrain or interfere with the exercise of any of the Granted Rights, it being my understanding that my sole remedy shall be the right to recover monetary damages with respect to any such breach.

F. Liquidated Damages: I agree that any breach or violation by me of any of the terms or provisions of this Agreement shall result in substantial damages and injury to Producer and/or the Network, the precise amount of which would be extremely difficult or impracticable to determine. Accordingly, Producer and I have made a reasonable endeavor to estimate a fair compensation for potential losses and damages to Producer and/or the Network which would result from any breach by me of any material term of this Agreement and, therefore, I further agree that, in addition to the remedies set forth herein-above, I will also be obligated to pay, and I agree to pay to Producer and/or the Network, the sum of One Million Dollars ($1,000,000) as a reasonable and fair amount of liquidated damages to compensate Producer and/or the Network for any loss or damage resulting from each breach by me of the terms hereof. I further agree that such sum bears a reasonable and proximate relationship to the actual damages that Producer and/or the Network will or may suffer from each breach by me.

G. Assignment: I acknowledge that I shall have no right to assign this Agreement or delegate any of my responsibilities hereunder to any third party. Producer shall have the right to assign this Agreement freely.

H. Relationship of Parties: I acknowledge and agree that my relation-ship to Producer is limited solely to that of a grantor of rights and not as an employee of Producer or of an independent contractor, I acknowledge and agree that I will be responsible for payment of all taxes and insurance applicable under existing law on all amounts paid to me hereunder (if any), including but not limited to, Social Security taxes, Federal, State and Local income taxes. I hereby agree to com-plete, execute and deliver, in person, to Producer all required forms necessary for identity and eligibility under the 1986 Immigration Reform and Control Act. I warrant and represent that I will make all necessary payments due governmental agencies to comply with the foregoing.

I. Applicable Law: This Agreement, and any exhibits and attachments hereto, together with the Participant Personal Release, Participant Medical and Psychological Examination Release, the Participant Confidentiality Agreement, the Videotape Release, and the long form Participant Questionnaire contain the entire understanding between the parties, and supersede all prior negotiations, understandings and agree-ments (whether written or oral) of the parties hereto relating to the sub-ject matter herein. This Agreement cannot be changed or terminated except by a written instrument signed by the parties hereto. This Agreement and all matters or issues collateral thereto shall be governed by the laws of the State of California applicable to contracts executed and performed entirely therein (regardless of the actual place(s) of performance). Any and all controversies, claims or disputes arising out of or related to this Agreement or the interpretation, performance or breach thereof, including, but not limited to, alleged violations of state or federal statutory or common law rights or duties, and the determination of the scope or applicability of this Agreement to arbitrate ("Dispute"), except as sat forth in subparagraphs B and C, below, shall be resolved according to the procedures set forth in subparagraph A, below, which shall constitute the sole dispute resolution mechanism hereunder:

1. Arbitration: In the event that the Parties are unable to resolve any Dispute informally, then such Dispute shall be submitted to final and binding arbitration. The arbitration shall be initiated and conducted according to either the JAMS or AAA arbitration services.

2. Other Matters: Any Dispute or portion thereof, or any claim for a particular form of relief (not otherwise precluded by any other provision of this Agreement), that may not be arbitrated pursuant to applicable state or federal law may be heard only in a court of competent jurisdiction in the state of Washington.

No waiver of any breach of or default under any provision hereof shall be deemed a waiver of such provision, or of any subsequent breach or default. If any provision hereof shall be invalid or unenforceable due to any law, said provision shall be modified to the minimum extent necessary to effect compliance with such law, and in any event such invalidity or unenforceability shall have no effect upon the remaining terms and conditions hereof. The grant of rights, representations, warranties, indemnities, restrictions on use of trademarks, and confidentiality obligations contained herein shall survive the expiration or earlier termination of this Agreement. The paragraph headings have been inserted herein for the purpose of convenience only and shall not be used in interpreting this Agreement. The provisions hereof shall be binding upon me and my heirs, executors, administrators and successors. I acknowledge that Producer has explained to me that an attorney prepared this Agreement and that Producer has recommended to me that I consult with my attorney in connection with this Agreement.

After Producer and I have signed this Agreement where indicated below, the foregoing shall constitute a binding and enforceable agreement between us.

DATED: _____ DATED: _____

_____ _____
Signature

Print Name: _____ By: _____
Address: _____ Its: _____
_____
Telephone: _____

THE LINGO

20/60/10/10 formula: A payment schedule pursuant to which talent (most commonly producers and directors) are paid 20 percent of the negotiated fee over the period of formal pre-production; 60 percent over the scheduled period of principal photography; 10 percent upon delivery of the director's cut, and 10 percent upon delivery of the final print of the film.

100/5: The promise to pay an additional 100 percent of a television writer's negotiated royalty over the first five repeat broadcasts of an episode. Twenty percent of the negotiated amount would be paid upon each of the first five repeat broadcasts of the episode.

100/50/50: A formula pursuant to which an individual rendering services in connection with a television film will be paid certain bonuses in the event that the film is released theatrically; i.e., an additional 100 percent of the original fee in the event that the television movie is exhibited theatrically in the United States prior to its television broadcast, an additional 50 percent of the original fee if the TV movie is released theatrically in the United States subsequent to its television broadcast, or an additional 50 percent of the fee if the television movie is exhibited in theaters overseas (whether before or after its initial television broadcast).

Abandonment: When a producer or studio ceases to develop a motion picture or television project, formally "passing" or abandoning such project.

Above-the-Line: Refers to specific elements of a production budget, generally appearing in the top portion of the budget (above an actual line separating such costs from other costs, known as below-the-line costs). These elements include rights payments, as well as fees to actors, directors, writers, and producers (all of whom are referred to as "above-the-line" talent).

Ad-Supported: Network wireless or broadband programming that is supported through advertisement sales.

Adjusted Gross Participation: Generally, the equivalent of a gross participation (a percentage of total revenue realized by a studio) less certain specified deductions, most notably a "reduced" distribution fee (i.e., a lesser fee than the studio charges to net participants).

Answer Print: The first finalized print made from the edited picture and sound-track, incorporating fades, dissolves, and other effects.

AVOD: Ad-Supported Video On Demand, referring to VOD (see below) that is streamed on the Internet and not available for permanent download. Such programming contains commercial breaks, which cannot be fast-forwarded.

Back Nine: The nine additional series episodes sometimes ordered by networks to reach a full season of twenty-two episodes (after initially committing to produce only thirteen).

Below-the-Line: Refers to costs of production other than those resulting from talent compensation and rights acquisitions (which are typically set forth in a discrete section of production budget and are known as above-the-line costs). Also refers to a production's crew members.

Bible: A term defined in the Writers Guild Agreement as a long-term story projection for a television series or miniseries.

Billing Block: Refers to the list of credits appearing (in block form) at the bottom of one-sheets and ads in newspaper ads, billboards, etc.

Blog: Shorthand for Web log, a Web site where an author creates an online journal. Blogs focus on personal commentary ranging from purely social (e.g., "the things I did on my vacation") to editorial (e.g., "I think that school budgets shouldn't be cut"). Blogs are typically considered "citizen news" sites, though corporations can launch blogs to express their own opinions.

Boilerplate: Standard contractual provisions that vary very little from agreement to agreement.

Breach: A default, or violation, of a particular contractual provision or deal point.

Business Affairs Department: The division at most studios and production companies responsible for negotiating talent and other production agreements on behalf of such studios and production companies. Business affairs executives are usually lawyers, but this is not always the case.

Ceiling: A maximum price, i.e., "no more than."

Chain of Title: The historical "chain" of ownership of a literary property, dating back to its creation.

Clear Field: Used in reference to a credit appearing during an end-title "crawl" (i.e., as credits scroll down the screen). At such time as said credit reaches the center of the screen, there will be sufficient space above and below such credit so that no other credit appears on screen at that moment.

Contingent Compensation: Compensation that is payable only upon the occurrence of one or more events (such as the film generating profits or achieving certain specified box-office levels).

Cover Shots: Alternate footage that is filmed to "cover" (i.e., replace) footage that may not be suitable for certain media (such as airline or network television exhibition). Most commonly, footage containing nudity or profanity are "covered."

Cuts: Edited versions of a film.

Dailies: Film footage shot over the course of a given day.

Daily Variety: A Hollywood trade publication (printed daily) that covers entertainment news and tracks the performance of many films and television programs.

Default: A breach, or violation, of a particular contractual provision or deal point.

Deferment: See "Deferred Compensation."

Deferred Compensation: Compensation that is not payable until the occurrence of a particular event, if ever.

Department Head: Refers to key below-the-line personnel engaged in connection with productions to run their respective departments. Examples of department heads are costume designers, production designers, editors, cinematographers (also known as "DPs"), and casting directors.

Depiction Release: A document conveying to a producer the right to depict or portray an individual or his or her life story in a film or television project (and to dramatize and fictionalize portions thereof).

Development Activities: Activities taking place during the development period, such as interviewing and hiring writers to write or rewrite scripts.

Development Fee: Fee paid to compensate talent for services rendered in connection with the development stage of a project.

Development Stage: The period during which development activities take place.

Distant Location: Generally defined as a locale more than one hundred miles from an individual's place of residence.

Distribution Fee: A fee charged by most film and television distributors (normally calculated as a percentage of receipts) as compensation for the selling or licensing of programming on behalf of producers. When distributors self-distribute their wholly-owned programming, a distribution fee is charged against revenues payable to profit participants, if any.

Double-Banger: A two-unit trailer, usually serving as dressing rooms for talent while on location.

DP: Director of photography, also known as the cinematographer.

DRM: Digital Rights Management. Technologies used to monitor and track content usage and provide content providers with control over access to material by protecting it from unauthorized access, use, disclosure, destruction, modification, or disruption.

DTO: Refers to content (such as a television episode) that is available for permanent download by the user, usually for a fee.

DVR: Digital Video Recorder. Device for time-shifting television content by recording shows or movies for later replay. TiVo is a well-known brand of DVR.

E & O: Errors and omissions insurance, purchased by studios and production companies to provide protection against defects in the copyright to a film project.

EST: Electronic Sell-Through. Refers to content (most often video content via the Internet) that is made available for permanent retention by consumers (for example, permanent copies on a consumer's hard drive). EST content is typically portable (i.e., the consumer may transfer it to a DVD or handheld device).

Exhibitors: Theater owners.

Fair Use Doctrine: Allows the use of copyrighted work (without obtaining consent) for specific purposes encouraged by public policy, such as criticism, news reporting, commentary, teaching, or research.

Favored Nations: An agreement to treat several parties in the same manner with respect to a particular issue, i.e., no one to be treated less favorably.

Final Cut: The ability or power to determine the final version, or "cut," of a motion picture.

First-Dollar Gross: A true first-dollar gross participation refers to a stake in any and all revenue received by the studio or distributor from the first dollar. Since true first-dollar gross participations are extremely rare, "first-dollar gross" typically refers to a stake in each dollar of revenue received by the studio/distributor *after* deducting a limited number of defined charges.

First Draft Screenplay: A first complete draft of any script in continuous form including full dialogue (per the Writers Guild Basic Agreement).

First Negotiation: The first opportunity to enter into negotiations to obtain rights or to secure employment, before any third parties are permitted to make offers. See also "Right of First Negotiation."

Fixed Compensation: Compensation that is guaranteed (subject to the individual's satisfactory performance of services) and is not conditioned on any contingent events (such as the film generating profits, for instance).

Floor: A minimum price, i.e. "no less than."

Force Majeure: An unexpected and disruptive event, such as an earthquake, flood, union strike, or act of war. The types of events qualifying as force majeure are usually set forth in the applicable contract.

Forced Call: When an actor is required to report to work before availing herself of the minimum rest period required under the applicable collective bargaining agreement (twelve hours, if SAG).

Free Weeks: Additional, contracted-for weeks beyond the stipulated term of services. These free weeks or days are not technically paid for, thereby allowing the individual's weekly "quote" to remain high.

Frontload: To modify a payment schedule so that a larger percentage of the total monies owed will be paid at an earlier point in time, such as upon commencement of services.

GAAP: Generally Accepted Accounting Principles.

Green Light: A formal commitment by the applicable studio to produce the project.

Gross Participation: This term generally refers to a percentage participation of a studio's gross earnings, less very limited deductions, such as taxes, trade dues, and residuals. Studios rarely, if ever, grant "true" gross participations (i.e, participations with no deductions whatsoever).

Guaranteed Compensation: See "Fixed Compensation."

Guaranteed Step: A writing step (such as first draft, rewrite, polish, etc.) with respect to which compensation is guaranteed, subject only to the writer's performance of the requisite services.

Guild: Union (such as the Screen Actors Guild).

Guild Signatory: See "Producer Signatory."

Hiatus: A scheduled break during or in between production periods.

Holdback Period: A specified period of time during which a rights holder is prohibited from exploiting some or all of his or her rights.

Hollywood Reporter: An entertainment news trade publication, similar to *Daily Variety.*

Hyphenate: An individual wearing two or more hats, i.e., serving in multiple capacities, such as writer/director.

Inducement Agreement: An agreement signed by talent stipulating that such individual will be bound by the terms of the agreement entered into by his or her loan-out company.

In the Black: Profitable; showing a profit.

In the Red: Showing a financial loss.

IPTV: Internet Protocol Television. Content (in the form of packets) provided by network operators over closed networks. Depending on how robust the system is, IPTV technology can also provide access to on-demand gaming, data services, digital music, and home security.

ISP: Internet Service Provider. A company that provides third-party access to the Internet (e.g., AOL, Earthlink, and NetZero).

Last Refusal: Also known as a matching right, this refers to a purchaser's right to match any third-party offers that the seller might be willing to accept.

Lead-Ins/Lead-Outs: Fifteen- to thirty-second "stay tuned" on-air spots.

Libel: The publication of defamatory matter by written or printed word.

License Fee: In television, this refers to the fee paid by networks to studios or production companies in exchange for the right to exhibit the applicable program.

Likeness Parity: Refers to a producer's obligation to include an actor's likeness in any item of advertising in which any other actor's likeness appears, in connection with a particular program or film.

Literary Option: The exclusive, irrevocable right to purchase a literary property or certain rights thereto during a specified period of time.

Loan-Out: A corporation set up by talent for tax purposes. The corporation then "loans out" such talent's services, and it, rather than the individual, will contract with the studio/producer.

Main Titles: Credits that appear before the first scene of the picture or program. In television, the main titles are usually accompanied by theme music.

Meal Penalties: Monetary fines imposed by SAG on producers who violate SAG's rules regarding regulated meal breaks for performers.

Minimums: Usually refers to guild- or union-prescribed minimum payments.

MPAA: The Motion Picture Association of America, a trade group representing the interests of most major motion picture producers and distributors.

Negative Cost: The actual cost of producing a movie (i.e., of producing a complete film negative of the motion picture).

Net Proceeds: A contractually defined term specifying the manner in which such defined proceeds shall be calculated and paid. Also known as "Net Profits" or "Project Net Profits."

Net Profits: See "Net Proceeds."

Novelization: The adaptation or conversion of a film or television program into a novel.

NVOD: Near Video On Demand. Video content that is scheduled to start at regular intervals and is available for purchase in advance. Portions of the video may be downloaded to a DVR to help in buffering or be entirely streamed.

On Spec: On speculation, i.e., rendering services without any promise of payment. Most commonly, writing a screenplay without any deal in place to write or sell such screenplay.

One-for-One Basis: In reference to series creators, the right to render consulting services for a number of years equal to those in which the writer rendered full-time producing or executive producing services.

One-Off: A one-time assignment, such as a script writing deal.

One-Sheets: Posters advertising upcoming films or television programs.

Option: The right, but not the obligation, to take a certain action, e.g., the right to acquire all motion picture rights in and to a novel, usually for a limited period of time.

Output Deals: An agreement pursuant to which one party agrees to acquire rights to all of the product created by the seller during the contract term. For example, HBO may agree to purchase the cable television right to all of the movies produced by Disney between 1990 and 2000.

Overages: Additional payments due to talent or crew because their services are required beyond the contracted-for term of employment.

Overall Deals: Agreements pursuant to which a studio or network pays a lump sum to a writer in return for an ownership interest or "first look" at any written material generated by such writer during the term of such agreement. Such deals may apply to television scripts only or to all written material. Most successful television series creators enter into an overall deal at some point in their careers.

Overbudget Penalty: Refers to a contractual provision that most commonly refers to the computation of contingent compensation for directors and producers. If the production is over budget (or over budget after a contractual cushion), the studio would be permitted to recoup some of the excess overbudget costs out of the contingent compensation otherwise payable to the producer or director).

Paid Advertising: Ads taken out and paid for by a studio to promote a particular film or television project.

Passive Payments: See "Royalty."

Pay-and-Play: The commitment by a studio or producer not only to pay the talent, but to actually utilize his or her services, barring unusual contractual contingencies such as force majeure or material default. In other words, the producer agrees that it will not produce the movie or television program without the talent's full participation.

Pay-or-Play: The commitment by a studio to pay the talent, regardless of whether the studio subsequently determines that such talent's services are no longer required. In other words, such talent will either render services or not, but will be paid regardless (again, subject to limited exclusions, such as the talent's breach of the agreement).

Per Diem: A daily expense allowance (intended as reimbursement for meals and incidental expenses).

Pilot: An initial, sometimes experimental episode of a potential series. Pilots that generate series orders are typically sent by networks to the major advertising agencies in an effort to generate interest among purchasers of network advertising time.

Pilot Option Period: See "Test Option Period."

Pilot Season: Generally mid-January to April, this is the period of time in which the broadcast networks produce (or finance the production of) the majority of their pilots, with the intention that some such pilots will yield series and air on the network in the fall.

Pilot Test Deals: See "Test Option Deals."

Pitch: An encapsulated version of a story, plot, or idea intended to entice a potential buyer. Such pitches may be written, but are often submitted verbally.

Points: Another term for a percentage of profits or net profits (i.e., 5 percent of net proceeds is colloquially referred to as "5 points"). In the music industry, points can refer to a soundtrack royalty.

Polish: A minor revision to a screenplay or teleplay.

Possessory Credit: A credit associating the project with a particular individual. This term most often refers to a director's "Film by" credit (e.g., A Martin Scorsese Film), but can also refer to films in which the author's name is included in the title, such as *Bram Stoker's Dracula* or *John Grisham's The Rainmaker*.

Preemption language: Contractual language that allows the talent to accept other job offers while a given producer has an option on their services, subject to that producer's right to preclude (or preempt) such talent from taking the other job by guaranteeing the talent employment and compensation.

Pre-Production: The period immediately preceding principal photography, where such activities as rehearsals, set designing, and final casting take place.

Prequel: A program (e.g., a television episode or motion picture) in which the characters from an existing program are depicted in events that predate the events portrayed in the original program. Under the WGA definition, sequels include prequels.

Presentation: A production falling short of an actual "pilot," i.e., a prototype episode not intended to be aired, but merely to allow the network to evaluate whether additional episodes should be produced. Nevertheless, presentations are sometimes subsequently "completed" and aired as pilots.

Previews: Test screenings, usually of a film or pilot. Researchers will often ask members of the audience to fill out evaluations or even to remain after the broadcast to discuss their views.

Prima Facie: Literally, "on its face," indicating that it is fundamentally or intrinsically proven.

Principal Photography: The period of production (i.e., taping or filming)—sometimes just called "photography."

Producer-Signatories: Producers, studios, and production companies that are signatory to the applicable collective bargaining agreements, such as those of SAG, WGA, and DGA.

Production Bonus: A monetary bonus paid in the event that a project reaches the production stage, most commonly paid to writers.

Professional Availability: At times, certain required services (such as the rendering of publicity services by an actor) will be subject to an individual's professional commitments, so that if an actor is filming a movie, he would not be required to render publicity services. Personal commitments would not negate such an obligation.

Project Net Profits: See "Net Proceeds."

Public Domain: Available for public use, either because the work is not copyrightable or because the term of copyright has expired.

Publisher's Release: A document intended to be executed by a book publisher that stipulates that the publisher does not own the rights that the book author purports to sell (usually film and television rights). This document, when signed, ensures that the purchaser is free to exploit such rights.

Quote: The individual's "going rate"—what he or she has been paid for similar services.

Release Patterns: The release or distribution strategy for a particular film, e.g., how many screens will the film appear on during its opening weekend, and how quickly will such release expand to appear on more screens in more cities?

Remake: A production other than the initial production based upon the property in question in which (i) the principal character(s) are principal characters in the property and (ii) said character(s) are shown as participating for the most part in the same events in which said character(s) participated in the first production based upon the property.

Reversion: The point in time, if ever, that ownership rights in or to a property revert back to its creator.

Rewrite: Also known as a "set of revisions," the act of reworking or revising a screenplay or teleplay.

Right of First Negotiation: The obligation (usually on the studio's part) to negotiate in good faith for the services of a particular individual, so that the studio is prevented from offering such employment to third parties prior to undertaking such negotiation. Thus, the "right" of first negotiation is granted to talent, as it obligates the studio to make an offer of employment to such individual. Studios sometimes grant networks a right of first negotiation in connection with television license agreements, so that upon expiration of the initial license term, the studio must negotiate with the original network before attempting to license future episodes of the series to a competing network. See also "First Negotiation."

Royalty: Also referred to as a "passive" payment, because actual services are usually not required in order to qualify for a royalty. These payments are most often promised to creators of programming in the event that their work generates subsequent productions. For instance, most pilot writers will be contractually guaranteed a royalty upon production of series episodes based upon such pilot.

Run of the Picture: The entire duration of principal photography, usually denoting the number of work days required of a particular film actor.

Scale: Minimum payments, as prescribed by the applicable union.

Schedule F: Refers to Schedule F of the Screen Actors Guild Agreement, which relates to terms of employment for the most highly compensated actors. Because such actors are paid above a certain SAG threshold, the employing producer is entitled to certain benefits and will be exempt from certain restrictions that otherwise apply to the engagement of lower-paid actors.

Script Doctor: A writer hired to "spruce up" or "fix" a script, usually by inserting jokes or otherwise adding some "juice." These highly paid writers are often hired by studios for brief periods of employment, most often to work on scripts that are very close to being "green-lit."

Separate Card: With reference to credit, a separate card (or frame of film) signifies that no other credits will appear on screen at the same time that the referenced credit appears.

Separated Rights: A specified set of rights that the WGA Agreement "separates out" from the rights that would otherwise be owned by the writer's employer and instead grants them to the writer (assuming certain conditions are met).

Sequel: The WGA defines the term "sequel," used with reference to a particular production, as a new production in which the principal characters of the first production participate in an entirely new and different story.

Series Regular: An actor that is contractually required to render services in connection with a television series as a regular, or continuing, character (as opposed to a guest star or a character that recurs only sporadically). An actor may be considered a series regular even if he or she does not appear in every single episode, but such "regulars" generally appear in a majority of episodes.

Series Sales Bonus: A monetary bonus paid by studios/producers to individuals (usually to pilot writers, and sometimes to pilot directors) in the event that a series is "sold" to the network—in other words, if the network orders the production of series episodes based upon the pilot.

Set of Revisions: Sometimes called a "rewrite," a reworking of a script, such as from first draft to second draft.

Set-Up Bonus: An additional fee payable to a rights holder in the event that the purchaser enters into an agreement with a studio, production company, or financier to develop the property (i.e., it is "set up" at a studio).

Shared Writing Credit: When the "Written by" credit is accorded to two or more writers (that did not write as a writing team).

Showrunner: The executive producer (or producers) who has day-to-day responsibility for a television series. The showrunner is frequently the creator of the original pilot and is the top dog on set, reporting only to the applicable studio and network executives.

Slander: The issuance of defamatory spoken words or gestures.

Sole Writing Credit: When the "Written by" credit is accorded to a single writer or writing team.

Spec Scripts: Scripts written on the "speculation" of a future sale, i.e., without the guarantee of compensation or a buyer.

Spin-Offs: Television series that evolve from preexisting television series. There are generally two types of television series spin-offs: generic spin-offs and planted spin-offs. A generic spin-off is one in which continuing characters from the original series serve as continuing characters in a new series (portraying the same characters). *Joanie Loves Chachi* was a generic spin-off of *Happy Days.* Another example is the short-lived *The Ropers,* which spun off from *Three's Company.* A planted spin-off refers to a situation in which characters from the new series are "planted" into an established series for a limited number of episodes in order to introduce them to as wide a viewership as possible. These characters are not regulars on the original series. *Melrose Place* was a planted spin-off, in that some of the *Melrose Place* cast appeared in several episodes of *Beverly Hills, 90210* prior to the series premiere of *Melrose Place.*

Spotting: When a cut of a film or television program is viewed (typically, by the composer, director, and certain producers) in order to identify places where music cues should be inserted.

Stop Date: A contractual date on which the applicable studio or producer agrees to release the individual (actor, director, producer) from his or her obligation to render continuing services—even if the project is not yet complete.

Streaming: Online media term for the delivery of media content over a packet network, which enables content to be read, heard, or viewed as it is being delivered.

Submission Release Form: Except when represented by a reputable representative, anyone wishing to submit unsolicited literary material to a potential buyer (studio, production company, etc.) or representative (agent, manager, etc.) will usually be required to sign this form. The form purports to release the recipient of any liability in the event that such recipient later becomes associated with a project that is alleged to be similar to the one submitted.

SVOD: Subscription Video On Demand. Video On Demand service offered at a flat (subscription) price that provides viewers with unlimited access to select programs from the libraries of featured cable networks.

Syndication: The sale of programming to individual television stations in cities throughout the United States and abroad.

Television Pilot: See "Pilot."

Term Deal: See "Overall Deal."

Test: In television, this refers to a formal audition for a role in a pilot or television series.

Test Option Deals: Also known as "pilot test deals," these are agreements for actors' services in television pilots and for up to seven years on a series. They are called "tests" because the actor must typically negotiate and sign a contract before being informed of whether he secured the role.

Test Option Period: The period of time in which a studio must decide whether to release an actor from its "hold" or commit to engage him or her as an actor in the pilot.

Theatrical Release Bonus: A monetary bonus paid to an individual in connection with his or her television services in the event that the television project is released theatrically.

Trades: Refers to the Hollywood daily trade journals, specifically *Daily Variety* and the *Hollywood Reporter.*

Treatment: A rough sketch or detailed outline of a screenplay or teleplay.

Turnaround: When a studio decides to abandon further development of a property, but allows the producer or other talent to shop such property to other potential buyers for a limited period of time. When a project is in turnaround, it is searching for a new home, as the initial studio had declared that it is not interested in producing the project.

Underbudget Bonus: A bonus payment that is sometimes negotiated in producer or director deals, where a portion of the budget savings (or a fixed dollar amount) would be payable to the producer or director as a reward for maintaining costs at a level that is below the budgeted costs.

Underlying Material: A property (whether book, movie, script, comic book, animated character, etc.) on which a film or television project is based.

Upfronts: The period of time (customarily commencing at the end of May) when the networks announce their upcoming Fall television schedules to the advertisers. The advertisers (through their agencies) then negotiate with the network sales departments for the purchase of advertising time. This period is known as the "upfronts," because the bulk of the network's ad spots are usually sold up front (i.e., at this time), with the remainder being sold on an ad hoc basis in the "scatter market," i.e., throughout the year.

Upset Price: A minimum sum of money, specified by the WGA, that must be paid to the writer of a pilot script in order for the purchaser to retain the ability to acquire the "separated rights" that would otherwise be retained by the writer.

Vertical Integration: The economies of scale (i.e., cost-efficiencies) realized by joint ownership of production entities and distribution outlets (e.g., networks and studios under common ownership, such as Disney/ABC).

Vesting Schedule: A schedule setting forth the points in time in which portions of an individual's compensation or other rights will be deemed "earned," and therefore due and payable.

VOD: Video On Demand. A system that allows users to select and watch video content over a network as part of an interactive television system.

Work-for-Hire: A work prepared by an employee within the scope of his or her employment, or a work specifically ordered or commissioned for use as a contribution to a collective work as a part of a motion picture or other audiovisual work.

Writers Guild of America (WGA): The union governing the employment of television and screenwriters when hired by signatory companies.

ABOUT THE AUTHORS

Dina Appleton is special counsel in the Entertainment, Media and Technology Practice Group at the law firm of Sheppard Mullin Richter & Hampton in Los Angeles, California. She previously ran business and legal affairs at Writers and Artists Agency for nine years. Ms. Appleton handles a wide range entertainment transactions for a diverse range of clients, including major film and television studios and production companies, independent producers, book authors, directors, actors, writers, talent agencies, and individual investors and financiers. She also teaches at UCLA extension and is a columnist for *Backstage* magazine.

Daniel Yankelevits is an attorney for Sony Pictures. He has served as Director of Business Affairs at Home Box Office and at New Line Cinema, and as co-chair of the Beverly Hills Bar Association Entertainment Section and the USC Entertainment Law Symposium Syllabus Committee. He also teaches a course entitled "Negotiating Talent Agreements" at UCLA Extension. Daniel is a graduate of Harvard Law School and resides in Los Angeles with his wife and two children.

INDEX

Books from Allworth Press

Allworth Press is an imprint of Allworth Communications, Inc. Selected titles are listed below.

Animation Development: From Pitch to Production
by David B. Levy (paperback, 6 × 9, 240 pages, 73 b&w illustrations, $24.95)

Splatter Flicks: How to Make Low-Budget Horror Films
by Sara Caldwell (paperback, 6 × 9, 224 pages, 22 b&w illustrations, $19.95)

The Filmmaker's Guide to Production Design
by Vincent LoBrutto (paperback, 6 × 9, 240 pages, 15 b&w illustrations, $19.95)

Producing for Hollywood: A Guide for Independent Producers, Second Edition
by Paul Mason and Don Gold (paperback, 6 × 9, 288 pages, $19.95)

The Screenwriter's Legal Guide, Third Edition
by Stephen F. Breimer (paperback, 6 × 9, 352 pages, $29.95)

An Actor's Guide: Your First Year in Hollywood, Third Edition
by Michael Saint Nicholas (paperback, 6 × 9, 272 pages, $19.95)

Screenplay Story Analysis: The Art and Business
by Asher Garfinkel (paperback, 5½ × 8½, 208 pages, $16.95)

The Health & Safety Guide for Film, TV & Theater
by Monona Rossol (paperback, 6 × 9, 256 pages, $19.95)

Documentary Superstars: How Today's Filmmakers Are Reinventing the Form
by Marsha McCreadie (paperback, 6 × 9, 28 b&w illustrations, $19.95)

Get the Picture? The Movie Lover's Guide to Watching Films, Second Edition
by Jim Piper (paperback, 6 × 9, 336 pages, 164 b&w illustrations, $24.95)

Your Career in Animation: How to Survive and Thrive
by David B. Levy (paperback, 6 × 9, 116 b&w illustrations, $19.95)

Starting Your Career in Broadcasting: Working On and Off the Air in Radio and Television
by Chris Schneider (paperback, 6 × 9, 256 pages, 21 b&w illustrations, $19.95)

To request a free catalog or order books by credit card, call 1-800-491-2808. To see our complete catalog, or to order online, please visit us at ***www.allworth.com***.